PATTON AT BAY

PATTON AT BAY

The Lorraine Campaign,
September to December, 1944

John Nelson Rickard

Foreword by Carlo D'Este

Praeger Series in War Studies

Westport, Connecticut
London

Library of Congress Cataloging-in-Publication Data

Rickard, John Nelson, 1969–
    Patton at bay : the Lorraine campaign, September to December, 1944
/ John Nelson Rickard ; foreword by Carlo D'Este.
        p.   cm.—(Praeger series in war studies, ISSN 1083–8171)
    Includes bibliographical references and index.
    ISBN 0–275–96354–3 (alk. paper)
    1. Patton, George S. (George Smith), 1885–1945.   2. World War,
1939–1945—Campaigns—France—Lorraine.   3. United States. Army.
Army, 3rd—History.   4. United States. Army—Biography.
5. Lorraine (France)—History, Military.   6. Generals—United
States—Biography.   I. Title.   II. Series.
D762.L63R53   1999
940.54 21438 092—dc21   98–36753

British Library Cataloguing in Publication Data is available.

Library of Congress Catalog Card Number: 98–36753
ISBN: 0–275–96354–3
ISSN: 1083–8171

First published in 1999

Praeger Publishers, 88 Post Road West, Westport, CT 06881
An imprint of Greenwood Publishing Group, Inc.

Printed in the United States of America

The paper used in this book complies with the
Permanent Paper Standard issued by the National
Information Standards Organization (Z39.48–1984).

10 9 8 7 6 5 4 3 2 1

Contents

A photo essay follows page 133

Illustrations

TABLES

Foreword

General George S. Patton, Jr.'s glowing reputation rests solidly upon his achievements in organizing, commanding, and leading into battle the first American tank force during World War I, and upon his exploits during World War II in command of II Corps in Tunisia, the Seventh Army in Sicily, and the Third Army in Northwest Europe. Now recognized as one of the pioneers of twentieth-century mobile warfare, Patton's triumphs during World War II are solidly etched in the history of the United States Army.

Patton's extraordinary success was rooted in his basic doctrine that, by always keeping the enemy off balance, he could control events and thereby achieve success on the battlefield. During late July and early August 1944, his Third Army spearheaded Operation Cobra, the great breakout from the Normandy bridgehead. In a matter of days what had been a troubling and potentially deadly stalemate turned into one of the most dramatic Allied victories of World War II. The German army in Normandy was shattered, and its survivors were forced to retreat in disarray, mostly on foot, behind the River Seine. Paris was soon liberated, and as British, American, and Canadian forces swept into Belgium and eastern France, there was an almost euphoric belief that the war was all but won.

During August 1944 the Third Army was a juggernaut that rolled virtually unchecked across southern Normandy and into the province of Lorraine. Rheims and the great champagne vineyards, Verdun with its gruesome reminder of the horror of an earlier world war, and the dreadful Argonne, where Patton had been wounded and nearly died in 1918—all fell to Third Army in late August and early September 1944. Patton's euphoria was that of a conquering hero. As one historian has noted, "To be Patton roaring across France was to feel more like a god than a man. . . . To grab all three on the run and keep moving was to triumph over History."[1]

Unfortunately, it became a classic catch-22 that the farther and faster Eisenhower's armies advanced, the more difficult it became to sustain offensive operations. The primary lifeblood of war is fuel and ammunition. However, the insatiable logistical appetite of three Allied army groups displaced from the Belgian coast to the Swiss border could not be rapidly satisfied from Normandy where virtually 95 percent of the required supplies were stored in supply dumps near the invasion beaches. As the Allies advanced farther from Normandy, they began to falter, the victim not of German resistance but of an acute shortage of the transportation required to move supplies forward. Even the renowned Red Ball Express could only fill a fraction of the Allied needs, and then for only a brief period.

By early September Third Army had ground to a virtual halt along the flooded Moselle River. In places, Patton's tanks and vehicles sputtered and literally ran out of fuel on the battlefield. The great Third Army advance was suddenly history. An angry and frustrated Patton raged to his superiors: "For God's sake give us gas!" What Third Army eventually received was too little, too late.

One of the most fought-over areas in military history, Lorraine was the shortest gateway to Germany and has for centuries been a traditional invasion route of invading armies. After the pursuit across southern Normandy, the only logical employment of Third Army was for it to advance into Lorraine. More importantly, this was in keeping with Eisenhower's blueprint to advance on the Third Reich on a broad front and eliminate its fighting units this side of the Rhine.

With German forces in total disarray at the end of August, a virtually undefended Lorraine beckoned like the Rhine sirens of mythology. Patton begged his boss, General Omar N. Bradley, the Twelfth Army Group commander, that if he could be allocated even four hundred thousand gallons of fuel, "I'll put you inside Germany in two days."[2] Time was crucial before the Germans inevitably reacted to prevent Patton from advancing to and penetrating the Siegfried Line guarding the German frontier. Instead, Third Army simply ground to a halt in the inhospitable terrain of Lorraine. "The conditions for a breakout and pursuit, which had carried it across the soft underbelly of Normandy, no longer existed in Lorraine. The war of movement that Bradley had ushered in with Cobra was already turning, even if imperceptibly as yet, into a war of position."[3]

The sudden turnabout from pursuit operations to static warfare within the space of a few days effectively ended any chance of rapidly cracking the Siegfried Line and, in Patton's view, possibly even ending the war in 1944.

Instead, from September until mid-December 1944 the master of mobile warfare was obliged to direct a frustrating and costly slugging match between Third Army and what was now the most powerful of the German armies in the West.

These events are the subject of John Rickard's well-researched account. All but forgotten between Patton's greatest triumphs, Normandy and the subsequent Battle of the Bulge, Lorraine has heretofore failed to attract much interest from military historians. In *Patton at Bay*, the author not only enhances our knowledge of Patton but admirably fills a void in the history of one of World War II's least-known campaigns.

Carlo D'Este*

NOTES

1. Geoffrey Perret, *There's a War to Be Won* (New York: Random House, 1991), 366.

2. Quoted in Carlo D'Este, *Patton: A Genius for War* (New York: HarperCollins, 1995), 660.

3. Ladislas Farago, *Patton: Ordeal and Triumph* (New York: Ivan Obolensky, 1963), 598–599.

*Author of *Patton: A Genius for War*, 1995.

Preface

The name George S. Patton, Jr. has become, in the years since the end of World War II, synonymous with fast, armored warfare. He is quite deservedly recognized as the master of American blitzkrieg. This reputation rests on his aggressive operations in Sicily, the brilliant exploitation of German weakness in Normandy and Brittany, and the amazing drive against the German flank during the Battle of the Bulge. Yet between the stunning victories in Normandy and the Bulge are his less glamorous operations in Lorraine from September to December 1944. This three-month struggle represents one of the grimmest campaigns fought by any Allied army in World War II. Horrendous weather conditions, difficult terrain, acute supply problems, and the hard-fighting German Army turned the campaign into a bitter and protracted contest of attrition. It was the toughest test of command and operational maneuver Patton faced during the war.

In order to pass judgment on Patton's part in the campaign, I have for the most part worked within the general guidelines suggested by B. H. Liddell Hart, who maintained that to make an accurate judgment on generalship, the historian had to consider conditions and relative resources along with those factors that lie outside a commander's control. Only then could one properly estimate the quality of his performance. I have kept in mind, however, the fact that the historian has to know when to stop qualifying his statements and offer a pronouncement. Uncontrollable factors must be given their proper weight, but the ultimate responsibility for success or failure on the battlefield lies with the commander's own decisions.

It may seem logical to some that war can only be legitimately discussed by those who have practiced it, but this is a fallacy. One need only look at the excellent work done by such civilian military historians as Stephen Ambrose, Russell F. Weigley, John Keegan, and others to convince one otherwise. My limited military experience has consisted of infantry exercises at the section, platoon, and company levels. I have heard live rifle shots whip overhead on the firing range and have taken part in simulated assaults and defensives, but I have never heard shots fired in anger. I have examined different battlefields from Gettysburg to Normandy and have even been to Bosnia where war could break out again at any time, but as John Keegan once said, I have never been in a battle. Yet even this barebones experience has taught me the truth of the old military adage that in war the seemingly most simple things can oftentimes be the most difficult. Though hardly the same as commanding an army, one need only try to control a ten-man infantry section in an advance over broken terrain covered with smoke and deafened by the cacophony of weapons firing to understand my point. I have kept the realization that Clausewitz's "friction of war" really does exist in mind, and it has served me well in preparing this work.

The Lorraine Campaign has been covered elsewhere. Hugh M. Cole's official history is a testament to the quality of the U.S. Army in World War II series, but it can be said without reservation that *The Lorraine Campaign* is primarily a small unit account. Anthony Kemp's *The Unknown Battle: Metz, 1944* deals with only one particular and salient aspect of the campaign; Christopher R. Gabel's short forty-page monologue, *The Lorraine Campaign: An Overview, September–December 1944*, is only the starting point for a fuller examination of the campaign. Other notable sources are Russell Weigley's *Eisenhower's Lieutenants: The Campaign of France and Germany, 1944–1945* and Chester Wilmot's *The Struggle for Europe*, but both fail to delve deep enough into Patton's decision-making. George S. Patton, Jr. has been called the greatest combat general of modern times, and it is hoped that this book will round out our understanding of Patton the fighting general.

In preparing this work, I have relied on numerous individuals. Frank Henner at the National Infantry Museum, Fort Benning, Georgia, provided me with Major General Manton S. Eddy's diary in the midst of a downsizing of his department, and I appreciate his promptness in getting the material to me. There are few military historians working on World War II today that do not owe Dr. Richard Sommers and David Keough at the Military History Institute, Carlisle Barracks, a debt of gratitude, and I am no exception. On two different occasions they answered my questions and retrieved documents for me. The staff of the Bird Library at Syracuse University and the staff at the Library of Congress Manuscript Reading Room were helpful in dealing with the papers of Major General John S. Wood and Patton respectively. Mr. Alan Aimone of the Special Collections Room at the West

Point Library provided the diaries of Patton and his chiefs of staff, Hobart Gay and Hugh J. Gaffey. I appreciated his lugging out the large, unwieldy Third Army After Action Reports, especially when I made the mistake of missing something and asking him to retrieve it once again. Most of the photos in the book are courtesy of Mr. Aimone and the West Point library. Thanks also to Mike Bechtold of Wilfrid Laurier University for providing me with valuable air force documents pertaining to the campaign. Lieutenant Colonel (Ret.) Henry G. Phillips of Penn Valley, California, was kind enough to discuss Manton S. Eddy with me and provided a copy of his work on the 9th Infantry Division in North Africa, and Dominick Graham freely gave me his views on Patton's abilities.

I must thank Professor Terry Copp, with whom I spent an enjoyable three weeks in the summer of 1995 on a battlefield tour of Normandy. Terry reinforced my belief in the absolute necessity of understanding how terrain affects military decisions while we examined the battlefields around Caen and Falaise. From Terry I have come to readily concede the fact that terrain is a primary document. This is partly why I spent a week in Lorraine once our Normandy tour was over. In this regard I should thank the little French boy who brought my well-traveled bicycle to me every morning while I inspected the battlefields around Metz.

In regards to the preparation of the manuscript, I have been particularly fortunate in that both Carlo D'Este and Martin Blumenson, two seasoned and gifted military historians, read it and offered perceptive insights into how to make it better. Martin Blumenson brought to my attention several errors that an author fails to detect after working with his material for a long time, and Carlo is to be thanked for commenting on an early draft and for writing the forward while suffering a bad back. Of particular mention must be Bill Traer, who literally spent hundreds of hours with me designing and correcting the numerous maps in the book. He graciously put up with my constant demands for changes and, in way of compensation, asked only for liquid refreshment at the campus bar. The University newspaper, *The Brunswickan*, allowed me to use more than my fair share of computer time, printer paper, and ink cartridges, and I thank Joe Fitzpatrick, the editor of the paper for allowing me virtually free access. Additional help was continually sought and freely given from the two secretaries in the History Department at the University of New Brunswick. Elizabeth Hetherington graciously put up with my constant requests for paperwork, and Carol Hines kept me out of administrative trouble.

I am indebted to Lieutenant Colonel (Ret.) Jack English for his favorable response to the idea of writing a book on Patton in Lorraine when I first suggested it to him at the Royal Military College of Canada in March 1994. As the military series advisor for Praeger Publishing, his assistance in getting the manuscript approved was also invaluable. On that note, I also thank Heather Ruland for her support during production of the book and Praeger for taking a chance on a young author.

The last person I need to mention is Dr. Marc Milner, director of the excellent Military and Strategic Studies Program at the University of New Brunswick, and my mentor. Without the funding of the Strategic Studies Program I would never have been able to travel to France to look at the ground or carry out my research at numerous repositories. Marc's assistance has been invaluable and his friendship appreciated.

Finally, I thank my faithful black lab mut, Rommel, for his constant companionship and for always agreeing with my conclusions.

Any errors or omissions in the text are mine alone.

Symbols

CCA — X — CCB	Brigade Boundary
4 Armd — XX — 80th	Divisional Boundary
XX — XXX — XII	Corps Boundary
First — XXXX — Fifth Pz	Army Boundary
B — XXXXX — G	Army Group Boundary

German *Army*	
German *Panzer Corps*	
German *Panzer Brigade*	
German *Volksgrenadier Division*	
German *Panzer Grenadier Division*	
American Infantry Division	
American Armored Division	

Chapter 1

A Philosophy of Battle

> War is a very simple thing, and the determining characteristics are self-confidence, speed, and audacity.
>
> —Patton[1]

Patton's great difficulty in the autumn of 1944 was an inability to reconcile his established notions of how battles should be conducted with the type of battle demanded by conditions in Lorraine. At times, he managed to bridge the gap, and in one instance he almost succeeded in imposing his own concepts on the battlefield. For the most part, however, he struggled to define and master this new way of fighting. Understanding Patton's established battle philosophy is an important step in assessing his performance in Lorraine.

It would not be correct to say that George Patton adhered to a battle doctrine. With its connotation of inflexible obedience to certain perceived rules of war, "doctrine" would not have accurately described his approach to fighting. In responding to criticism concerning a violation of rules during the Louisiana Maneuvers of 1941, he announced that he was unaware of the existence of any rules in warfare.[2] In this regard, he reflected the thinking of Field Marshal Helmuth Graf von Moltke, the "Elder," who declared, "From the beginning of operations, everything in war is uncertain. . . . Universal rules and the systems built upon them therefore can have no possible practical value."[3]

Patton used certain basic "concepts" in practicing his particular style of the operational art during World War II and did not always think in terms of linear sequence when applying those concepts to the battlefield. He utilized them in varying patterns much like a painter reaching for different shades of paint at a moment of inspiration. What is discovered after extensive analysis of Patton's battle "philosophy" are contradictions, especially between his theoretical writings and marginal notations in books he read, and his practical experience. This is understandable because Patton began an intensive study of the military art at an early age. As he matured as a professional soldier, revisions in his thinking were inevitable.

If one had to isolate the most important factor underpinning Patton's battle philosophy as practiced in World War II it would invariably be his long association with traditional horse cavalry. The connection between Patton and the cavalry is so widely known that few people probably realize that he agonized over which branch of service to choose during his last year at West Point in 1909. Patton rejected the artillery outright because it did not satisfy his thirst for personal combat. The infantry offered more rapid promotion, but the cavalry best suited his southern heritage and a belief that this branch contained the better class of gentleman. The lure of horses, a lifelong love, played an important part in his eventual selection of the cavalry as well.[4] The fundamental influence of the cavalry on how Patton perceived tactics cannot be overstated. He enthusiastically referred to German armor in the Polish Campaign as having been "utilized exactly as Murat used his cavalry corps in the days of Napoleon."[5] He continued to believe in the inherent abilities of horse cavalry long after it became obsolete on modern battlefields.

When the tank began to supersede the cavalry in World War I as the principal instrument of mobility on the battlefield, Patton was prepared for the change for two reasons. First, according to William J. Woolley, he had a "curiosity . . . which made him quite receptive to new ideas and new things" and "sufficient intellectual integrity to ensure an honest evaluation of whatever he encountered."[6] Moreover, Patton possessed a "highly developed imagination which was vital in dealing with mechanization. . . . The new concepts of the mechanizationists had never been tried in combat, so they could be evaluated only on the basis of imaginary constructs, an area in which most empirically-minded military professionals felt fairly uncomfortable, but in which Patton moved with great ease."[7] Prior to heading off to Europe, he commented that "new ideas are what are winning this war."[8] The second reason for his smooth transition from cavalry to tanks was his recognition of the real similarities between the horse and the new armored fighting vehicles being produced.

Patton quickly identified himself with tanks while commanding the 1st Tank Brigade during the Saint-Mihiel and Meuse-Argonne offensives in World War I. Having taken a chance that promotion would come quicker in the newly formed armored force, he left the cavalry and threw himself into mastering the nuts and bolts of tanks and developing his own ideas regarding their proper employment. Even at this stage in the development of armor, states Carlo D'Este, he "grasped the enormous potential of the tank as a potentially decisive factor on the modern battlefield."[9]

American armored forces faced deep cuts in the postwar army reductions, but Patton remained a keen student of the new technology. The National Defense Act of 1920 ruined any hopes of an independent tank arm and placed tanks in the infantry. Seeing this as the end of independent armored formations, Patton returned to the cavalry.[10] Promoting the potential of tanks in the postwar army was tantamount to professional suicide. Patton's close friend, Dwight D. Eisenhower, was threatened with court-martial for his dangerous views on tanks. As Eisenhower noted, "George, I think, was given the same message."[11] Though his advocacy of tanks (not his interest) would decline during the interwar years due to chastisement from senior infantry officers and lack of government funding for experimental development, Patton never let the concept of armored forces die in his own mind.

In the interwar years Patton expanded his theoretical thinking on armored warfare. By 1928 he had developed his understanding to such an extent that he could predict the powerful combination of airplane and tank characteristic of blitzkrieg. "The tanks and attack planes or a large proportion of them," he wrote, "should be held as a reserve to be used after a general battle had developed the enemies [*sic*] plans and sucked in his reserves. Then . . . this force should be launched ruthlessly and in mass."[12] Eisenhower did precisely this when he purposely held Third Army back until Bradley had finished the "general infantry battle" in Normandy. Then Patton "ruthlessly" pushed his armor behind the crumbling German lines while constant air cover protected his spearheads.

With the basic concepts of the cavalry deeply entrenched in his mind from almost thirty years of hands-on experience, Patton developed his battle philosophy further by an exhaustive professional and private study of the military art that extended over the same period. Napoleon had once said that the only means of acquiring the secret of the art of war was to study the campaigns of the great captains.[13] If any general ever took Napoleon's advice literally and to great effect, it was George Patton.

Patton combined a massive personal reading program with attendance at various army service schools, but it appears that of these two pillars of his training, the former had the greatest influence on his development. His abilities as a combat general probably owed more to his enormous private military library than to the army schooling system.[14] Whereas Patton served little more than four years in student and faculty time at the Army's various service schools, his less-creative contemporaries averaged more than ten. He was, however, an honors graduate of every service school he attended, though the value of that training is in question.

Patton and other successful World War II commanders, like John S. Wood and Lucian K. Truscott, excelled *in spite of* such schools as Leavenworth with its "school solutions" to tactical problems.[15] Patton noted prior to attending Leavenworth, while he and Eisenhower were working on tactical problems from previous years, that the school's authors were overcautious and their solutions "much too timid. Time is wasted [*sic*]."[16] Martin Blumenson declared that by failing to stimulate the best students, "the Army forced them to learn on their own, which may have enhanced initiative and resourcefulness."[17]

Certainly, most senior American officers kept up with their professions by reading, but few equaled Patton's mastery of an enormous range of military history. His reading was eclectic and analytical, focusing primarily on leadership, tactics, and operations, but he read widely in memoirs, biographies of the great captains, studies of men in battle, campaign histories of the Civil War and World War I, intelligence, and the future of warfare. In so doing Patton proved to be an extremely critical reader. He frequently questioned the author's conclusions, substituted his own analysis and inserted historical examples in the margins to support his assertions.[18] Prior to heading off for World War II, Patton had read or heard of nearly every treatise on mobile warfare that had been produced in English since World War I whether they had been written by advocates of cavalry, infantry, air power, or mechanization. The intelligence community's latest reports also drew his constant attention.[19] There was a great deal to learn from the writings of innovative officers from foreign armies.

Patton paid special attention to the writings of Germany's foremost armored expert, Heinz Guderian. Although certain philosophical differences between them are apparent, Patton would certainly have agreed with Guderian's observation that only those armored leaders who were prepared to act with daring would be blessed by victory in a future war.[20] Patton had actually come to the same conclusion in 1918 when he wrote that "boldness is the key to victory, the tank must be used boldly. It is now and always has the element of surprise."[21] In a post–World War II recollection, Brigadier General Holmes E. Dager, commander of a combat command in the 4th Armored Division in Third Army, shared this view and wrote of Patton that "armor gave him the surprise element his active mind so constantly sought."[22]

When Patton once again transferred from the cavalry to mechanized forces in July 1940 and took command of a brigade in the newly formed 2nd Armored Division, he brought with him the cavalry theories of speed, maneuver, flank and rear attack, firepower, and shock action.[23] His concept of shock action was not contingent on massed formations but was achieved by a combination of speed and surprise. By the time American forces entered combat in World War II, Patton had solidified his belief in the virtue of surprise and other concepts of mobility to become America's leading spokesman for a bold armored doctrine.

Keeping in mind Patton's fundamental faith in the virtues of the cavalry, his professional study added a unique twist to his battle philosophy and brought him into direct opposition with traditional U.S. Army methods of waging war. The American army that fought World War II struggled to combine the two principal legacies from its past—mobility and sheer power. The border wars against Indians and Mexicans required great mobility to cover the vast stretches of the American West; and the Civil War strongly suggested that sheer power was the best formula for successful war-making.

The Civil War had a profound impact on U.S. Army doctrine. One philosophy in particular survived the Civil War to be taken up by American officers for the wars of the twentieth century. "Despite the veneration of R. E. Lee in American military hagiography," states Russell Weigley, "it was U.S. Grant whose theories of strategy actually prevailed."[24] Grant chose to offset Lee's Napoleonic *manœuvre sur les derrières*, brilliantly conducted at Second Manassas and Chancellorsville, by locking Lee's army in continuous battle where a trade-off in casualties favored his superior resources of men and equipment. Grant's strategy of attrition was virtually codified into Army doctrine in the years between the world wars by the various service schools.

As the American Army followed the British lead and began to codify principles of war, highest priority was placed on one particular principle, that of the objective. Grant's principal objective had been to destroy the main Confederate force, Lee's Army of Northern Virginia. American doctrine thus came to reflect Clausewitz's teaching that the ultimate objective in war is the destruction of the enemy's main body. The American concept differed markedly from the Europeans in one important aspect, however. Weigley notes that in comparison to the Germans, the American doctrine was different in the "extent to which they expected overwhelming power alone, without subtleties of maneuver, to achieve the objective."[25] By 1939 a commentator on the revised army field manual FM 100–5, which outlined the army's doctrine, could declare with little thought of professional censorship that "no matter what maneuver is employed, ultimately the fighting is frontal. . . . One must accept the formula or not wage war."[26] Here was a blatant belief in the correctness of Grant's strategy. Patton the cavalryman did not accept the formula.

Patton was well acquainted with the teachings of Clausewitz, having fully annotated his copy of *On War* by 1926. His notation that one should always "go the limit" in the destruction of the enemy's forces[27] reflected Clausewitz's principal thesis. Similarly, he wrote in Herbert Sargent's *The Strategy on the Western Front* that "the only end of war and strategy is the destruction by battle of the enemy army."[28] Yet he was never swayed by those in the army advocating frontal assaults as the only means to cripple an opponent and achieve the objective. He believed frontal assaults were justified only when circumstances dictated no other course of action. Specifically, they became valid operations beyond circumstantial necessity when used to flank an opponent.

In Moltkean terms, a frontal assault designed for this purpose was a "fixing" attack. In Pattonesque terms, this became Patton's famous dictum, "Hold them by the nose and kick 'em in the ass." Moreover, Moltke noted that "which attack [the frontal or flanking] is to be viewed as the main attack and which as the secondary attack will depend on the general operational intention, the disposition of hostile forces, and the terrain."[29] Patton, however, clearly favored flanking movements.

The key to avoiding limited tactical situations where frontal assaults offered the only solution was mobility, but the lesson was so obvious that few picked it up. The vast bulk of Patton's contemporaries adopted the attrition strategy of Grant, and therefore, according to Blumenson, were "bland and plodding . . . workmanlike rather than bold"[30] in their operations in World War II. Patton, however, though he would display Grant's bulldog tenacity, leaned more towards the indirect approach of Stonewall Jackson and William Tecumseh Sherman. British historian and theorist B. H. Liddell Hart suggested that Sherman's methods of fighting "fired Patton's imagination—particularly with regard to the way that they exploited the indirect approach and the value of cutting down impedimenta in order to gain mobility."[31]

Patton's early thoughts on the indirect approach suggest that he did not like the concept. In 1926 he wrote in British Major General W. D. Bird's *Direction of War: A Study of Strategy* that "a maneuver is valueless which fails to cause a fight."[32] He repeated this position by writing "This would be a useless campaign" beside Clausewitz's suggestion that a campaign may be conducted with great activity and virtually no combat. Yet this was not a rejection of indirect means. Patton was careful to underline Sun Tzu's statements that "all warfare is based on deception" and "in all fighting . . . indirect methods will be needed in order to secure victory."[33] However, he was not philosophically predisposed to playing a cat and mouse game, giving up territory to effect an operation at another point the way Jackson had done in the Shenandoah Valley in 1862. His brand of the indirect approach was not as subtle as Jackson's. For Patton, speed and maneuver acting in unison were enough to exploit enemy weakness.

Patton's belief in the feasibility of the indirect approach was proven when the German blitzkrieg was unleashed on Poland in 1939. In a lecture given to officers of the 2nd Armored Division in September 1940, he noted how the Germans, when encountering resistance, developed two options. If strong resistance was discovered in prepared positions, the panzer forces were withdrawn for attack on another axis. If a continuous line was encountered, the armor "broke through the intervals between the centres of resistance and swamped the enemy back areas." The isolated pockets were left to the following motorized infantry while the armor, noted Patton, "plunged swiftly forward, sometimes as much as fifty miles ahead of the advance guards of the main body."[34]

The success of the German blitzkrieg relied chiefly on avoiding lengthy battles and utilizing speed to the fullest extent. Patton agreed. In preparing Third Army for battle in April 1944, he stated that he intended to "use the means at hand to inflict the maximum amount of wounds, death, and destruction on the enemy" and finished by adding the vital qualifier, "in the minimum time."[35] For Patton, this was the "only tactical principal [*sic*] which is not subject to change." He continually cautioned his troops that the number of casualties they sustained was directly related to the amount of time they spent under fire and used this reasoning to spur them to great efforts in the short run. As Nye contends, "Patton's expertise lay in his effective use of military force to stop fighting as quickly as possible."[36]

If Patton ever seriously thought in terms of basic dogma, the importance of continuous movement on the battlefield might have been his first principle. He reiterated this point whenever possible. To troops of his 2nd Armored Division during the 1941 Tennessee maneuvers he stressed that "we must always keep on moving, do not sit down, do not say, 'I have done enough,' keep on, see what else you can do to raise the devil with the enemy." He added that "if you can't think of anything else to do, throw a fit, burn a town, do *something*" [emphasis added].[37]

Field Marshal Sir Harold Alexander, who commanded Patton in Tunisia and Sicily, recorded a conversation between Patton and General Omar N. Bradley in Tunisia where Patton asked "Why are we sitting down doing nothing? We must do something!," at which point Bradley inquired what he had in mind. "Anything," responded Patton, "rather than just sit here on our backsides!" Alexander quickly gauged the difference between Patton and Bradley, noting "the one impatient of inaction, the other unwilling to commit himself to active operations unless he could clearly see their purpose."[38]

Patton's obsession with continuous movement was designed to serve a specific purpose. Brigadier General Oscar W. Koch, Patton's G-2, pointed out that although the idea of constant activity was not unique (Napoleon stressed *activitée, vitesse, vitesse*), Patton's application of the concept was. "He figured enemy reactions in simple formulae," stated Koch, "applying the tactical concept that it would take a certain minimum of time for a large enemy force to react." He sought to "catch his enemy in the act of maneuvering to react" to his initial move by "progressively following up his first action" with a second operation "in less than that minimum."[39] By displacing enemy strength out of the time-space relationship on the battlefield with slash-and-run tactics against the rear, Patton hoped to cut off and immobilize that strength without conducting attrition-type battles.

This perpetual motion could become a pursuit in the right circumstances once the enemy had been initially knocked off balance. Stonewall Jackson believed that after the enemy had been routed, the attacker should "never let up the pursuit so long as your men have strength to follow; for an army routed, if hotly pursued, becomes panic-stricken and can then be destroyed by half their number."[40] The development of Patton's own views on the pursuit are interesting. Upon reading Sun Tzu's advocacy of not pressing "a desperate foe too hard," Patton's marginal note held the odd comment, "especially in the pursuit."[41] Clearly, here is further evidence of the evolution of his thoughts on war-fighting because no one would be a greater advocate of pursuing the Germans in Normandy, surrounding them at Falaise, and cutting them off in the Bulge than he.[42]

For all his training as a cavalryman and his desire to bypass serious opposition, however, Patton fully recognized the importance of hard fighting to success on the battlefield. After reading Herbert Sargent's *Napoleon Bonaparte's First Campaign*, he wrote that "this campaign illustrates the predominance of *Man* over men and things; it shows the virtue of hard fighting and the determination to win or die."[43] In his belief that man possessed an ascendancy over weapons in war, he was not alone; his great rival in World War II, Sir Bernard Law Montgomery, held the same view.[44] Ultimately,

Patton recognized the simple fact that "war means fighting and fighting means killing,"[45] but long, attrition-type battles were not compatible with his mobile philosophy.

Patton's views on operational planning were a significant part of his battle philosophy. His freewheeling opportunistic tactical style meant that he approached the art of planning from a radically different perspective than did the methodical Montgomery or the overly cautious Bradley. His planning style, like the rest of his battle philosophy, was a synthesis of his cavalry experience and his professional study. His expertise in World War II manifested itself on the level of grand tactics, or the operational level of warfare. He was concerned with the big picture, on both the strategic (he always insisted that his intelligence staff show him how his current operations fit in with other Allied operations) and tactical levels. Yet on the tactical level, where success, as he put it, was crucial to fulfilling strategy, he strained to project himself as far forward as possible. This had important repercussions for his planning.

In an exploitive situation, Patton considered distant objectives rapidly obtainable with armored forces. Detailed planning at a high operational tempo is not only difficult but probably counterproductive. In such situations, Patton relied on the initiative and ingenuity of his corps and divisional commanders, especially those commanding armored units. He demanded independent judgment and a high level of tactical daring from them.[46] He firmly believed that the essence of cavalry combat lay in spontaneous leadership.

One historian has noted that Patton's decision to lead Third Army's August breakout in Normandy with armor turned the battle into a free-for-all. The speed of the attack and its constantly changing direction confused the Germans, but it was hard to discern a purposeful maneuver.[47] This is debatable, for Patton's operations positively affected Allied strategy. What is apparent from Third Army's fast, mobile operations in Normandy is the validity of Bradley's observation that Patton improvised operational plans as he went along.[48] He had made sound estimates of tactical situations while at Leavenworth, but improvisation became his *modus operandi* during the war because he was "content to just bull ahead."[49]

In comparing the operational methods of Patton and General Courtney Hodges, the commanding officer of the First U.S. Army, Bradley noted that "whereas Patton could seldom be bothered with details, Hodges studied his problems with infinite care and was thus better qualified to execute the more intricate operations."[50] Patton did not believe that a commander had the time to study a problem with "infinite care," and it is obvious from Hodges' performance in the Hurtgen Forest that he was not as qualified as Bradley had suggested. Still, there is no question that Patton often sacrificed detail for rapid execution.

In 1930 Patton read General Hans von Seeckt's *Thoughts of a Soldier* and agreed with the author's view that in war "the essential thing is action" and that action has three stages: "the decision born of thought, the order or preparation for execution, and the execution itself."[51] Patton's belief that speed was essential in the *execution* of a plan once decided upon is clear, but more crucially, speed had to be a factor in the *conception* of the plan itself. Whereas Montgomery hesitated to move until every gallon of gasoline and every shell was accounted for, and talked of "balance" and properly "teeing-up" a battle, Patton insisted that "a good plan violently executed *now* is better than a perfect plan next week."[52]

In real time and space, he had no faith in perfect plans and operated on the premise that there was "no approved solution to any tactical situation." Battles were simply "an agglomeration of numerous small actions and practically never developed according to pre-conceived notions."[53] Because a commander could never be absolutely sure how a battle might develop, Patton believed that "one does not plan and then try to make circumstances fit those plans. One tries to make plans fit the circumstances."[54]

In instructions issued to his subordinate commanders in March 1944, Patton made his point another way: "Plans must be simple and flexible," he wrote, and "you build as necessity directs or opportunity offers."[55] Specifically, he stated that formal orders "will be short, accompanied by a sketch—it tells what to do, not how." Beyond formal orders, fragmentary orders allowed maximum flexibility and would be delivered "in writing, or orally, by phone or personally."[56] Despite his insistence that plans be flexible, it appears that this was only the case in mobile operations. In tough circumstances, Patton held the counterview. During the battle to break through the German defenses in Tunisia, he stated that one had to be wary of "ever changing a plan."[57]

Inherent in an approach based on improvisation is a considerable degree of risk, but Patton avoided blind risk like he did the enemy's main strength—although there were exceptions. Rommel once stated that a bold operation was one "in which success is not a certainty but which in case of failure leaves one with sufficient forces in hand to cope with whatever situation may arise." A gamble, however, could "lead either to victory or to the complete destruction of one's force."[58] When Patton pushed two corps through the Avranches corridor in August to begin Third Army's breakout, he gambled. Troy Middleton, the VIII Corps commander, reflected that "you couldn't work it out on paper; you could never have gotten by with saying that it could be done at any of the service schools—an automatic F would have resulted."[59] Patton noted that "There was no plan, because it was impossible to make a plan. . . . It was a hazardous operation, because the troops were jammed head to tail for miles."[60] He admitted that "if a jam occurred . . . our losses, particularly with truck-borne infantry, would be terrific."[61]

Rommel further realized that the commander could not "creep about the battlefield anxiously taking all possible security measures against every conceivable enemy move." He felt it much more advantageous to "operate on the grand scale."[62] Patton would have agreed completely. He firmly believed in Stonewall Jackson's old motto "Do not take counsel of your fears" and fully believed that he could always "pull something out of the hat" to drive back an enemy penetration. Patton possessed great confidence in his ability to read enemy situations and the flow of battle. In order to become a great soldier, he once wrote, it was vital to become "so thoroughly conversant with all sorts of military possibilities that whenever an occasion arises he has at hand without effort on his part a parallel."[63] Yet the heart of his own security measures was grounded in a keen understanding of the role of up-to-date intelligence in attempting to bridge the gap between boldness and an operational gamble. Moreover, he relied on the timely intervention of air power to delay the enemy while he adapted to the situation.[64]

Part of Patton's ability to make instantaneous decisions, such as those required at Avranches, was the result of the excellent relationship he enjoyed with his staff, particularly his two chiefs of staff, Major General Hugh J. Gaffey and Brigadier General Hobart Gay. Although he had once questioned the need for a chief of staff, he subsequently authorized both men to issue orders in his name.[65] It was an additional benefit that both Gay and Gaffey thoroughly understood his battle philosophy and planning style. Patton admitted that the Avranches operation was only "made possible by extremely effective use of veteran staff officers" who managed to "improvise under pressure."[66]

George Patton put his faith in speed, mobility, and continuous movement. Centered around the relentless push of armor through the enemy's Achilles heel toward distant objectives, he created a style in World War II fluid enough to take rapid advantage of sometimes fleeting opportunities in a wide-ranging, fast-paced environment. He was clearly one of the army's deepest thinkers during the interwar years. His writings leave little room for doubt. The result of this intense study was, according to Nye, the creation of "a kind of warfare that was so fast and so destructive of the enemy that the battle could be won with a minimum of friendly casualties and expenditure of materiel."[67] He became a master of the mechanizationists' style of warfare by blending it with his own traditional perspective. The end product was a modern approach to battle based on proven past concepts. If his battle philosophy at times contained contradictions, they were indicative of his earnest attempt to understand the modern battlefield as it stood on the verge of World War II.

It has also been suggested that Patton's opportunistic operational method did not prevent him from "meticulously" planning anticipated campaigns.[68] Yet there was nothing "meticulous" about Patton's preparation for operations in Lorraine. In the fall of 1944 he was exuberant about his August successes where his tactical formula had worked to perfection. He would never cease in his attempt to impose the notions of the old cavalryman on the battlefield in Lorraine even when the circumstances demanded new methods.

NOTES

1. George S. Patton, *War as I Knew It* (Boston: Houghton Mifflin, 1947), 273.

2. Carlo D'Este, *Patton: A Genius for War* (New York: HarperCollins, 1995), 396.

3. Daniel J. Hughes, ed., *Moltke on the Art of War: Selected Writings* (Novato, Calif.: Presidio, 1993), 46.

4. Martin Blumenson, *Patton: The Man behind the Legend, 1885–1945* (New York: William Morrow, 1985), 59.

5. George S. Patton, "Armored Operations in Poland," lecture given to officers of the 2nd Armored Division, Fort Benning, Georgia, September 4, 1940, Box 62, Patton Papers (PP), Library of Congress (LC), Washington, D.C.

6. William J. Woolley, "Patton and the Concept of Mechanized Warfare," *Parameters: US Army War College Quarterly* XV, 3 (1985): 73.

7. Ibid., 73–74.

8. Martin Blumenson, *The Patton Papers* (Boston: Houghton Mifflin, 1974), II: 30–31.

9. D'Este, *Patton: A Genius for War*, 245.

10. Blumenson, *Patton: The Man behind the Legend*, 122.

11. Dwight D. Eisenhower, *At Ease: Stories I Tell to Friends* (Garden City, N.Y.: Doubleday, 1967), 173. D'Este noted that Patton "retreated into the conventional ideas of the time and sought a different approach that would educate his fellow officers in other aspects of leadership and soldiering. In so doing he forfeited an opportunity to become the father of the American armored force of World War II, a role that was taken over by other visionary officers." D'Este, *Patton: A Genius for War*, 299.

12. D'Este, *Patton: A Genius for War*, 245. Patton's concept of "mass" at this point was probably stimulated by his experience during the final tank action of the Saint-Mihiel offensive where he thought that a genuine breakthrough could have been accomplished if only he had sent in a larger tank force.

13. David G. Chandler, *The Military Maxims of Napoleon* (London: Greenhill, 1994), 240.

14. Roger H. Nye, *The Patton Mind: The Professional Development of an Extraordinary Leader* (Garden City, N.Y.: Avery Publishing, 1993), 161. Nye's work is based on a careful examination of several hundred of Patton's books that George S. Patton IV donated to the West Point Library. Nye noted that although others—such as Eisenhower, Bradley, MacArthur, Collins, Taylor, and Ridgway—all read extensively, little conscious thought was given to recording their ideas on what they read. Patton was the great exception because he "left behind the most complete record of exhaustive professional study of any World War II General—or any general in American history, for that matter."

15. Martin Blumenson, "America's World War II Leaders in Europe: Some Thoughts," *Parameters: US Army War College Quarterly* XIX, 4 (1989): 8–11.

16. D'Este, *Patton: A Genius for War*, 298.

17. Blumenson, "America's World War II Leaders in Europe," 9. Much debate continues over the value of Leavenworth and other army schools in preparing officers for command in World War II. Bradley, who finished first out of eighty students in the class of 1915, thought instruction methods were less than stellar, although he admitted that the courses were intellectually challenging. "Lightning Joe" Collins thought instruction to be first rate. Ernest N. Harmon, whom Patton thought extremely highly of, felt the courses "intensive and imaginative." Timothy K. Nenninger, "Leavenworth and Its Critics: The U.S. Army Command and General Staff School, 1920–1940," *The Journal of Military History* LVIII (April 1994): 204–205.

18. Steve E. Dietrich, "The Professional Reading of General George S. Patton, Jr.," *The Journal of Military History* LIII, 4 (1989): 390. Dietrich's article, like Nye's book, is based on Patton's annotated collection of books at West Point.

19. Nye, *The Patton Mind*, 129.

20. Major General Heinz Guderian, *Achtung Panzer: The Development of Armoured Forces, Their Tactics and Operational Potential* (London: Arms and Armour Press, 1993), 212.

21. George S. Patton, "Notes on the Co-operation between Tanks and the Other Arms especially Infantry," 1918, Box 48, PP, LC.

22. Item by General Dager about General George S. Patton, September 10, 1950, Holmes E. Dager Papers, United States Army Military History Institute (USAMHI), Carlisle Barracks, Pennsylvania.

23. Nye, *The Patton Mind*, 113.

24. Russell F. Weigley, *Eisenhower's Lieutenants: The Campaign of France and Germany 1944–1945* (Bloomington: Indiana University Press, 1981), 4.

25. Ibid., 4.

26. Ibid., 7.

27. Dietrich, "The Professional Reading of General George S. Patton, Jr.," 403. Patton would write of Clausewitz upon his first reading of *On War* in 1910 that he "is about as hard reading as any thing can well be and is as full of notes of equal abstruseness as a dog is of fleas."

28. Nye, *The Patton Mind*, 59.

29. Hughes, *Moltke on the Art of War*, 56. Moltke believed that a frontal attack in this manner had to be carried out with great energy so as to hold the attention of enemy forces while the flanking maneuver was being carried out. The best modern example of Patton's dictum occurred in the Gulf War. While the various Arab contingents, along with two U.S. Marine divisions and a brigade from the U.S. 2nd Armored Division launched a frontal attack against dug-in Iraqi forces in Kuwait, the U.S. VII Corps and the U.S. XVIII Airborne Corps flanked Iraqi positions and attacked Republican Guard reserves.

30. Blumenson, "America's World War II Leaders in Europe," 3. Blumenson noted that few of their operations could be considered brilliant, but those that were—namely the thrust to Palermo and Messina, the breakout across France, and the rescue of Bastogne—could "usually be traced to a single actor," meaning, of course, Patton.

31. B. H. Liddell Hart, *The Strategy of Indirect Approach* (London: Faber and Faber, 1941), 298.

32. Dietrich, "The Professional Reading of General George S. Patton, Jr.," 404.

33. Patton's annotated copy of Sun Tzu, Box 61, PP, LC. Upon completing his reading of Sun Tzu, Patton wrote at the end "A very good field service regulation."

34. Patton, "Armored Operations in Poland," 15.

35. Patton, *War as I Knew It*, 314.

36. Roger H. Nye, "Whence Patton's Military Genius?," *Parameters: US Army War College Quarterly* XXI, 4 (Winter 1991–1992): 73.

37. D'Este, *Patton: A Genius for War*, 394.

38. John North, ed., *The Alexander Memoirs, 1940–1945* (London: Cassell, 1962), 44.

39. Oscar W. Koch, *G-2: Intelligence for Patton* (Philadelphia: Whitmore, 1971), 158.

40. Robert U. Johnson and C. C. Buel, eds., *Battles and Leaders of the Civil War* (Secaucus, New Jersey, no date), II: 297.

41. Dietrich, "The Professional Reading of General George S. Patton," 398.

42. Ibid.

43. Nye, *The Patton Mind*, 30.

44. B. L. Montgomery, *The Memoirs of Field Marshal the Viscount Montgomery of Alamein* (London: Collins, 1958), 86. Montgomery wrote, "It is clear

that my whole working creed was based on the fact that in war it is 'the man' that matters."

45. Nye, *The Patton Mind*, 71.

46. Martin Blumenson, *Breakout and Pursuit,* U.S. Army in World War II: European Theater of Operations (Washington, D.C.: Department of the Army, 1961), 349.

47. Ladislas Farago, *Patton: Ordeal and Triumph* (New York: Ivan Obolensky, 1963), 461.

48. Omar N. Bradley and Clay Blair, *A General's Life* (New York: Simon and Schuster, 1983), 100.

49. Bradley's Commentary on World War II, as recorded by Chester Hanson, Omar Bradley Papers, 16–b s-o, USAMHI.

50. Omar N. Bradley, *A Soldier's Story* (New York: Henry Holt and Company, 1951), 358.

51. Nye, *The Patton Mind*, 91.

52. Patton, *War as I Knew It*, 273.

53. Blumenson, *The Patton Papers*, II: 433, 436.

54. Patton, *War as I Knew It*, 90.

55. Ibid., 310.

56. Ibid.

57. Blumenson, *The Patton Papers*, II: 203.

58. B. H. Liddell Hart, ed., *The Rommel Papers* (London: Collins, 1953), 201.

59. Frank J. Price, *Troy H. Middleton: A Biography* (Baton Rouge: Louisiana State University Press, 1974), 186.

60. Patton, *War as I Knew It*, 295.

61. Ibid., 76.

62. Liddell Hart, *The Rommel Papers*, 201.

63. Nye, *The Patton Mind*, 18.

64. Patton, *War as I Knew It*, 296.

65. Nye, *The Patton Mind*, 90. When von Seeckt wrote that the general had to "leave the wearisome daily routine to the Chief of Staff in order to keep his own mind fresh and free for the great decisions," Patton wrote "Bull." This attitude changed dramatically by World War II.

66. Patton, *War as I Knew It*, 295.

67. Nye, *The Patton Mind*, 162.

68. Ibid., 54–55.

Chapter 2

From Theory to Practice

IN CASE OF DOUBT, ATTACK!; we can conquer only by attacking; continued ruthless pressure by day and by night is vital.
—Patton to Seventh Army, June 1943[1]

Patton's first opportunity to test his theories on mechanized warfare came during the large-scale army maneuvers of 1941 in Tennessee, Texas, Louisiana, and Carolina. The maneuvers were the ultimate testing ground, other than actual battle, for American officers seeking high command before the United States entered the war. Though many failed miserably, Patton succeeded brilliantly and proved that his interwar years of study had paid dividends. He had thoroughly mastered mechanized warfare.

Prior to the start of the exercises, Patton attempted to intervene in the selection of umpires to guarantee that he would not be penalized for his armored tactics because he had already settled on what he considered the proper employment of tanks. "[T]he primary function of an Armored Force," he wrote, "is to disrupt [enemy] command, communications, and supply."[2] Moreover, he believed that tanks "should be used as quail-shooting weapons and not as buffaloes," an analogy Blumenson has interpreted as meaning "mobility and firepower were more important than shock action," which Patton compared to a buffalo stampede.[3] He had actually toyed with the idea of an armored corps, consisting of two or three armored divisions and possibly one mechanized division in late 1940. He even visualized a "situation in which several armored corps would be organized into an armored army."[4] But he never pursued the idea in Normandy, no doubt because of the fact that there were not enough armored divisions on the continent to allow more than one per corps.

Massed armored formations would have restricted his operational freedom and made it more difficult to maneuver such a concentration to avoid pitched battles. He announced prior to the maneuvers that "so far as tactics are concerned, it is the doctrine of this division [2nd Armored] to attack weakness rather than strength."[5] He wanted the division to focus its effort on attacking the enemy's rear. Patton considered it the "greatest compliment" when he was reprimanded for not launching his armor in mass (buffalo stampede) during the maneuvers. His belief that the use of tanks in mass was "futile" and perhaps even "suicidal" differed fundamentally from Guderian's concept of *"Nicht kleckern, sondern klotzen"* ("Not a drizzle, but a downpour"), meaning tanks, their mobility, and firepower had to remain concentrated.[6] Guderian thought that armor would be needed *en masse* to break long fortified zones characteristic of World War I. Patton wanted to avoid fortified zones.

In the rugged, hilly terrain of Tennessee in June, Patton showed great adeptness in maneuvering his 2nd Armored Division into position in the dark and succeeded in routing his opponents. During the initial stages, he quickly bewildered the 5th Infantry Division by cutting in behind it and captured its command post. In the last phase of the exercise, Patton cut the enemy's lines of communication and captured the principal defended city. Although the umpires tried to slow him down, his tactics were so successful that the exercise was called off after only twelve hours.[7]

Patton's exploits in Tennessee had been impressive but it was in phase II of the Louisiana exercises that he truly displayed his talent for covering ground (see Map 2.1). As part of the Blue Third Army, Patton's mission was to attack Shreveport, Louisiana, defended by the Red Second Army, from the west. To effect such an attack, Patton crossed the border into Texas at Orange and, after reaching Beaumont, proceeded to relentlessly drive his division northward through Woodville and Nacogdoches until he arrived at Henderson. This drive, accomplished in twenty-four hours, brought Patton some two hundred miles from the initial crossing at Orange. True to his belief in the futility of assaulting prepared positions, he then avoided a frontal attack upon Red forces guarding Greenwood and chose to carry his flanking movement even further north around Caddo Lake to come in behind the Shreveport defenses. He then proceeded to attack the northern Red defenses on the outskirts of the city and in combination with other Blue offensives, succeeded in having the exercise called off twenty-four hours ahead of schedule.

Patton's bold actions brought severe criticism from General Leslie J. McNair, Chief of Staff of the General Headquarters, who declared that

Map 2.1
Patton's 2nd Armored Division, Louisiana: Phase II

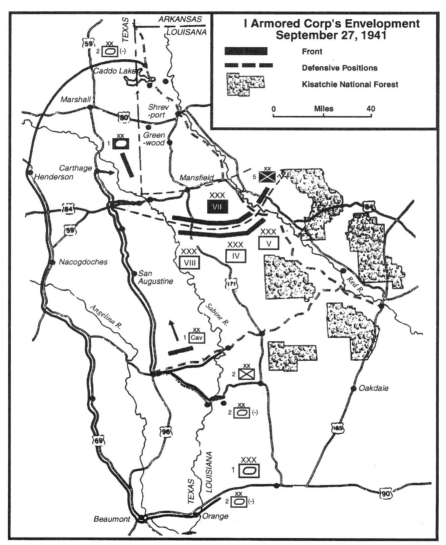

Source: Base map taken from Christopher R. Gabel, *The U.S. Army GHQ Maneuvers of 1941* (Washington, D.C.: Office of the Chief of Military History, 1991), 104. Altered by Bill Traer.

Patton's methods were "no way to fight a war." Specifically, McNair believed that his tactics occupied ground but did not destroy enemy forces on
an appropriate scale. He had wasted his strength on "too many piece-meal
attacks" spread out much too far over the combat area.[8] One historian con-
cedes this point, noting that despite his marvelous dash through Texas "Patton's force, virtually isolated from the rest of the Third Army at the end of a
300–mile supply line, held at best a tenuous position on Shreveport's outskirts."[9] The commander of I Armored Corps in which Patton served, Major General Charles L. Scott, saw great potential in such tactics, however.
He advised Patton and General Bruce Magruder, commander of the 1st Armored Division, that "the attack and destruction of forward elements are
merely incidental" and that the armor had to "advance rapidly to critical lo-
cations in rear of the hostile front lines."[10]

McNair could not see that Patton desired semi-independent actions over
the battlefield. In 1929 Patton prepared written reports on the 1st Cavalry
Division maneuvers at Fort Bliss, Texas. Dealing with the command and
control of mobile and dispersed units, he wrote, "So far as I can see control
and mobility are inimical. We should admit this and . . . let the two principal
elements work independently."[11] In responding to criticism received during the Tennessee maneuvers, Patton noted that coordination was a "fine
old military word" best used to describe the operations of Alexander or Napoleon but "it was not quite the same for armored divisions." He compared
coordinating armored forces to throwing hand grenades in that "you can
only give them initial impetus and direction. You cannot control (coordinate) these missil[e]s during flight."[12] He did note, however, that during the
maneuvers, the divisional elements always managed nonetheless to arrive
where they were supposed to and on time.[13] Scott had nothing but praise for
Patton's coordination of his far-flung units, observing that "when the enemy was pressing from all sides, when our own and the enemy's tactical
dispositions were obscure, and when exacting and intricate night movements were ordered, I could always count on you and all the elements of
your command being in the right place at the right time to meet effectively
any hostile opposition."[14]

Patton came away from the 1941 maneuvers having convinced many
people that he represented the epitome of the aggressiveness of the United
States Army. Scott labeled him "energetic and capable" and a commander
who was "quick in his decisions and vigorous in their execution."[15]
Weigley, however, put Patton's operational method, as developed by the
end of the 1941 maneuvers, in perspective. "Patton's was an aggressiveness
of speed and mobility," notes Weigley, "not of the application of over-

whelming power to crush the enemy. The most aggressive senior American commander remained a soldier of saber and spurs."[16]

Patton's aggressiveness on the battlefield has been well recognized, but one of the chief criticisms directed towards his generalship over the years is that he achieved his success in World War II against "questionable" opposition. In much the same fashion that Alexander the Great's military triumphs have been tarnished by historians pointing to the inherently rotten structure of the Persian empire, so too have Patton's victories been subjected to the same standard. He either fought weakened elements of the Wehrmacht or hopelessly outclassed Italians. There is good evidence to support this claim, but it must be measured against his philosophical attitudes about avoiding enemy strength. Moreover, virtually none of his experience in North Africa, Sicily, and Normandy had offered him any sustained opportunity to flesh out his thoughts on slugging matches characteristic of set-piece battles. It is accurate to describe his operations up to Lorraine as quick and decisive.

Although Patton was the most seasoned American commander in Europe by the time he entered Lorraine at the beginning of September 1944, his first test in battle, the November 1942 invasion of French North Africa, ended too quickly to be considered anything but a skirmish. Despite sustaining 530 killed, 650 wounded, and over 100 missing, his fight for Morocco was hardly a pitched battle. As D'Este notes, "Torch was unlike any other battle Patton would ever fight. It was not a 'hold them by the nose and kick 'em in the ass' type of battle, but rather an unconventional fight against 'friends.' "[17] After a short defense, French forces surrendered within four days.

His first period of sustained combat came during the fighting in Tunisia during early March and April 1943. Eisenhower had great confidence in Patton's fighting ability and leadership. When Lieutenant General Lloyd R. Fredendall faltered in command of the U.S. II Corps, Patton was brought in to reestablish morale and combat effectiveness in preparation for supporting Montgomery's Eighth Army as it attempted to drive Rommel out of the Mareth Line. Patton found II Corps badly shaken after the disaster at Kasserine Pass where in eight days, Rommel inflicted some 6,700 casualties and destroyed two hundred tanks.[18]

Patton had little opportunity to display his battlefield abilities in this support role because General Harold K. Alexander, commander of the Eighteenth Army Group to which II Corps was assigned, kept him on a short leash.[19] Alexander even commented to Montgomery that Patton, although a "good man," was "not a highly trained commander."[20] If Alexander had certain misgivings about Patton, he had serious reservations about the fighting quality of American troops after Kasserine. As a result, the objectives assigned the Corps were intended as confidence builders. The March 18th occupation of Gafsa by the 1st Infantry Division, accomplished with minimal fighting, is characterized in the official history as being "an encouraging exercise rather than a hard battle."[21] Despite the lack of confidence from his British superiors, Patton succeeded brilliantly in infusing II Corps with a new fighting spirit as evidenced by the performance of the 1st Infantry Division against the veteran 10th Panzer Division and an Italian infantry division near El Guettar on March 23. The American infantry firmly held their ground against the crack German armored unit even though the psychological disaster at Kasserine lay less then a month in the past.[22]

Patton's toughest moments in Tunisia came when he attempted to break through the Eastern Dorsal to Gabes in order to sever the link between the Afrika Korps and the Fifth Panzer Army. It represented the first real chance of the war for him to maneuver his armor on a large scale. In fact, the role he envisioned for the Corps was much more ambitious than that outlined by Alexander.[23] In Tunisia, Patton first displayed his intent to break the rules to achieve success. His grand plans were frustrated, however, by the failure of Major General Orlando Ward's 1st Armored Division to break through the German defenses at Maknassy. The incident is illustrative of Patton's battle philosophy. General Jurgen von Arnim sent the 10th Panzer Division in against II Corps to protect his rear on March 22 and encountered Ward's 1st Armored at the Maknassy Pass. Instead of exhibiting Patton's ruthless desire to speed forward and forestall enemy action, Ward regrouped the division for an attack the following day.[24] The battle quickly became an old-fashioned breakthrough operation.

Patton ultimately relieved Ward for lack of aggressiveness, and D'Este correctly identified the reason. "The 1st Armored Division," he noted, "had been von Arnim's prime victims at Sidi-Bou-Zid, and Rommel's at Kasserine Pass, and Patton rightly considered its leadership too timid and in need of a solid jolt to restore both morale and confidence."[25] The operation also gives some indication of how Patton proposed to handle set-piece attacks. The battle at Maknassy Pass was Patton's first sustained attempt to deal with a prepared position that could not be flanked. Before Ward was relieved Patton ordered him to lead an attack in person even if he sustained losses of 25 percent. He commented, "I feel quite brutal in issuing orders to take such losses," but believed that "wars can only be won by killing."[26] This was not the "Blood and Guts" Patton as so often portrayed by his detractors. His concepts of speed and surprise had failed. All that was left to do was slug it out.[27] Though Patton commanded II Corps only for the space of some forty days, he had learned a few things. After the campaign in Tunisia, he wrote Senator Henry Cabot Lodge that he had had several changes of heart. "I believe in heavy field artillery," he said, "and I am strong for telephone wires instead of radio."[28] As Nye observed, "Heavy artillery and wire were barely the tools of the attacking cavalryman, but they were essential to sustained attack in heavily defended positions."[29]

It is also possible that Patton was influenced in some small way by Montgomery. Patton had access to a small pamphlet entitled "Tactical and Training Notes," dated March 1943, and it is obvious from the content that it was a reproduction of Montgomery's Address to the Middle East Staff College in Haifa during September 1942. Patton had met Montgomery in Tripoli in mid-February 1943 before he took command of II Corps. In attending Montgomery's "Tactical Talks" he had an opportunity to listen to the views of the man he described as "the best soldier—or so it seems—I have met in this war."[30]

Monty, in analyzing the Battle of Egypt, stated that the only solution to the problem of attacking a strong position with no open flank was "to attack frontally and 'break-in.' " He characterized the type of fighting required as a "dog-fight."[31] Perhaps Montgomery's views on the subject of tackling fortified positions influenced Patton or reinforced his own views on the necessity of aggressive frontal assaults when options were scarce. He certainly agreed with the importance Montgomery placed on centrally controlled artillery against strong points. When it came to maneuver warfare, however, he and Montgomery were worlds apart. In "Tactical and Training Notes," Montgomery wrote that the first step towards achieving battlefield success is to have armor secure ground that dominates the battle area. "This ground," he observed, "is required as a firm base from which to operate offensively and upon which subsequently to reorganize." Most importantly, the ground has to be "so important to the enemy that he will be forced to attack our armor on it, i.e. on ground of our own chosing."[32] Patton, however, never saw armored warfare in stages or armor as a defensive weapon. Armor would be wasted if it was not continually pushed forward.

In Sicily, during July and August 1943, Patton maneuvered the U.S. Seventh Army along the principles he had worked out before the war. He possessed much wider operational control than he had exercised in Tunisia and, like Montgomery, frequently ignored Alexander's directives. Patton received a far rougher reception on the initial beachhead at Gela than he had on the beaches in Morocco, but it was not unexpected. He had purposely replaced the inexperienced 36th Infantry Division with the veteran 1st Infantry Division in anticipation of the kind of resistance offered by the vaunted Hermann Goering Panzer Division.

Although the official history applauded Patton for a "masterful job" in creating a battleworthy field army, it also recognized the fact that his great armored dash to Palermo, in the northwestern corner of the island, was a "relatively empty" objective.[33] His swift operations in the western part of the island were hardly comparable to the "dog-fights" Montgomery's troops were forced to endure on the Plain of Catania in the east. Seventh Army's toughest fighting occurred during the drive along the north coast to Messina, the only strategic spot of any value on the island. II Corps, commanded by Lieutenant General Omar Bradley since the latter stages of the Tunisian Campaign, managed to capture the well-fortified walled city of Enna in five hours. When the 45th Infantry Division ran into the 29th Panzer Grenadier Division, however, the advance bogged down. For a solid week the 45th fought some of the bitterest American engagements of the campaign. As in Lorraine the adverse terrain made it difficult to maneuver. The Germans took maximum advantage of this factor and in combination with a skillful use of artillery, mortar and tank fire, and occasional counterattacks, succeeded in breaking Patton's momentum.[34] Patton's only other real fight developed between the 1st Infantry Division and the 15th Panzer Grenadier Division defending the town of Troina. Poor intelligence had suggested that the town could easily be taken, but as D'Este notes, it took "six days of savage combat against a desperate and skilful enemy who had launched twenty-four counterattacks against 1st Division units."[35] Patton hardly enjoyed being on the defensive.

His response to the German delaying actions was typical, but novel, for he employed amphibious "end runs" to flank his opponents. Though D'Este suggests that these operations might have been conducted on a larger scale, Patton's motivation was sound. In bypassing the dug-in German defenders, he hoped to maintain momentum. Ultimately, it is questionable whether a week here and six days there of tough fighting in the hills of Tunisia and Sicily was enough time for Patton to fully assimilate any lessons for future set-piece battles. He did, however, manage to impress Montgomery with his ability to handle armor in "terrain wholly unsuitable for tank warfare" in Sicily.[36] Even greater accomplishments with armor came a year later.

When Patton activated Third Army in Normandy on August 1, 1944, he was perfectly situated to execute mobile operations. Bradley's First Army had done the hard fighting to breach the German defenses during Operation "Cobra," and when Patton began pressing the exposed German left flank, it readily gave way despite a desperate but futile counterattack at Mortain on the 8th. Subsequently, the static fighting of June and July shifted to fast, maneuver warfare, the kind of opportunity Eisenhower always envisaged Patton exploiting. As Blumenson noted, this situation was "exactly suited to his unique talent of driving forward with outright abandon, with seeming recklessness, to far-off targets."[37]

The speed of Patton's advance, some four hundred miles by August 26, was based on his prime directive to his subordinates, "Don't stop." He wrote to his old friend Kenyon Joyce in early August that his advance thus far was a "typical cavalry action in which, to quote the words of the old story, 'The soldier went out and charged in all directions at the same time.' "[38] Yet Third Army's rapid advance was due in large measure to the conscious avoidance of fighting.[39] Third Army did inflict a large number of casualties on the Germans during August, but in proportion to the extent of ground covered they were not significant.[40] Cleaning out isolated pockets was not what Patton had in mind. He knew that the bigger prize, the potential entrapment of the entire German Seventh Army, was possible through maneuver.

Patton's ability to cover ground was an exceptional trait. Well-known Civil War historian Bruce Catton once made the simple comment that Sherman thought geographically and Grant thought in terms of the enemy army.[41] Perhaps the best way to describe Patton's operational method is in terms of geography. Yet even though this is undoubtedly true, it is equally true that Patton's armored exploits prior to Lorraine were a function not only of his philosophy of avoiding strong points but also of the limited resistance he frequently faced. Bradley pointed out the downside of such swift operations. "Patton's great and dramatic gains, beginning in Sicily and continuing through Brittany and on across the Seine," he observed, "had been made against little or no opposition. Until now Patton had not really had a serious fight on his hands, and I was certain that sooner or later Patton was going to have one. I was not sure how good a tactician he would be in a tough fight. None of his divisions had ever been put to the real test."[42] Without any substantial experience fighting sustained setpiece battles, Patton entered Lorraine dependent on his tried and proven formula of speed, mobility, and continuous movement. His great successes in Sicily and Normandy had reinforced his views on maneuver warfare. Success does not usually lead to revisions in thinking.

NOTES

1. Roger H. Nye, *The Patton Mind: The Professional Development of an Extraordinary Leader* (Garden City, N.Y.: Avery Publishing, 1993), 136.

2. Martin Blumenson, *The Patton Papers* (Boston: Houghton Mifflin, 1974), II: 29.

3. Ibid., 32.

4. George S. Patton, Letter to Lieutenant Colonel Earl F. Cress, December 2, 1940, Box 62, Patton Papers (PP), Library of Congress (LC).

5. Blumenson, *Patton Papers*, II: 33, 39.

6. Major General F. W. von Mellenthin, *German Generals of World War II: As I Saw Them* (Norman: Oklahoma University Press, 1977), 89.

7. Christopher R. Gabel, *The U.S. Army GHQ Maneuvers of 1941* (Washington, D.C.: Office of the Chief of Military History, 1991), 52.

8. Ibid., 108. The presence of large numbers of anti-tank weapons helped Patton make his decision.

9. Ibid., 110. Patton had sustained his columns by refueling at commercial stations along the route.

10. Ibid., 122.

11. Nye, *The Patton Mind*, 86. In responding to observations that there was little control of units during the exercise, Patton wrote that "in war we shall have much less control than at maneuvers. The sooner we accommodate ourselves to this fact and arrange our methods of war so that they will function despite lack of information, the better we'll be off."

12. Blumenson, *Patton Papers*, II: 37.

13. Ibid. In the various maneuvers, Patton continually broke rules to effect desired results. McNair had even told the umpires that Patton was not to be allowed to run all over the battlefield, which is exactly what he did. He was especially criticized for leaving his command post and prowling the front lines and, for all things, running "roughshod" over his opponents. Omar N. Bradley and Clay Blair, *A General's Life* (New York: Simon and Schuster, 1983), 99.

14. Blumenson, *Patton Papers*, II: 44–45.

15. Ibid., 36.

16. Russell F. Weigley, *Eisenhower's Lieutenants: The Campaign of France and Germany 1944–1945* (Bloomington: Indiana University Press, 1981), 245.

17. Carlo D'Este, *Patton: A Genius for War* (New York: HarperCollins, 1995), 435.

18. Martin Blumenson, *Patton: The Man behind the Legend, 1885–1945* (New York: William Morrow, 1985), 181.

19. Bradley, *A General's Life*, 151. Patton also had the 5th Armored Field Artillery Group, seven battalions of tank destroyers, a British reconnaissance squadron, and air cover from the XII Air Support Command.

20. Stephen Brooks, ed., *Montgomery and the Eighth Army* (London: Army Records Society, The Bodley Head, 1991), 188. Alexander to Montgomery, March 29, 1943.

21. George F. Howe, *Northwest Africa: Seizing the Initiative in the West*, U.S. Army in World War II: European Theater of Operations (Washington, D.C.: Department of the Army, 1957), 560–562.

22. Ibid., 548. Patton noted that "The 1st Infantry Division in repulsing this strong German attack from positions which had been prepared in a relatively short time demonstrated clearly the ability of Infantry, properly supported, to withstand armored attacks supported by air, provided the defending unit has the will to stay and fight." II Corps After Action Report (AAR), April 10, 1943, PP, LC, 5.

23. D'Este, *Patton: A Genius for War*, 472.

24. Ibid., 474.

25. Ibid., 476.

26. Ibid.

27. Blumenson, *Patton Papers*, II: 230.

28. Nye, *The Patton Mind*, 138.

29. Blumenson, *Patton Papers*, II: 171.

30. Brooks, *Montgomery and the Eighth Army*, 137.

31. "Tactical and Training Notes," March 1943, Box 62, PP, LC, 6.

32. Ibid., 9.

33. Albert N. Garland and Howard McGraw Smyth, *Sicily and the Surrender of Italy*, U.S. Army in World War II: European Theater of Operations (Washington, D.C.: Office of the Chief of Military History, 1965), 426. Bradley did not think much of the decision to capture Palermo. Even though the port was required to supply Seventh Army (a debatable point according to Lucian Truscott), Bradley noted that "except for that single port there was little to be gained in the west. Certainly there was no glory in the capture of hills, docile peasants and spiritless soldiers." Omar N. Bradley, *A Soldier's Story* (New York: Henry Holt and Company, 1951), 140.

34. Carlo D'Este, *Bitter Victory: The Battle for Sicily, 1943* (New York: HarperCollins, 1988), 452. D'Este described the fighting at this point as a "bloody business" where the German tactics continually "forced the Americans into costly and time-consuming battles."

35. Ibid., 468.

36. Ibid., 558.

37. Blumenson, *Patton: The Man behind the Legend*, 229.

38. Blumenson, *Patton Papers*, II: 502.

39. Weigley, *Eisenhower's Lieutenants*, 244.

40. Ibid.

41. Bruce Catton, *The Centennial History of the Civil War*, Vol. III, *Never Call Retreat* (Garden City, N.Y.: Doubleday, 1965), 317.

42. Bradley, *A General's Life*, 317.

Chapter 3

Orders of Battle

Here the First German Army was being rebuilt to a strength of eight divisions and, while Patton's six divisions were halted on the Meuse . . .
these fresh forces had established themselves on the Moselle. . . . This
was the only sector of the entire Western Front where von Rundstedt's
troops could meet the Allies on more or less equal terms.
                                   —Chester Wilmot, *The Struggle for Europe*[1]

The condition of the German Army in late August 1944 was the worst it had
been since the war began. The months of June, July, and August had been
particularly bad, very nearly witnessing the complete collapse of Germany's Western and Eastern fronts. During these three grim months the
German Field Army suffered 916,860 dead, wounded, and missing in Russia. In the West, where fewer divisions were engaged, the casualty numbers
since D-Day ran to 293,802, and the total losses swelled to over a half mil-
lion when the 230,320 officers and men surrounded in the various coastal
fortresses were added.[2]

For a time in Normandy, it looked as though the army might actually turn
the campaign into a stalemate, but after Operation "Cobra" in late July, the
tide turned and the German Seventh Army was virtually destroyed in the attempt to escape the Falaise Pocket. By late 1944 only 10 percent of the
Wehrmacht was mechanized, and the crushing defeat in Normandy and the
Falaise Pocket had "destroyed what was left of the German mechanized
army after its mauling on the eastern front."[3] The Seventh and Fifteenth Armies had fought in Normandy with only 14,500 trucks and 67,000 horses
because of severe shortages of fuel and tires. By September, Germany was
down to a mere 150,000 tons of oil, less than half the monthly total needed
to keep the army in the field.[4] During the Normandy campaign, half the

horses and most of the trucks were lost along with 2,200 out of 2,300 tanks.[5]
During 1944, German industry produced only 88,000 trucks, but the field
army lost over 100,000 trucks between January and August. By comparison, in the same year, the United States produced 600,000 army trucks.[6]
The German army fighting in Lorraine, and on all other fronts, depended to
an exceptionally high degree on horse-drawn transport.

Despite the massive losses, the best available calculations place the
strength of the German army in the West at the beginning of September at
close to fifty divisions with a cumulative strength of over 700,000.[7] But it
was an army in retreat, without cohesion and firm leadership. Field Marshal
Gerd von Rundstedt had presided over the defense of Normandy as
Commander-in-Chief, West until Hitler relieved him in early July for his
failure to stem the Allied advance. By early September Field Marshal Walter Model was acting as both Commander-in-Chief, West and the commander of Army Group B. When he reported that he could not do both jobs
simultaneously, Hitler reinstated Rundstedt to resurrect a badly shaken
command structure and a front on the verge of complete collapse.[8]

Rundstedt's title of Commander-in-Chief hardly bore the weight it im-
plies, and it is apparent that the appointment was meant as a stabilizing factor in the army. As one historian has noted, Hitler "certainly did not propose
literally to entrust Rundstedt with the Western Front."[9] Indeed, Hitler had
long since assumed virtual command of all operations from his field mar-
shals. Rundstedt's comment about Hitler's constant interference during the
Normandy battle is instructive. He wrote sarcastically that "my sole pre-
rogative was to change the guard in front of my gate."[10]

By the time of the Lorraine campaign, Hitler's control had filtered down
to the smallest operational detail, and the result was predictable. John Strawson stated that by insisting that he retain control of low-level tactical operations, Hitler "made it certain that he had neither the facts on which to make a
sound decision nor the time to make any decision quickly enough for it to be
effective."[11] Rarely in Lorraine, or anywhere else, would a German general
have the freedom to assess and act upon battlefield possibilities as he saw
them. Hitler was particularly protective about armored reserves and retained an iron hold on their commitment and withdrawal. His interference
in operations cannot be ignored because the effect was debilitating.

Although Rundstedt's reappointment was window dressing, Hitler did
institute important measures in late August to address the growing crisis in
the West. Many authors point to his September 2 instructions for the creation of an operational reserve of twenty-five divisions ready for deployment
between October and December as the beginning of his quest to regain the

initiative in the West. Most of the new divisions being formed were Volks-grenadier (People's Grenadier) divisions, smaller in size than a traditional infantry division. This reflected the tendency since 1943 of reducing man-power and increasing firepower in German divisions.[12]

A Volksgrenadier division had a standing strength of ten thousand men organized into three regiments, but each regiment contained only two battalions. The additional battalion in each regiment was replaced with a gun company and an antitank company. Each division had an artillery regi-ment made up of one battalion of 75-mm, one battalion of 150-mm, and two battalions of 105mm guns.[13] This distribution represented a more than 30 percent reduction in artillery assets over previous German infantry divisions. Other problems with this type of division were reduced reconnaissance capabilities and a serious lack of training time prior to actual deployment.[14] These divisions represented the last reserves of German manpower and were formed from replacement units, shattered divisions, and other low-quality personnel.[15]

Hitler also attempted to replace the weapons of the army, most of which were destroyed in Normandy. He gave the West priority on all new artillery and assault guns, a move followed by a transfer of artillery units in the Bal-kans back to France.[16] German artillery, though certainly not poor, still util-ized guns that had been in service for several years prior to World War II, and piece for piece, was inferior to American artillery. The standard divi-sional piece was the 105-mm le FH 18, which had a maximum range of only 11,675 yards. Various modifications after the outset of the war extended the range to 13,479 yards.[17] To match the American 155-mm M1 Howitzer, the Germans possessed the 150-mm sFH 18, capable of reaching 14,490 yards, but almost 2,000 yards less than the M1. An attempt was made to improve this model by introduction of the 150-mm sFH 36, but the scarcity of light alloy forced production to cease in 1942.[18] In terms of heavy artillery, the Germans experimented with all sorts of calibers but found that the 170-mm K 18 was the best heavy piece because its range of 32,371 yards made it a formidable weapon.[19]

Probably the most effective piece of artillery possessed by the Germans was the 8.8-cm Flak gun better known as the "88." Neither the British nor American armies had a weapon comparable to the German 8.8-cm gun for physical and moral effect.[20] The legendary "88," originally a high-velocity antiaircraft gun, had been employed since early in the war in a direct fire role against ground targets. With a maximum range of 16,202 yards, it was highly effective when utilized in an antitank screen.[21] With their penetrating power, the 88s were potent weapons against Allied tanks and could also fire devastating shell bursts against infantry.[22]

German field artillery in Lorraine was also augmented by the numerous batteries still functioning within the defensive system of the fortified city of Metz on the Moselle River. The calibers ranged from light to heavy, and despite chronic ammunition shortages, these guns were capable of giving effective fire over a vital area of the river south of Metz. Despite the limitations of German artillery in Lorraine (including the fact that much of it was horse-drawn), it was still capable of providing reasonable support for assaults. It, like American artillery, also performed well in beating off attacks. Though possessing nowhere near the number of guns or destructive effect of its opponent, German artillery played an important part in the overall defense of Lorraine.

To address the devastating armored losses in Normandy, Hitler also gave the Western Front priority on tank production, and by September 1, ten new panzer brigades built around a battalion of Mark IVs and a battalion of Mark V Panthers were either forming or going into action. Several of these brigades were destined for Lorraine. Based on the Normandy losses, Hitler decreed a one-for-one ratio in the production of the Mark IVs and Vs in hopes of redressing the armored imbalance posed by the number of Shermans the Allies could put on the battlefield.[23]

By 1944 the German Panzer force had three types of main battle tanks: the PzKw IV, the Mark V Panther, and the Mark VI Tiger. The PzKw IV, an excellent overall design, had gone into service before the war and was utilized until the war's end as the mainstay of the German army. Its quality was evident in the fact that it was successfully upgunned throughout the war without radical redesign.[24] Armor for the PzKw IV was also continually upgraded, usually with fitted plates until a universal thickness was incorporated into production. The front and sides of the last version of the tank to go into production, the *Ausfuhung J*, had a maximum thickness of 80-mm and 30-mm respectively. At twenty-five tons this tank could travel at forty kilometers per hour (kph) with a 210-mile radius of action.[25] Despite some minor problems from additional weight on the same chassis, the PzKw IV was mechanically reliable and slightly superior to the American M4 Sherman medium tank. The only striking difference between the two was that the former had a 75-mm high-velocity KwK 40 L/48 gun, whereas the latter mounted a 75-mm low-velocity gun. The higher-velocity gun allowed for greater penetration of armor plate at greater distances. At 1,000 yards, the Mark IV could penetrate 99 mm of armor, but the Sherman at 1,000 yards could penetrate only 60 mm.[26]

After the PzKw IV experienced difficulty in coping with the heavier and more-powerful Russian tanks first encountered in 1941, Hitler demanded heavy, technically complex machines as a countermeasure. The result was the introduction of the Panther and Tiger designs. Of the two, the Panther proved to be the more mechanically reliable. The Mark V Panther, classified as a medium tank, was developed to counter Russia's sturdy T-34. After a horrendous performance at the battle of Kursk in July 1943, where its teething troubles were clearly evident, the Panther became perhaps the best tank of the war. Most of the Panthers that fought in Lorraine were right off the assembly lines and hence were the upgraded and final active version of the tank, the *Ausfuhung G*.

At 45 tons, this design mounted a 75-mm KwK 42 (long-barreled) high-velocity gun. At 1,350 yards the Panther's gun could penetrate 99 mm of armor at a sixty degree angle and an incredible 145 mm at a ninety degree angle.[27] Its own enhanced armor package of 100 mm on the front made it virtually invulnerable to fire from that direction. Side armor went as high as 50 mm.[28] Completely outgunned, American tanks consistently went for side shots on the Panther. One of the chief drawbacks of the Mark V was the lack of an electric turret like that found in the Shermans. A hydraulic (pedal operated) system and a handwheeled turret ensured that the Panther could not traverse its gun as quickly as its opponent.[29] Moreover, although it was capable of speeds of up to 55 kph, there were several instances in Lorraine where Shermans, with their inferior speed of 40 kph, raced around the Panthers. The principal strength of the Panther in Lorraine was that, like in Normandy, it was a formidable weapon when concealed to fire across open areas. When it was committed to a fast moving battle, its weakness in mechanical reliability and mobility vis-à-vis comparable American armor was apparent. The Tiger design was even more powerful in the defensive role because of its superior gun, but it appears that few if any fought in Lorraine.[30] The design had two basic variants, the Tiger E and the Tiger IIB (King Tiger, Royal Tiger), both formidable machines at 68.7 tons with an 88-mm high-velocity gun. But the production run of the former ended in August 1944. Of the latter only 484 were built by the war's end.[31]

It may prove impossible to argue with the conclusion that the Allies won the war because they overwhelmed the Wehrmacht with sheer numbers and volume of matériel, but in Lorraine the odds were somewhat more even. The terrain restricted mass deployment of armored formations, and weather conditions interfered significantly with American air power. German troops were not continually annihilated *en masse* from the air like they had been in Normandy. By late 1944 the German soldier had become accustomed to (if not used to) fighting without a friendly aircraft in sight and diminishing quantities of tanks, armored fighting vehicles, and artillery. One historian has argued that the growing German deficiencies in these areas were the result of progressive "demodernization" of the heart of the armed forces. What permitted the German Army to remain an effective fighting force despite being outnumbered in all forms of weaponry by a huge margin was the gradual switch from offensive to defensive firepower as a result of the defeats in Russia.[32]

At the beginning of September, although planting the seeds for a future counteroffensive, Hitler's immediate concern was defense. He ordered the retreating German armies to hold in front of the frontier defensive system known as the West Wall at all costs until that line could be properly prepared. It had fallen into disrepair after the fall of France. Hitler's holding line ran from the Dutch coast, through northern Belgium, and along the western border of Lorraine. To gain room for operational maneuver, he ordered Rundstedt to take the offensive against Patton's right flank near Nancy and Neufchateau, an operation Rundstedt saw little hope or value in. On September 7, reflecting much of Model's warnings a few days earlier, he reported that the Allies had fifty-four divisions, all "thoroughly mechanized and motorized," on the continent. He described his own forces as "burned out" and requested a further ten infantry and "several" panzer divisions,[33] a request that fell on deaf ears. He did, however, agree with Hitler on where the principal threat to the West Wall lay.

According to Cornelius Ryan, Rundstedt considered Patton a "far more dangerous opponent" than the "overly cautious, habit-ridden and systematic" Montgomery.[34] Based on this assessment of his opposition, he knew that the greatest threat to his weak line in the West in early September was Third Army's hard charge toward the Saar industrial region. He therefore committed his best troops against Patton.[35] The principal force Rundstedt possessed to hold Patton in front of the West Wall was First Army, commanded by General der Panzertruppen Otto von Knobelsdorff. First Army was the southernmost element in Army Group B at the beginning of September and held a front extending from Sedan, north of Luxembourg, to slightly south of Nancy.

During the last days of August, First Army retreated across the Meuse River with only nine battalions of infantry, ten tanks, two batteries of field guns, three flak batteries, and ten 75-mm antitank guns.[36] Complete annihilation was avoided at Falaise when the Allies failed to completely cut off the retreating columns. Despite the dire material situation, a nucleus of recovery remained because the Germans extricated their corps and divisional headquarters largely intact. These organizations quickly absorbed the heterogeneous replacements streaming into the line from all over the front, from Germany, and from other theaters.[37]

The process of assimilating such diverse units, especially the ones in retreat, was not easy. One officer stated:

The complete confusion of the armies withdrawing from France rendered them useless to us. We discounted them in our plans and took their appearance as a gift; they would come streaming back in great disorder and suddenly show up at one of our installations always lacking their equipment. Therefore, we rushed up all sorts of miscellaneous units from deep within Germany . . . everything but organized units.[38]

Yet whatever their status, these heterogeneous units represented manpower, precisely what the German Army needed at the end of August. The respite offered by the Allied failure to maintain the momentum gave sufficient time for reorganization and reequipping.

Reinforcements started to arrive September 1 from behind First Army lines. Elements of the 559th Volksgrenadier Division detrained east of Metz, the entire 553rd Volksgrenadier Division unloaded at Saarbruecken and headed for Nancy, and the 106th Panzer Brigade detrained its new Panthers at Trier.[39] This reinforcement brought First Army's combat strength to an estimated three and a half divisions. Remarkably, that figure jumped to nearly eight divisions only four days later, making First Army the strongest German army in the West. It was therefore in Lorraine in early September that the West Wall was reconstructed and the best of the German army was mustered to fight.

The army commander, Knobelsdorff, had seen extensive campaigning in the East, and his XLVIII Panzer Corps had performed well in its relieving attempt of Sixth Army at Stalingrad. In July 1943 his corps was the cutting edge of Hermann Hoth's Fourth Panzer Army during the fight to recapture Kharkov and liquidate the Kursk salient. Knobelsdorff had experienced the horrible weather and ground conditions caused by the twice yearly thawing, known as the *rasputitsa*, which turned Russia's dirt roads into quagmires.[40] Thus the deteriorating conditions in Lorraine through the fall of 1944 probably came as no surprise. F. W. von Mellenthin served as Knobelsdorff's Chief of Staff in the XLVIII Panzer Corps and has written that his former commander was "flexible and broad-minded."[41] A man of solid armor background, and several times wounded, Knobelsdorff, according to Cole, was nevertheless "physically weakened by the rigors of long months on the Eastern Front" by the time Third Army initiated its Lorraine operations.[42]

Knobelsdorff's two corps, the XLVII Panzer Corps and the XIII SS Corps, aligned themselves roughly opposite the advance of Patton's XII and XX Corps respectively in early September. The XLVII Panzer Corps was commanded by General der Panzertruppen Heinrich Freiherr von Luettwitz, a commander Patton would have found much in common with. Luettwitz was an expert horseman and former cavalry officer and had fought in Poland and Russia before returning to France to command what Patton called the best German armored division in the West, the 2nd Panzer Division. Despite having his division virtually destroyed in the Falaise Pocket, General Luettwitz had a reputation as an outstanding armored tactician.[43] At the moment, however, he possessed no armor but did have two divisions experienced in tough mountain fighting.

The German divisions on the Western Front in September 1944 were all classified according to the standards of the Oberkommando der Wehrmacht (OKW). Kampfwert I meant that a division was capable of a sustained all-out attack; Kampfwert II indicated a limited offensive capability. Because almost no German division was capable of an all-out sustained attack in September, the best divisions at the time were usually given the second classification.[44] Though some of the divisions available to Knobelsdorff would perform well, none was given a Kampfwert I.

Luettwitz's best division, and probably the best division in the entire army, was General Hans Hecker's "battle-tested" 3rd Panzer Grenadier Division. Hecker brought his division into the line north of Nancy in fairly good condition despite air attacks during the trip from Italy. The division's ranks were nearly full, and the men were still outfitted in tropical uniforms. Because a 1944 panzer grenadier division numbered some 14,446 men, with 12,963 in the combat arms, the 3rd probably approached these figures in strength.[45] The divisional artillery assets were also nearly full, but the organic tank battalion and engineers had not yet arrived from Italy. All in all, the division was in excellent shape with high morale.[46]

Generalleutnant Eberhard Rodt's 15th Panzer Grenadier Division was Luettwitz's other experienced division, but after having fought through ten months of continuous combat in Italy and suffering losses on the rail journey north from air attacks, it was sorely depleted. At the time of its deployment north of Nancy, the division mustered just 50 percent of its normal strength, around seven thousand men. Its tank battalion was still en route, leaving Rodt with perhaps seventeen tanks and assault guns. Though dangerously understrength, higher command still felt the 15th capable of carrying a Kampfwert II designation.[47] The 553rd Volksgrenadier Division, with no combat experience, was the unknown quantity in the XLVII Panzer Corps. Still, this, and other Volksgrenadier divisions deployed in Lorraine would perform fairly well despite their limited makeup. To augment its position in and around Nancy, the 553rd was given large numbers of replacement and school troops from the First Parachute Army.

At the start of the campaign along the Moselle, the LXXXII Corps controlled First Army's center from Thionville to just south of Metz. However, the presence of large numbers of Waffen-SS units in the area caused control to pass on September 7 to Generalleutnant der Waffen-SS Herman Priess's newly activated XIII SS Corps. One important aspect to be considered regarding the presence of SS divisions and SS generals is the tension that almost certainly existed between them and their Wehrmacht counterparts. Bonn points out that SS units were usually better supplied with both replacements and weapons and that this situation prompted "resentment" and led—along with diametrically opposite ideological, political, and social views—to disputes "between commanders of adjacent army and SS units—all adding to totally unnecessary friction on the battlefield."[48]

Priess had gained an excellent reputation while commanding the elite "Death's Head," 3rd Panzer Division in Russia and now commanded four divisions. His principal corps element was the "exhausted" 17th SS Panzer Grenadier Division of Generalleutnant der Waffen-SS Werner Ostendorff deployed west and south of Metz.[49] SS panzer grenadier divisions had an additional one thousand men in their battalions compared to army panzer grenadier divisions, but Ostendorff's division was probably below strength despite having absorbed large numbers of replacements from two panzer grenadier brigades in early September.[50]

Priess also had Generalmajor Kurt Freiherr von Muehlen's new 559th Volksgrenadier Division. Despite the deficiencies already identified in these divisions, the 559th was a fairly good unit. Originally intended for the Russian Front, the division was officered by young veterans from the East, and 60 percent of the enlisted personnel were in their twenties.[51] The least effective German division in XIII SS Corps, and First Army, was Generalleutnant Carl Casper's weak 48th Infantry Division. After suffering severely in the August retreat, the division had been reduced to a "demoralized and burned-out" unit and was placed north of Thionville. This division was the weakest link in an already weak chain.

At the other end of the spectrum, another excellent division available to Priess and Knobelsdorff was the unit charged with the defense of Metz—Division Number 462. Commanded by Generalleutnant Walther Krause, the core of this heterogeneous unit was the young officer cadets from the Metz service schools, 3,300 men divided into two regiments. These cadets were highly trained and fanatical, and their resistance during the campaign would be of the highest quality. The remainder of the division numbered among its ranks a security regiment, four companies of Waffen-SS Signal School troops, two replacement battalions, a machine gun company, two Flak battalions, one artillery battalion, an engineering battalion, and a few Luftwaffe troops—which altogether totaled some fourteen thousand men.[52] Though such a patchwork of assets would have been a nightmare to handle in the open field, the relatively static nature of the defense of Metz maximized their usefulness.

The last element in Knobelsdorff's reconstituted army was his operational reserve, the new 106th Panzer Brigade. It boasted one battalion of forty-nine Mark IVs and one battalion of forty-nine Mark Vs. The Panthers had come straight from the assembly lines, and training amongst the crews was minimal. The 106th Panzer Brigade constituted First Army's only large collection of armor. While Knobelsdorff's forces arranged themselves in orderly fashion along the Moselle, to his immediate south stood the loose elements of Generaloberst Johannes Blaskowitz's Army Group G, whose principal element was General der Infanterie Frederich Weise's Nineteenth Army. On September 8, Knobelsdorff's First Army would also be placed under Blaskowitz's command.

Blaskowitz, a sixty-one-year-old Prussian and good friend of Rundstedt, had served in the army for forty-three years. During the Polish Campaign, he commanded the small Eighth Army and was given the difficult task of protecting the right flank of Field Marshal Walther von Reichenau's fully mechanized Tenth Army. In the process he withstood a major Polish attack into his northern flank but managed to turn a potential crisis into a crushing German victory. As a reward, he was allowed to capture Warsaw. His biographer, Richard Giziowski, has pointed out that within the army Blaskowitz was "considered one of its best generals," but he soon fell out of favour with Hitler when he protested SS atrocities in Poland.[53] Although originally scheduled to command the Ninth Army for the invasion of France, Blaskowitz was relieved at the last moment by Hitler. His next command was Army Group G in southern France, where, notes Giziowski, he faced "a situation of virtually insurmountable difficulty" in trying to halt the American landings on August 15.[54] Yet he managed to orchestrate the retreat of the Nineteenth Army and elements of the First Army from south and west France respectively with considerable skill and determination.

Blaskowitz's task in early September was equally daunting. From Nancy southward, and generally forming a west-reaching salient, stood Weise's army, the northern wing of which was open-ended. The LXVI Corps, containing but one division, the 16th, struggled to close the holes existing there before Patton started his offensive. It was not until September 4 that Knobelsdorff and Weise made even the slimmest of tactical links.[55] Weise, an infantryman, had seen action as a corps commander in the East and was transferred directly from the Russian Front to take command of Nineteenth Army in June 1944. His handling of the retreat showed good tactical ability,[56] and his tenacity in holding Lieutenant General Alexander Patch's American Seventh Army in the Vosges Mountains would allow the reinforcement of Knobelsdorff's army with Nineteenth Army assets.

The ability of the German Army to recover from the disaster of Normandy and Falaise has been called the "Miracle of the West." In reality the miracle was the result of a logistical crisis for the Allies. Nevertheless, it was a prodigious effort by the Germans. As the Allied momentum stalled from Antwerp to Switzerland, Hitler threw every unit he could find west and managed to organize a continuous defense on the borders of the Reich. When Patton finally advanced once more, he confronted a German army that had stopped retreating. At the same time, just when he needed a full strength army to fight his toughest campaign, his own fighting power was whittled away to reinforce First and Ninth Armies.

The army that Patton took into Lorraine on September 5, 1944 fielded only half its original strength of August 1, the day it was fully committed on the continent. In Normandy and Brittany, Third Army was a powerful force, consisting of four corps, totaling twelve divisions. But on September 5 Major General Troy Middleton's VIII Corps, which had remained in Brittany when the rest of the army rolled east, came under the command of the newly operational U.S. Ninth Army. Patton lost a solid corps commander and Major General Robert W. Grow's excellent 6th Armored Division. Major General Wade H. Haislip's XV Corps, including the excellent French 2nd Armored Division of Major General Jacques Leclerc, was also removed from Third Army after it crossed the Seine River in mid-August. Haislip was probably the best corps commander Patton ever had while commanding Third Army. The heart of Third Army now consisted of two corps, the XII and XX, which between them contained six divisions, four infantry and two armored. By comparison, Lieutenant General Courtney Hodges' First Army was more than twice the size of Patton's command and contained a far greater quantity of armor.

With Middleton and Haislip gone, Patton was left with two very different corps commanders. Major General Manton S. Eddy, the commander of XII Corps, had participated in the Aisne-Marne and Meuse-Argonne offensives in World War I and finished the war as a machine-gun battalion commander. He later commanded the 9th Infantry Division in North Africa and Sicily in commendable fashion, but it was in Tunisia that Bradley first noted that although Eddy was "a good leader and a well-schooled tactician," he was "inclined to be cautious."[57] Eddy received the Distinguished Service Cross (DSC) for his handling of the 9th Infantry Division at Cherbourg,[58] but he could not be considered aggressive or opportunistic. Working at the pace of the infantry, he rarely understood what Patton was trying to accomplish in Lorraine.

XX Corps was commanded by a man who better understood Patton's style of fighting. Major General Walton H. Walker had fought in France in 1918 as an infantryman but later transferred to tanks. He preached continuous activity the way Patton did but was often "dissatisfied and irritated," according to Blumenson, when results were not immediately forthcoming. "Bulldog," as he was sometimes called because of his build and tenacity in battle, was a great admirer of Patton. He emulated his boss in his mannerisms, dress, and philosophy.[59]

One factor Patton had little option but to accept was that, like Knobelsdorff, he had to rely on the fighting ability of several untested divisions in early September. Of his six divisions under command on September 5, only two had previously been engaged in high-intensity battle. Bradley's comment that none of his divisions had ever been put to the test was more or less correct. One battle-tested division was Major General Paul W. Baade's 35th Infantry Division, a National Guard formation serving in Eddy's XII Corps. Baade had commanded the division since January 1943. The 35th landed on the continent during the second week of July, where it seized Hill 122 from the 352nd Division near St. Lô. The division suffered "severe" losses in the fighting there and during the subsequent Mortain counteroffensive.[60]

The other experienced division was the 90th Infantry Division, a Texas-Oklahoma draftee unit. It had taken an even greater beating in its first baptism of fire in the Cotentin peninsula. Within six weeks of arriving, the division's losses exceeded 100 percent, and in the rifle companies that figure sometimes jumped to 400 percent. Poor leadership has been identified for the division's heavy casualties, and after going through two divisional commanders, Troy Middleton turned the unit over to then Brigadier General Raymond S. McLain.[61]

In September 1944 the 90th was in Walker's XX Corps, and with McLain, the division finally had a real leader. McLain, destined for corps command later in the campaign, had fought in the Meuse-Argonne offensive in World War I. Patton had awarded him the DSC for his performance in command of the 45th Division's artillery in Sicily. He also took part in the Salerno and Anzio operations, which gave him a good education in tough, nasty fighting.[62] Patton was sufficiently impressed with his ability that he specifically requested him to command the 90th Infantry Division.[63]

Patton's remaining two infantry divisions had little battle experience. Major General S. Leroy Irwin had been at Kasserine Pass where as the commander of the 9th Infantry Division artillery he had stopped the German attack. But as commander of the 5th Infantry Division, a Regular Army unit assigned to XX Corps, he had thus far not experienced any grueling combat. Casualties in the division since its commitment in mid-July were small.[64] Major General Horace L. McBride's 80th Infantry Division, serving in XII Corps, had also sustained few casualties. McBride had been a field artillery battalion commander in World War I and took over the 80th Infantry in March 1943. He completed its training before it was brought to Europe and then led it through the Falaise Pocket battles.[65]

Both of Patton's armored divisions became operational on the continent once the breakout had begun and sustained minimal casualties during the pursuit. The 7th Armored Division of Walker's corps was commanded by Major General Lindsay McD. Silvester. He had fought in World War I as an infantry officer and won the DSC, but his infantry background affected his performance in command of the division and Patton was never happy with him. On August 26 and September 6 Patton expressed dissatisfaction with Silvester's aggressiveness. Despite his own misgivings and Walker's recommendation that Silvester be relieved, Patton retained him in command.[66] In no way was Silvester comparable to Patton's other armored commander, Major General John Shirley Wood. Wood, who commanded the 4th Armored Division in XII Corps, was by far Patton's favorite subordinate, not simply because of lifelong friendship but because of their common views on armored warfare. Blumenson wrote that Wood was "probably the most intelligent disciple of Patton and the most vigorous exponent of his method of tank warfare."[67] Geoffrey Perret has called Wood "one of the most impressive soldiers anywhere" and that "there was no division better trained than the 4th Armored."[68] In Wood, Patton possessed a hard-driving, relentless, and tactically proficient subordinate to execute his operations.

The strength returns for Patton's six divisions in early September totaled 76,260 men,[69] but his cutting edge was far less. The total rifle strength of a

1944 American infantry division with a Table of Organization (T/O) strength of 14,253, was 5,184.[70] Patton's four infantry divisions thus had a real rifle strength of less than 21,000 men. The fighting power of Third Army was in the twenty-seven rifle companies of the infantry division, and it was also the infantry that sustained, by far, the highest percentage of casualties among the combat arms. American estimates for infantry casualties were placed at 70 percent prior to D-Day but had to be raised to 83 percent after the battle of the hedgerows and raised yet again to 90 percent for the hard fighting during the Mortain counteroffensive.[71] The infantry strength figure of 21,000 for Third Army becomes all the more crucial when one realizes that Patton, by the time he was forced to suspend active operations once more on September 25, had accumulated a manpower deficit of 2,077 (see Appendix C). This translated into ten rifle companies, three battalions, or more than one full regiment. The replacement system failed to keep his divisions up to strength during September and would prove even more inadequate in the later November offensive. Patton would be forced to make maximum use of such assests as his cavalry squadrons to fill long portions of the front so as to release the core infantry fighting elements for action elsewhere.

In terms of heavy equipment, Third Army was trimmed from its juggernaut days of August. Though counting some 650 medium tanks in its ranks, it averaged 150–200 fewer medium tanks than First Army during the month of September. Each armored division had 186 medium tanks, and the combined strength of the five separate tank battalions attached to the army added another 265.[72] It had long been standard practice to attach a tank battalion to each frontline infantry division for close support on an almost permanent basis.

The backbone of Patton's armored force was the M-4 Sherman, a highly reliable machine from a mechanical perspective. At thirty-plus tons the Sherman was nonetheless underarmored and undergunned compared to German tanks. Offset against the tank's obvious weaknesses was its great mobility, at least on solid ground. The Sherman's greatest asset was the fitting of a gyrostabilizer for the gun and power traverse for the turret, which produced more flexibility and a greater rate of fire than its foe. This superior rate of fire was essential to keeping a Sherman in a firefight because of the difference in gun velocities. Only late in the campaign did the new 76-mm guns for the Shermans begin to appear.[73] Nonetheless, Cole rightly concluded that the Americans fought the Lorraine tank battles with a "relatively obsolescent weapon."[74]

American tank destroyers for the most part were also outclassed. The only comparable weapon Patton had in regards to firepower against the Panthers was the twenty-eight-ton M36 tank destroyer mounting a 90-mm gun. Standardized in July 1944, the M36 quickly proved to be the best American antitank weapon against the superior German armor.[75] The M18 Hellcat was a solid design, fast, and equipped with a 76-mm gun, but the M36 represented a significant step forward in killing power. Of the twelve tank destroyer battalions that served with Third Army in Lorraine, five were fully equipped with M36s, two were equipped with the M18 Hellcat, four underwent outfittings from the M10 to the M36, and one was a towed anti-tank battalion (see Appendix A). During the latter stages of the campaign, the tank destroyers fired chiefly in support of the infantry. In December, the tank destroyers of Walker's corps fired 27,289 rounds in direct fire and only 900 rounds in indirect fire.

Though clearly outgunned in armored firepower against the heavy German tanks, Patton did enjoy a decisive advantage in artillery. The purpose of artillery is to provide close and continuous fire support for attacking formations, to provide long-range fire to interdict enemy movement, and to engage enemy artillery assets by counter battery fire. In all these requirements, American artillery excelled. In 1940 American artillery had been about a full generation behind other leading nations in development, but by 1942 that had changed dramatically. Its success in World War II was the product of numerous factors. It possessed robust prime movers, bore-safe fuses, powerful ammunition, FM radio, and its own observation planes. The artillery probably had the best communications of any combat arm in the world along with great mobility and the ability to quickly achieve Time on Target (TOT) concentrations.[76] TOT was the coordination of the fire from several guns to strike a target simultaneously. The effect was immensely destructive. The Germans, both during and after the war, held American artillery up as an object of high praise, noting especially its ability to speedily coordinate concentrations. Bryan Perrett noted that veterans of the Eastern Front who later fought in the West were "shocked by the volume, accuracy, flexibility and rapid response of . . . American artillery which was able to switch its fire . . . in a manner hitherto unknown."[77]

The American light artillery piece, the M2A1 105-mm howitzer, was a solid design with a maximum range of 12,205 yards and became the standard divisional piece in March 1940.[78] Making up three of the four field artillery battalions in an infantry division, the M2A1s were the backbone of an infantry division's organic fire support. The medium M1A1 155-mm gun ("Long Tom") was also a high-quality weapon with a maximum range of 16,355 yards.[79] All of Patton's 155s were drawn by high-speed tractors, an essential requirement in the mud of Lorraine. American heavy artillery consisted of the excellent "Black Dragon" M1 240-mm Howitzer hauled by an 18–ton tractor. This weapon fired a massive 360-lb HE shell to a maximum distance of 25,225 yards.[80] The number of heavy artillery battalions increased in the American army after the bitter struggle at Cassino in Italy proved that aerial bombardment could not replace heavy artillery.

At the start of the Lorraine Campaign, Patton had fifty-one field artillery battalions under command. Each infantry division had one 155-mm battalion and three 105-mm battalions with 12 guns per battalion. The armored divisions possessed three battalions of 18 105-mm guns. Taken together, Patton's six divisions, with twenty-two artillery battalions, had 252 105-mm and 48 155-mm guns. An additional twenty-nine battalions were held at corps level. A fairly reasonable estimate of their strength is approximately 348 105-mm, 155-mm and the heavier 240-mm guns. Thus Patton had well over 600 artillery pieces of 105-mm or better on September 5.

With over 1,000 tanks and tank destroyers and 600 artillery pieces, Third Army was still a potent force, and air power rounded out its arsenal. Brigadier General Otto P. Weyland's XIX Tactical Air force (TAC) was specifically designed to support the mobile operations of Third Army. Of Weyland's 600 aircraft in August, nearly 85 percent were fighter-bombers.[81] At the start of the Lorraine campaign, he still had the eight fighter-bomber groups and the 10th Photo Reconnaissance Group from August, but by September 25 his command would be reduced to five groups. Each fighter-bomber group averaged seventy aircraft, usually the P-47 Thunderbolts and the P-51 Mustangs. Weyland and Patton became fast friends during August when Patton's spearhead armored columns were supported by P-47 fighter-bombers of XIX TAC.[82] The friendship nurtured between these two men was a great benefit to Patton, who could expect the best Weyland had to offer at all times in all conditions. Air support would be crucial to Patton's campaign in Lorraine.

Though certainly not possessing anywhere near Third Army's strength in field guns and tanks, it does appear that based on loose calculations, Knobelsdorff's First Army held at least a ratio of 1:1 against Patton in manpower during September. In the first few days, Knobelsdorff may actually have enjoyed a slim numerical superiority. Patton's numerical inferiority would not last for long, but he was initially handicapped by the dispositions of his army on September 5. He held a seventy-mile front with six divisions, but his frontline strength was further diminished because he had to position Baade's entire 35th Infantry Division to guard the south flank of the army

from Nancy to Neufchateau. Further, the V Corps of Hodges' First Army
had yet to catch up on Patton's left flank. This forced Patton to deploy
McLain's 90th Infantry Division echeloned in a depth of almost twenty
miles to cover the gap. The forward strength of the division was thus only a
fraction of its potential.

This numerical tinkering brings the forces available to Patton in early
September to attack a river line defended by eight German divisions of
varying quantity and quality down to a little more than four divisions. Because it is generally accepted among military professionals that the attacker
requires a 3:1 superiority over his opponent to ensure victory, the rough parity enjoyed by Knobelsdorff with Third Army makes Patton's offensive
against the Moselle line problematical. Yet it is wrong to suggest, as some
have done, that he could not have achieved greater success during the opening days because of a numerical weakness in infantry. He possessed the inherent mobility (at least during the relatively good weather of September)
of his army to achieve what Clausewitz called "relative" superiority even
though he was initially inferior across the front. That he chose not to create
local superiority for a penetration of the Moselle defenses is indicative of
the way he perceived the forthcoming battles developing.

In the final assessment, Knobelsdorff was not commanding a ragtag
army burdened with obsolescent weaponry but one that was still capable of
using the good to excellent weapons it had to great effect, and Third Army
was no longer the potent force it had been in August. At times, the techno-
logical disparity was blatant, as when the American artillery could achieve
a TOT almost at will. Yet at other times, the critical ammunition shortage
suffered by Third Army early in the campaign brought artillery duels down
to more-even levels. Moreover, the uneven victory of Patton's armor during
the great tank battles of September was as much a function of untrained
German crews as it was of disparity in tank quality.

NOTES

1. Chester Wilmot, *The Struggle for Europe* (London: Collins, 1971), 482.
2. Hugh M. Cole, *The Lorraine Campaign*, U.S. Army in World War II:
European Theater of Operations (Washington, D.C.: Center for Military History,
1984), 31.
3. Richard Overy, *Why the Allies Won* (London: Johnathan Cape, 1995),
218, 227.
4. Ibid., 232.
5. Ibid., 227.
6. Ibid., 225.

7. Cole, *Lorraine Campaign*, 32. Because of the mass chaos commensurate with the German retreat, casualty figures were mere estimates. Tables compiled at the time indicated that the fighting strength on September 1 was 543,000, but they did not count the division and army troops and the separate replacement battalions sent to the front.

8. Correlli Barnett, ed., *Hitler's Generals* (New York: Grove, Weidenfeld, 1989), 202. Earl F. Ziemke, who wrote the chapter on Rundstedt, pointed out that Rundstedt was the logical choice because of the great respect he enjoyed throughout the army.

9. Ibid.

10. Wilmot, *The Struggle for Europe*, 189.

11. John Strawson, *Hitler as Military Commander* (New York: Batsford, 1971), 235.

12. Cole, *Lorraine Campaign*, 33. The Germans had reduced the strength of the standard infantry division from roughly 17,000 to 12,500.

13. James Lucas, *The Last Year of the German Army: May 1944–May 1945* (London: Arms and Armour Press, 1994), 43, 48.

14. Keith E. Bonn, *When the Odds Were Even: The Vosges Mountains Campaign, October 1944–January 1945* (Novato, Calif.: Presidio, 1994), 46–48. These divisions only trained for ten weeks before being committed to battle. Hitler also sent eighty of approximately one hundred fortress battalions to the Western Front.

15. Major General F. W. von Mellenthin, *Panzer Battles: A Study of the Employment of Armour in the Second World War* (Norman, Okla.: Oklahoma University Press, 1971), 314, note 5; Matthew Cooper, *The German Army 1933–1945: Its Political and Military Failure* (New York: Bonanza, 1984), 489.

16. Cole, *Lorraine Campaign*, 35.

17. Ian V. Hogg, *German Artillery of World War Two* (London: Greenhill, 1997), 49–50.

18. Ibid., 69–70.

19. Ibid., 91–92.

20. Ibid., 167.

21. Max Hastings, *Overlord: D-Day, June 6, 1944* (New York: Simon and Schuster, 1984), 189–190.

22. Ibid., 190.

23. Cole, *Lorraine Campaign*, 34.

24. Bryan Perrett, *Knights of the Black Cross: Hitler's Panzerwaffe and Its Leaders* (New York: St. Martin's Press, 1987), 105.

25. Walter J. Spielberger, *The Spielberger German Armor and Military Vehicles Series*, vol. IV: *Panzer IV and Its Variants* (Atglen, Pa.: Schiffer Military History, 1993), 157.

26. Ibid., 152; Hastings, *Overlord*, 189.

27. Walter J. Spielberger, *The Spielberger German Armor and Military Vehicles Series*, vol. I: *Panther and Its Variants* (Atglen, Pa.: Schiffer Military History, 1993), 233.

28. Ibid., 237.

29. Ibid., 161.

30. Stephen Ambrose stated that Hitler had assigned nearly "all the 400 new Panthers and Mark VI tanks available for the western front to a counterstroke against Patton," but his source, Chester Wilmot's *The Struggle for Europe*, clearly identified Panthers and Mark IVs, not Mark VI Tigers. Stephen E. Ambrose, *The Supreme Commander* (New York: Doubleday, 1970), 521; Wilmot, 536. The Third Army After Action Report (AAR) cited Tigers as having been engaged in "Comparative Charts—Losses of Material." According to the chart, Third Army destroyed 186 Tigers in September, 16 in October and 27 in November. The chart made no reference to Mark V Panthers, and one cannot help but think that the Tiger statistics actually represent the number of Panthers destroyed. Third Army AAR, Special Collections, United States Military Academy Library, West Point (WP), I: 93, 116, 147. Despite this evidence, Cole nonetheless cited the 11th Panzer Division as possessing four Mark VIs on November 15. Cole, Lorraine Campaign, 450, footnote 1.

31. Perrett, *Knights of the Black Cross*, 158.

32. Overy, *Why the Allies Won*, 215, 218.

33. Cole, *Lorraine Campaign*, 42–43.

34. Cornelius Ryan, *A Bridge Too Far* (New York: Simon and Schuster, 1974), 55.

35. Ibid., 55, 281.

36. Cole, *Lorraine Campaign*, 47.

37. Ronald Andidora, "The Autumn of 1944: Boldness Is Not Enough," *Parameters: US Army War College Quarterly* XVII, 4 (December 1987): 76.

38. ETHINT 37, "Defense of the West Wall," an Interview with Maj. Herbert Buechs, Luftwaffe aide to Genobst Jodl, September 28, 1945, Donald S. Detwiler, with Charles B. Burdick and Jurgen Rowher, eds., *World War II German Military Studies* (New York: Garland Publishing, 1979), III.

39. Cole, *Lorraine Campaign*, 47.

40. Robin Cross, *Citadel: The Battle of Kursk* (New York: Barnes and Noble, 1994), 10, 14.

41. Mellenthin, *Panzer Battles*, 175.

42. Cole, *Lorraine Campaign*, 46.

43. Ibid., 49.

44. Ibid., 80.

45. Martin van Creveld, *Fighting Power: German and U.S. Army Performance, 1939–1945* (Westport, Conn.: Greenwood Press, 1982), 54.

46. Cole, *Lorraine Campaign*, 60.

47. Ibid., 96–97.

48. Bonn, *When the Odds Were Even*, 48.

49. Cole, *Lorraine Campaign*, 47.

50. Bonn, *When the Odds Were Even*, 68.

51. Cole, *Lorraine Campaign*, 125, footnote 5.

52. Ibid., 125, footnote 6; Christopher R. Gabel, *The Lorraine Campaign: An Overview, September–December 1944* (Fort Leavenworth, Kans.: Combat Studies Institute, 1985), 19.

53. Richard Giziowski, *The Enigma of General Blaskowitz* (London: Leo Cooper, 1997), 143, 222.

54. Ibid., 315.

55. Cole, *Lorraine Campaign*, 52.

56. Ibid., 46.

57. Omar N. Bradley and Clay Blair, *A General's Life* (New York: Simon and Schuster, 1983), 136.

58. Cole, *Lorraine Campaign*, 16.

59. Martin Blumenson, *The Battle of the Generals: The Untold Story of the Falaise Pocket—The Campaign That Should Have Won World War II* (New York: William Morrow, 1993), 189.

60. Geoffrey Perret, *There's a War to Be Won: The United States Army in World War II* (New York: Random House, 1991), 337; Cole, *Lorraine Campaign*, 16.

61. Perret, *There's a War to Be Won*, 327–329.

62. Cole, *Lorraine Campaign*, 17–18.

63. Carlo D'Este, *Patton: A Genius for War* (New York: HarperCollins, 1995), 387.

64. Cole, *Lorraine Campaign*, 17.

65. Ibid., 16.

66. Martin Blumenson, *The Patton Papers* (Boston: Houghton Mifflin, 1974), II: 529; George S. Patton, *War as I Knew It* (Boston: Houghton Mifflin, 1947), 98.

67. Martin Blumenson, *The Patton Papers* (Boston: Houghton Mifflin, 1972), I: 545.

68. Perret, *There's a War to Be Won*, 364–365.

69. Third Army Daily Casualty Report No. 36, September 5, 1944, PP, LC. 5th Inf Div, 14,116; 35th Inf Div, 13,689; 80th Inf Div, 13,562; 90th Inf Div, 13,774; 4th Armd Div, 10,713; 7th Armd Div, 10,406.

70. Shelby L. Stanton, *World War II Order of Battle* (New York: Galahad, 1991), 9–10. The division total of 14,253 includes attached medical, chaplain, and band units. A standard infantry regiment as of February 26, 1944, contained 3,257 officers and men. A standard infantry battalion contained 871 officers and men. Calculating the cutting edge of the division by multiplying the regiment by three (9,771), or the battalion by nine (7,839), would be incorrect. The cutting edge of the division resided in the twenty-seven rifle companies, which gave the final figure of 5,184.

71. Omar N. Bradley, *A Soldier's Story* (New York: Henry Holt and Company, 1951), 445–446.

72. Stanton, *World War II Order of Battle*, 18–19. In 1942 the American armored division was classified as "heavy" and contained 390 tanks, 232 medium, and 158 light, and a strength of 14,620. In September 1943 the armored divisions were reorganized with the exception of the 2nd and 3rd, which retained the old organization. Of the 263 tanks in the new division, 186 were mediums and 77 were light.

73. Cole, *Lorraine Campaign*, 604; Richard M. Ogorkiewicz, *Armoured Forces: A History of Armoured Forces and Their Vehicles* (New York: Arco Publishing, 1970), 166, 197–198.

74. Cole, *Lorraine Campaign*, 604; Ogorkiewicz, *Armoured Forces*, 198.

75. George Forty, *World War Two Armoured Fighting Vehicles and Self-Propelled Artillery* (London: Osprey, 1996), 144.

76. Perret, *There's a War to Be Won*, 93. As Perret noted, "American artillery officers had stood back and looked at modern battle whole. They had not tried to beat the enemy gun for gun. They had made a mental leap. What they were ready for now was to fight system against system, their organization of artillery firepower against anyone else's. On that basis, they were a generation ahead."

77. Perrett, *Knights of the Black Cross*, 202.

78. Ian V. Hogg, *British and American Artillery of World War 2* (London: Arms and Armour Press, 1978), 62.

79. Ibid., 68.

80. Ibid., 161–162.

81. Perret, *There's a War to Be Won*, 367.

82. Ibid.

Chapter 4

Strategy, Logistics, and Perception

A hierarchical superior can control his subordinate by determining the goals which the subordinate is to pursue, controlling the resources available to the subordinate, or doing both.

—Samuel P. Huntington[1]

I am impatient with my friends for not letting me go faster, as I am sure—although people do not agree with me—that the Boche has no power to resist.

—Patton, September 1, 1944[2]

In the fall of 1944, the one great inhibiting factor in the successful Allied exploitation of German weakness after the defeat in Normandy was insufficient logistical support. Ninety to 95 percent of all the supplies on the continent, including crucial gasoline stocks, lay in the base depots near the invasion beaches with barely any stocks between Normandy and the forward army dumps some three hundred miles away.[3] It was a classic case of strategic overstretch. The original "Overlord" plan had called for a general regrouping of the Allied armies at the Seine River once the Germans had been driven from Normandy, but the rapid German collapse after Falaise had taken Eisenhower by surprise.[4] Quickly realizing that the enemy could not be allowed to retreat and consolidate unmolested, Eisenhower ordered the armies across the Seine on August 19 in pursuit.

From the 19th onward, Eisenhower fell back on the strategy advocated by the Supreme Headquarters Allied Expeditionary Force (SHAEF) planning staff prior to D-Day. They outlined an advance north and south of the Ardennes for advantages of maneuver and for the ability to shift the main weight of attack. The reasoning was that if the Germans had to thin out their already weakened forces to cover threats in the Metz Gap and Maubeuge-Liege areas, as well as fortifying the Channel ports, the entire front would become extremely vulnerable to several penetrations.[5]

The SHAEF planners identified the Rhur industrial region as the key to the entire advance, an objective Eisenhower agreed with because he believed that German forces would gravitate to defend this vital area. His overriding objective was the destruction of the enemy's field forces, and he intended to accomplish this west of the Rhine so that he could strike directly into the heart of Germany virtually unopposed. Eisenhower further agreed with the planner's assessment that it was dangerous to advance on a narrow front because it would invite a concentrated counterattack. His solution, known to historians as the "Broad Front" strategy, sought to make the major Allied effort north of the Ardennes in Montgomery's Twenty-First Army Group sector, supported by a secondary push in Bradley's Twelfth Army Group zone south of the Ardennes.

Eisenhower viewed Patton's position south of the Ardennes on a Metz-Frankfurt axis as the secondary front. Apart from the less important Saar industrial region and the two principal cities of Metz and Nancy, Lorraine offered few significant military objectives.[6] Montgomery's area, however, contained the great port of Antwerp, which offered the only real hope of long-term relief for Allied logistical difficulties. Moreover, the launching sites for the V-1 and V-2 rockets were located in the Pas de Calais and represented a powerful political component in Eisenhower's overall strategy.

Another important aspect of Allied strategy in late August was the stand taken by Omar Bradley against Montgomery's insistence that the bulk of Hodges' First Army support Twenty-First Army Group in its drive on the Channel ports, Antwerp, and the Rhur. Though Bradley had apparently agreed to such a plan on the 17th of August, he also envisioned striking due east for the Rhine with both First and Third Armies. On the 23rd he proposed that Twelfth Army Group could drive through the Saar Valley all the way to Frankfurt.[7]

Montgomery, somewhat taken aback by Bradley's about face, solicited support from Eisenhower on the same day and believed that he had won his argument for a single thrust on the Rhur. But Eisenhower had merely effected a compromise. In a directive of the 29th, he ordered Bradley to support Montgomery's drive northeast to open the channel ports while simultaneously building up American forces "generally east of Paris" in preparation for a "strike eastwards towards the Saar Valley."[8]

Patton was already moving east towards the Saar. Bradley sent him forward to Reims on the 25th with wide latitude as to how he carried out his orders. In fact, Bradley was having a change of heart concerning his former boss in Tunisia and Sicily. He had originally wanted nothing to do with him. "Had it been left up to me," he stated, "I would not have included Patton in Overlord. I did not look forward to having him in my command."[9] Indeed, according to Harry Semmes, "one of Bradley's prime missions was to keep a restraining hand on him, sometimes by order, or sometimes by diversion of supplies, or troops."[10]

There is ample evidence to support Semmes' claim that higher command got jumpy when Patton achieved free reign. Eisenhower had assured Chief of Staff George C. Marshall after the slapping incidents in Sicily that the "volatile, offensive-minded Patton would always serve under the more even-handed Bradley."[11] Hard evidence suggesting that Bradley and Eisenhower purposely kept him down is less evident, however. In fact, Bradley and Patton saw eye to eye on flaws in Eisenhower's strategy. Dominick Graham and Shelford Bidwell assert that by the end of August Bradley had decided upon a "settled policy of winks and nods at Patton's defiance of SHAEF directives." In addition, they stated that Bradley freely "aided and abetted" Patton in drawing crucial supplies away from First Army for his own attacks upon the Moselle.[12] Bradley was disillusioned with Eisenhower's ambiguous directives and the apparent deference to Montgomery.

Bradley was not impressed with Montgomery either at this stage and loathed working with him. He exhibited acute anger over Eisenhower's decision to throw the weight of Twelfth Army Group behind the British and was "enraged" at Montgomery's megalomania.[13] Patton could be difficult, but at least he was an American—and someone Bradley could pretend to control. The elevation of Montgomery to the rank of Field Marshal on September 1 (a move intended to assuage Montgomery and the British public when Eisenhower assumed command of ground operations on the same day), did not endear Montgomery to Bradley either. According to Patton, the promotion made them both "sick."[14]

By August 30 Patton had reached the Meuse River, but his spectacular dash across France came to an abrupt halt the next day due to a critical shortage of gasoline, the lifeblood of modern mechanized armies. Eisenhower had given supply priority to Hodges' First Army to support Montgomery's advance. Yet Eisenhower never had any intention of abandoning his Broad Front strategy. As Forrest Pogue pointed out, his "decision to shift the First U.S. Army northward temporarily during the British advance from the Seine to Antwerp was accompanied by a firm resolution to return as soon as possible to the early SHAEF policy of advancing toward Germany by routes north of the Ardennes and south of that area through the Metz Gap."[15]

On the last day of August the bulk of Third Army became immobilized, although cavalry patrols continued to operate all the way to the Moselle River until they, too, ran out of fuel on September 2.[16] Patton's tanks and trucks had consumed some 350,000 to 400,000 gallons of gasoline per day during the August pursuit, but on August 30 only 31,975 gallons arrived at Third Army fuel dumps. Sustainable offensive operations could not be mounted with such meager supplies since one armored division required 100,000 gallons per day to engage in rapid cross-country fighting.[17]

Just as Patton was slowing down, Montgomery was driving his forces eastward as fast as they could go. From August 29 to September 4 British forces advanced two hundred miles and liberated Brussels and Antwerp.[18] No matter how well Montgomery did, however, Eisenhower was always reluctant to give him everything. Strategically, Eisenhower believed in his Broad Front approach, but there was also American public opinion to consider, which would not accept the bulk of First Army placed under Montgomery's control and Third Army stranded for lack of supplies. Patton had to play a part, and Eisenhower gave him his chance at a meeting of the top American commanders at Versailles on September 2.

Although Eisenhower apparently chewed out Patton for stretching his line too far and creating supply problems, Patton was undaunted. In fact, he managed to convince the Supreme Commander that great opportunities lie in the Saar Valley. The result was that Eisenhower reserved stocks of fuel for Third Army and also gave Patton permission to attack east toward Mannheim, Koblenz, and Frankfurt.[19] As Norman Gelb stated, Eisenhower "had no wish to slow his old friend down when he was doing so well."[20] But in the end, no matter how much he may have wanted to support Patton, Eisenhower nevertheless recognized the vital importance of the objectives in Montgomery's sector.

Eisenhower stipulated in a directive of September 4 that Patton's drive to the east was contingent on the success of the northern thrust, which had priority of supplies.[21] One way of looking at Patton in Lorraine is to make the comparison to Montgomery's role as a magnet for German forces in Normandy while Bradley worked to create the breakout. In Lorraine, Patton would attract large armored forces and numerous German divisions away from Montgomery, who now was to achieve the decisive breakthrough. Eisenhower made it clear just how much Patton was helping Montgomery on September 20 when he informed the Field Marshal that Third Army had captured nine thousand prisoners and destroyed 270 tanks during Operation

"Market Garden," Montgomery's botched attempt to secure bridgeheads over the Rhine.[22]

On September 4, Patton's gasoline shortage found some relief with the arrival of 240,265 gallons. He received 1,396,710 gallons during the next three days, and by September 10 the period of critical shortage had ended.[23] However, uncertainty over continued supply persisted in Third Army. Eisenhower's Broad Front strategy was still stretching the Allied support structure to the limit. By mid-month, gasoline would be rationed at 5,000 gallons per day for the infantry divisions and 25,000 gallons per day for the armored divisions, and even then deliveries were "highly unpredictable." Gasoline receipts would continue to fall short of requirements until late October.[24]

Patton's supply problems did not end there. Twelfth Army Group determined that each division plus its supporting corps and army troops required a minimum of 600 tons of supplies per day during offensive action.[25] This figure dropped to 300–350 tons per day when the division was in pursuit.[26] Divisions, it should be noted, required not just supplies for the current day but also needed a certain volume of logistical support to create reserves. By the end of August reserves in forward army dumps were practically nonexistent, and sustained operations "became entirely dependent on daily replenishment from the rear."[27]

Third Army's stated minimum requirements for early September were 6,665 tons per day, a figure that obviously reflected the need for reserves. Based on the Twelfth Army Group estimates, Third Army's six divisions needed only 3,600 tons per day to carry out operations. Third Army's allotted tonnage for early September fell well below this figure. On August 30 Bradley allocated 2,000 tons of supplies to Third Army per day while giving First Army, charged with assisting Montgomery's advance on the Rhur industrial area, 5,000 tons per day. In theory, Patton achieved parity with Hodges at 3,500 tons per day on September 5, but in actuality, during the period September 3 to September 9, Third Army averaged only 2,620 tons.[28] This situation left Patton's forces on September 5 logistically starved. His Deputy Chief of Staff, Brigadier General Hobart Gay, noted later in September that "on 3,500 tons per day the Third Army cannot attack," even though at times it would fight with a lot less.[29] There can be little doubt that Eisenhower's strategy for continuing the war into the fall of 1944 influenced both the type and scale of warfare Patton conducted in Lorraine.[30] He was at the mercy of Eisenhower as the Supreme Commander struggled to please his two vocal subordinates, himself and Montgomery, while trying to press home the success hard won in Normandy. Indeed, despite the obvious problems associated with the logistical crisis, everyone, including Patton, was still somewhat mesmerized by that stunning success.

Patton's early operations in Lorraine reflected to a large extent his perception of the state of German defenses and his own army. He was now forced to jump-start his advance from a dead stop with cold engines against an enemy he continually underestimated. Third Army had no natural momentum heading into Lorraine like it had in Normandy. This had a resounding impact upon the start of the campaign because Patton failed to recognize that the great pursuit had finally come to an end.

As early as August 21 Patton had sensed German weakness. If consistent pressure were placed on the retreating columns, he felt that they would crack and the war could be concluded swiftly. At this time he conceived a general scheme of advance, which, in modified form, later served as his basis of advance in Lorraine. This involved advancing two corps abreast and a third echeloned to the right rear. Patton felt confident that he could punch through to the Rhine in ten days deployed this way. To accomplish this task, the three corps involved needed a cumulative strength of six infantry and three armored divisions.[31] This calculation is interesting because he stated that "it can be done" with this force, almost suggesting that it could not be executed with anything less. It did not seem to bother him, however, that on September 5 the entire Third Army contained only six divisions.

He announced on the last day of August that the faster he started moving across the Moselle and Rhine "the less lives and munitions it will take" and that "no one realizes the terrible value of the 'unforgiving minute' except me."[32] But in reality, from August 21 onward, Patton saw a window of opportunity and never stipulated in absolute terms when he thought it might close. At the meeting with Eisenhower at Versailles on September 2 he still perceived an opening. "Eisenhower kept talking about the future great battle of Germany," he noted, "while we assured him that the Germans have nothing left to fight with if we push on now. If we wait, there *will* be a great battle of Germany."[33] Yet he had already been waiting for two full days. The evidence suggests that Patton clung to this optimistic estimate right up to September 5 and probably well beyond. According to Cole, this explains why he showed so little concern for what rallying German forces might have accomplished on Third Army's front from September 1 to 5.[34]

Ladislas Farago disagreed with Cole on this point, claiming a "baffling contrast between Patton's boisterous outward behavior and the sober rationale of his inner thoughts."[35] He stated that Patton's true gut feeling led him to "realize that the spurt was at an end."[36] This seems highly unlikely. Patton's words and actions strongly refute Farago's undocumented assertion. With the exception of Deputy Chief of Staff, Hobart Gay, Patton's staff likewise displayed little apprehension about German activity in the lull. Gay prophetically asserted in his daily diary at the time that "it may be that this delay will have given the enemy time to entrench himself on or generally west of the Siegfried Line."[37]

To a degree Patton's assumptions were understandable. Eisenhower had seriously questioned the ability of the Allies to advance even in the face of weak opposition on August 20, but over the next ten days the troops continued to make steady progress. This sustained success created the impression that the Wehrmacht was finished as an effective fighting force. Eisenhower's G-2, Brigadier General Kenneth Strong, assessed the situation on August 23 in that vein: "The August battles have done it and the enemy in the West has had it. Two and a half months of bitter fighting have brought the end of the war in Europe within sight, almost within reach."[38] There could hardly have been a more optimistic assessment than this. It was not just Eisenhower's intelligence people spreading notions of imminent victory. First Army's intelligence section agreed with the appraisal, and the Combined Intelligence Committee announced that "no recovery is now possible" for the German field army.[39] Eisenhower reiterated these judgments on September 5, the very day Patton ran into strenuous resistance at the Moselle. "For some days it has been obvious that our military forces can advance almost at will," he wrote, "subject only to the requirement for maintenance."[40]

Underlying Eisenhower's optimism was the intelligence gathering system known as "Ultra." According to Ralph Bennett, Ultra gave the Allies the ability to "outline the strategy of the German withdrawal and to indicate where the enemy most feared sudden attack while still off balance and before a defense could be prepared."[41] In late August, Ultra revealed that the Germans considered the Moselle valley from Metz to Trier as their Achilles heel. The Germans were fully aware that a strong thrust by Third Army into this area at the beginning of September would cut off the escape route for the one hundred thousand Wehrmacht personnel and other stragglers Blaskowitz was trying to move back to Germany from south and southwest France.[42] Eisenhower's operations staff had no doubt utilized Ultra's revelations on this point when it indicated on September 1 that "there may be an opportunity to breach the Siegfried Line by rapid, aggressive movement by the Third Army on the Saar and thence on Frankfurt."[43] On September 1 there was definitely an opportunity, but by the 5th the window had been effectively closed.

Patton had always been skeptical of Ultra. The intelligence decrypts had been available to Allied officers at and above the rank of army commander since the early days of the war; he had received Ultra in Sicily, but its value to him there had been meager.[44] He had great faith in his own deductive abilities, and as Captain Harry C. Butcher, Eisenhower's naval aide, noted, Patton felt that he possessed a sixth sense and could "guess the intentions of the enemy better than a staff of G-2."[45] In early August, however, he came to see the true value of Ultra.

After Ultra accurately predicted Hitler's great counteroffensive gamble at Mortain, with the intention of cutting off Third Army, Patton gained a healthy respect for its capabilities. Because of Ultra, he was able to successfully guard his flank and thwart the German offensive. Thereafter, he solicited the knowledge of his Ultra representative, Melvin Helfers, every day and gave him special leeway to present valuable intelligence on short notice.[46] His new faith in the ability of Ultra to detect serious threats to his right flank (and the prescence of the XIX TAC) during August gave him the confidence to storm across France without giving that matter more than cursory attention.

Patton was always ready professionally to adopt ideas that had proven themselves in the test of battle. Harold Deutsch has suggested that as a zealous student of military history and the art of war, "it was inconceivable that he could have adopted one or another of the more negative attitudes toward intelligence."[47] Kenneth Strong once commented that Patton displayed "an extraordinary desire for information of all kinds. He . . . would quiz me on details about the enemy, usually to satisfy himself that the risks he intended to undertake were justified."[48] Patton fully appreciated the role of intelligence in war, and there is little reason not to believe that he had full confidence in what Ultra was telling him at the end of August, that the German high command had serious reservations about the quality of front it could establish in the path of Third Army.

The reassuring picture painted by Ultra's contribution reinforced Patton's optimism in early September. Cole's statement that Third Army faced the advance into Lorraine with a "contagious feeling that the final victory of World War II was close at hand" reflected Patton's attitude as much as it did the rank and file.[49] Many of his statements at this time suggest that he bordered on feelings of invincibility. This point is further illustrated by his attitude towards the findings of intelligence assets within Third Army.

Patton's own G-2, Brigadier General Oscar W. Koch, has recorded that Third Army's daily intelligence briefings were "a most fruitful exchange of ideas" between the army commander and his intelligence staff.[50] This is certainly accurate, but it requires a degree of modification, for Patton never abandoned his faith in his own sixth sense no matter how good Ultra and other intelligence sources might have been. Deutsch's estimate of the workings of Patton's intelligence team is more on the money. "In a sense," states Deutsch, "he was his own intelligence analyst. His staff would furnish him with the 'when, where, why, and what' of things and he would take it from there."[51]

As early as August 28 Koch warned Patton that the continuing German retreat did not have the characteristics of a rout or mass collapse. He stated that the enemy "has been able to maintain a sufficiently cohesive front to exercise an overall control of his tactical situation," and that barring insurrection within the Wehrmacht, the "German armies will continue to fight until destroyed or captured."[52] Koch offered proof for his assessment. The weather would soon deteriorate, thus lessening the effectiveness of the XIX TAC as a close escort for Third Army's armored columns. Moreover, the German retreat and the Third Army's advance had an inverse relationship when it came to supplies. German logistical lines would become shorter while Patton was already immobile due to overextension. Finally, the terrain ahead of Third Army would become less and less conducive to rapid movement by armor.[53]

A day later Patton "went carefully over the situation" and seemingly dismissed Koch's appraisal by casually stating that "There is no real threat against us from anywhere so long as we do not let imaginary dangers worry us."[54] He felt that any resistance ahead would be a thin crust because the enemy possessed no effective reserves. His perspective was completely contrary to Koch's estimation that "numerous new identifications in contact in recent days have demonstrated clearly that, despite the enormous difficulties under which he is operating, the enemy is still capable of bringing new elements into the battle area and transferring some from other fronts."[55] Though the divisions being assembled in Knobelsdorff's First Army did not possess high offensive ratings, they nevertheless represented a legitimate threat to Third Army's projected advance on the Rhine. Patton, however, rejected this possibility outright. On September 1, as he sat idle with empty gas tanks, he confidently asserted that "although people do not agree with me . . . the Boche has no power to resist."[56] One German officer who agreed with Patton's estimate was General Siegfried Westphal, Rundstedt's Chief of Staff. He stated that "the overall situation in the West was serious in the extreme." The Allies could have punched through at any point "with ease" until mid-October and "would have been able to cross the Rhine and thrust deep into Germany unhindered."[57] Westphal's first observation was valid,

but his second went too far. By September 5 it was apparent that Knobelsdorff, although far from content with his situation, was capable of mounting
a significant defense on the Moselle.

When Patton was questioned at a press conference on September 7 about
why he felt he could quickly breach the West Wall, his first response was
"My natural optimism," but on further prodding, he put his feelings in
harder terms. He stated that the smashing victories of August had had a profound impact upon the enemy. "You can't have men retreating," he declared, "for 300 or 400 miles and then hold anything." There was a
"psychological result in long retreats" that worked to his advantage.[58] Even
the West Wall would not be enough to stem the rout because he believed
that "as soon as a man gets in a concrete line, he immediately says to himself, 'The other man must be damn good, or I wouldn't have to get behind
this concrete.' "[59]

His belief in German weakness may have been connected to the ease
with which the Allies pushed through the old World War I killing fields.
The feat of covering in hours what had taken years and thousands of lives to
achieve inspired great optimism. But Patton had missed an obvious lesson.
The Red Army had retreated eight hundred miles from their positions in Poland to Stalingrad where they did indeed manage to "hold." In the case of
Knobelsdorff's scrambling First Army, Patton failed to realize, or con-
sciously refused to accept the fact, that it had retreated within immediate
range of its own soil. The retreat brought Knobelsdorff's forces onto good
defensive terrain and into strongly fortified areas.

During the great pursuit across France in early August, Patton's mobile
battle philosophy benefited greatly from the vast stretches of open territory
that lay in front of his racing armored spearheads. Under such circumstances he was able to exploit enemy weakness in four directions simultaneously. For a time he fought on two fronts 500 miles apart while protecting a
485-mile right flank. In twenty-six days he advanced 400 miles and liberated 47,829 square miles of France (see Map 4.1).[60] In stark contrast, as he
sat on the western border of Lorraine in early September, his multiple axis
of attack had suddenly been canalized into one front: straight ahead.
Squeezed between Hodges' First Army on his left and the rapid approach of
Lieutenant General Alexander Patch's Seventh Army on his right, Patton
had lost a large measure of his coveted maneuverability. He had also run out
of good tank country.

Patton had a reasonably good understanding of the main military topog-
raphical features of the area from landscape studies prepared on September
5 by his engineers. Lorraine offered the most direct route from France into

Map 4.1
Third Army's Advance, August 1–September 5, 1944

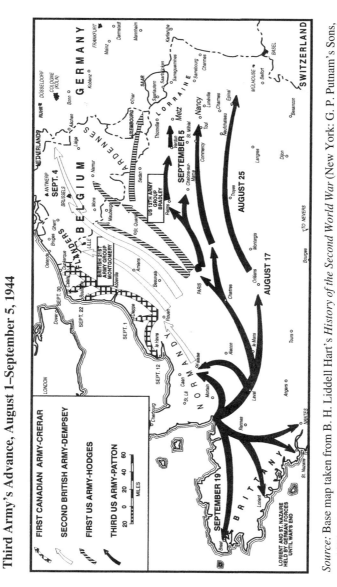

Source: Base map taken from B. H. Liddell Hart's *History of the Second World War* (New York: G. P. Putnam's Sons, 1970), 554–555. Altered by Eric Drummie and Bill Traer.

Germany and had been used as a traditional invasion corridor between the two countries for hundreds of years.[61] It was a self-contained battlefield with its western border running along the Moselle River and its eastern border following the Saar River. The Ardennes Forest and Luxembourg hemmed it in on the north, and the Vosges Mountains stood to the south. A man-made barrier, the Marne-Rhine Canal, between sixteen and twenty yards in width, bisected the southern portion of Lorraine, running from just south of Nancy to Sarrebourg, Saverne, and Strasbourg. In general terms, Lorraine sat on a plateau rising from west to east with elevations of 600 to 1,300 feet. Any advance across the Moselle from the west required the negotiating of a long natural slope and deep river trench, beyond which stood further heights with significant tactical importance.[62] These tactical heights gave Patton's attacking infantry a rough go in the opening stages of the campaign.

The initial obstacles to overcome in any assault across the Moselle were the two principal cities of the area, Metz and Nancy. Described as the "outposts of Lorraine," they were essentially anchor positions. The fortified city of Metz was the larger component of a system of defenses tied in with Thionville farther north and known as the Metz-Thionville *Stellung*. The French had lost these positions to Germany during the period of 1870 to 1914 and again in 1940. The Germans had added new fortifications at D'Illange and Koenigsmacker to extend the defense of the east bank of the Moselle even farther north,[63] and they oriented their additions to face west, not east. The defense of Metz was further strengthened by the Seille River, which flowed generally southeast from the city. This natural barrier prevented a quick envelopment from the south.

Patton had directed his G-2, Oscar Koch, to focus all intelligence planning on Metz as far back as March 1944 when Third Army was still in England. According to Farago, he "anticipated some complications" with the Metz forts at the time, and he and Walton Walker saw it as "potentially dangerous to bypass such a strong-point while thrusting some 150 miles ahead."[64] However, efforts to deduce the true nature of the Metz fortifications proved wholly inadequate. By the time Third Army closed up on them in September, Koch could provide little useful intelligence and Patton's attitude had changed from curiosity to a deferral of the problem posed by the position onto the shoulders of Walker. His belief in the weakness of the German defenses undoubtedly sparked his sudden disinterest in Metz.

Whereas the most-modern parts of the Metz fortifications faced west, Nancy generally faced east and had never been designed as a defensive bastion. The French had always utilized it as a bridgehead through which they could move east, and natural barriers were Nancy's only real defense. On the east, it was nominally protected by rugged terrain features. On the west the Moselle swung well wide of the city, and at the apex of this loop the city of Toul guarded passage across the river. Nancy's best defense was the rugged Forêt de Haye, which occupied the area between the western loop of the Moselle and the city. Despite these natural advantages, however, Nancy was vulnerable to a flanking attack.

The area between Toul and Epinal, known as the "Charmes Trough" or "Nancy Gap," represented a western entry into Lorraine and a means of outflanking both the Metz-Thionville position and Nancy. Relatively flatter than other sectors, the major impediment to an eastward exit from the gap was the succession of streams blocking the way in traverse. Extending from Nancy in a southeasterly direction ran the Mortagne, Meurthe, and Vezouse Rivers. Once past Metz and Nancy, an attacker had to deal with more natural impediments such as the swampy and heavily forested impassable sector west of Sarrebourg,[65] and man-made fortifications.

Mirroring the German frontier and the positions of the West Wall were the fortifications of the Maginot line (see Map 4.2). Designed to defend against a German attack from the east, the line was at a disadvantage defending against Patton advancing from the west. All easily removable parts, especially artillery, had long been removed from the line for use in Hitler's Atlantic Wall, leaving the position with limited defensive capabilities. What the Maginot line did offer the First Army was a series of well-constructed casements and bunkers from which defending infantry could delay Third Army's advance.[66] But the Germans made little tactical use of these positions as they retreated across Lorraine in November.

One of the most important aspects of topography from a military perspective is the presence of a good road net. Contrary to Anthony Kemp's assertion that Lorraine possessed few roads running west-east to the Saar and Rhine,[67] Terrain Area Analysis No. 10 clearly stated that "routes in the area, both road and rail, are adequate for any military movement."[68] Two main highways stretched across Lorraine. The first followed a Metz to Saarbruecken to Mannheim route; the second led from Nancy to Strasbourg. In general, an adequate road net covered most of the area east of the Moselle.[69]

From simply studying a road map (probably a Michelin), Patton determined that the weakest portion of the West Wall resided east of the Nancy Gap because good roads ran in this direction. He felt that "if you find a large number of big roads leading through a place, that is the place to go regardless of enemy resistance. It is useless to capture an easy place you can't move from."[70] Yet despite the good road net, Patton's choice of advance

Map 4.2
Location of the West Wall and Maginot Line

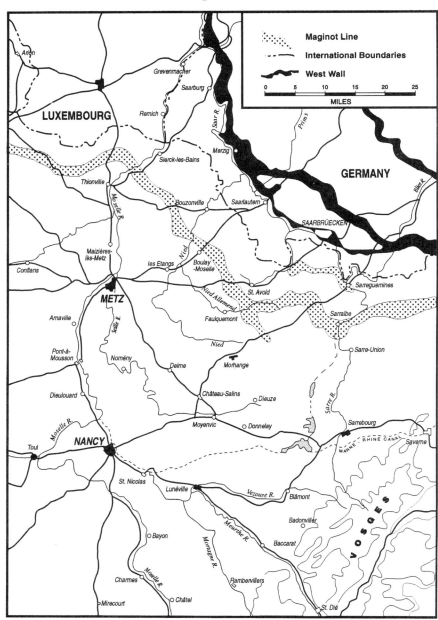

would be somewhat limited due to certain confining features of the terrain. Cole noted that "since the Lorraine plateau narrows as it approaches its eastern terminus, hemmed in as it is by the middle and lower Vosges and the western German mountains, there is not enough room to accommodate a modern army in advance on a wide front. As a rule, therefore, any advance east of the Moselle will tend to move diagonally toward the northeast on a constantly narrowing front."[71] Patton's operational directives during the campaign would consistently reflect this hard fact of military topography.

The most obvious obstacle to Patton's advance to the Rhine, apart from the Moselle and Metz, was the West Wall, a system of fortifications that followed the east bank of the Saar River. The line was strongest in the area of the Saar industrial region where it reached a depth of three miles in places. Running along the forward edge of the position was an antitank obstacle consisting of concrete dragon's teeth, curved steel rails, ditches, and escarpments. Mine fields supported the antitank obstacle in front with the purpose of canalizing the attack onto the strongest portion of the defenses.[72]

The numerous small concrete forts that made up the line behind the tank obstacle were designed to support each other with a closely interlocked zone of fire. Intelligence at the time was lacking, but three main types of forts were discernible from air photos and included machine-gun forts, antitank forts, and unarmed shelters. None of the types were very large, being on the average thirty-five by forty-five feet and capable of holding ten men each. As for the strength of the individual positions, the thickness of the concrete walls and roofs ranged from five to over six feet.[73] The dispositions of the West Wall guaranteed a significant challenge because the Germans had designed it with a keen eye for terrain. Where cross-country movement with armor was possible, the defenses were strongest; where the defenses were moderate, the terrain was formidable.[74]

Patton had never considered man-made fortifications to be worth much, and even in the face of this terrain study, he remained adamant that the West Wall could be breached with armor.[75] He rejected the theory that terrain supposedly limited the effectiveness of tanks, stating that although some types of terrain were more suitable than others, armor had and could function in any environment.[76] His persistent belief in the plausibility of this course of action was probably enhanced by what Ultra intelligence decrypts were telling him about the West Wall in September. General Westphal knew so little about the dispositions of the fortifications that he requested details of its course around Trier on September 3. Though Patton knew through Ultra that the West Wall was not ready in early September, he was equally informed that instructions had long been issued for the raising of emergency garrisons and construction crews, the latter of which reached 150,000 men by September 12.[77]

Whereas many American officers, with the exception of Patton, overestimated the strength of the West Wall, most German officers in postwar interviews continually disparaged the fortifications. One officer, who stated that the wall was a big bluff (in accordance with Patton's thinking), nevertheless pointed out that the wall gave the Germans three important advantages. It provided a physical installation to which they could tie in their reserves and stabilize the front, offered protection from American artillery, and adversely affected American troop morale.[78] Whatever the merits of the last suggestion, there is no question that the West Wall was an obstacle not to be taken lightly. It would take massive quantities of artillery and manpower, supported by air power, to crack the West Wall when Patton finally reached it in December.

The entire Lorraine battlefield was a formidable area to advance through, and the compartmentalizing effect cannot be overstated. The Moselle and Saar Rivers presented significant obstacles, and the lesser streams when flooded could be just as difficult. The extensive fortifications of Metz and the West Wall were strong defensive positions that would severely test the endurance of Patton's forces, and the forests and tactical heights at times severely constrained movement. The Lorraine battlefield did not offer much prospect for quick success.

Ultra may have been giving Patton intelligence on a strategic level, but as Third Army closed on the borders of Lorraine, it provided less and less hard tactical information. The failure to uncover the precise layout of Metz was one example. Corps intelligence assets could penetrate at best only fifteen thousand yards behind enemy lines.[79] The problem lay in the proximity of Third Army to the German frontier. In August, fleeing German units had depended heavily on highly vulnerable radio traffic for communications, but Lorraine was more secure because it had been colonized by Germany. The partially hostile population and the presence of German field forces proved inhospitable for Free French activities. Military Intelligence interpreter teams discovered fewer and fewer knowledgeable sympathizers willing to divulge important information.[80] Yet despite these intelligence deficiencies, several signs were quite visible signifying the enemy's decision to stand and fight, at least on the front covered by Walker's corps.

Cavalry patrols from XX Corps had lost contact with the enemy on August 29 but regained it on September 2. Even on this latter date there were signs of stiffening German resistance in front of the patrols. The Free French of the Interior (FFI) reported that German troops had entered Metz and were strengthening positions south of the city near Arnaville.[81] Patton, of course, exaggerated the truth for effect when he informed Bradley on September 2 that patrols from the 3rd Cavalry Group had entered Metz the day before.[82] Cole clearly refutes this: "Contrary to rumors that later circulated through the Third Army, no American cavalry were able to enter Metz or its environs."[83] They were not able to enter because German units had moved out from the city proper to erect outposts. The XX Corps Operations Report for this period noted that the enemy was observed setting up a defensive screen west of the Moselle in the Thionville area.[84] By September 4, defensive positions west of the river were being "rapidly manned and . . . fairly well coordinated."[85]

The erection of a defensive screen should have sparked something in Patton. Here was a clear example of German recuperation; a badly shattered army would certainly have retreated straight back into the confines of the West Wall as quickly as possible. There is no reason to believe that Patton would not have known of this German activity. He prided himself on the creation of his "Household Cavalry," formerly the 6th Cavalry Group until he gave it the official title "Army Information Service" in Normandy. Bypassing regular communications channels, the service coordinated and condensed information and sent it directly to the Army advance command post.[86]

The scattered German outposts had turned into real numbers by September 6, the day Walker began his advance. The Corps G-2 estimated that Knobelsdorff could bring a maximum of 38,500 men and 160 tanks and assault guns against XX Corps in the Metz area in a series of piecemeal commitments. The 17th SS Panzer Grenadier and 3rd Panzer Grenadier Divisions had been clearly identified, but some intervention by the 21st Panzer and Panzer Lehr Divisions was anticipated as well.[87] The reasoning behind this estimate was that the Metz-Luxembourg area constituted an important rallying point for German regrouping and reinforcement on the Western Front.[88]

XX Corps possessed limited reliable intelligence about what was in front of them, but XII Corps was even worse off. FFI and cavalry reports indicated that the enemy was not disposed in sufficient strength to make a stand on the east bank of the Moselle. However, Cole's assessment that the strength and location of German forces east of the Moselle was unknown to General Eddy is much more likely.[89] The resulting setback when the corps did attack is proof enough. Patton showed no obvious concern for what lay in front of or beyond the Moselle in Eddy's zone (nor in Walker's despite the presence of the two panzer grenadier divisions), for on September 3 he visited Eddy to discuss methods of attacking the West Wall.[90] Assaulting the Moselle in the face of his engineer's declaration that this natural barrier constituted a "major" obstacle did not weigh on him to any great extent.[91] His eyes were on the Rhine.

Patton retained his belief that only thinly deployed reserves would stand in his way at the Moselle. This was a serious mistake on his part and looks even worse when all the ingredients were present for him to make the right assessment. If Ultra was telling him how desperately Rundstedt feared a major breach in the Metz-Trier area, then surely he should have deduced that every available man and vehicle would be thrown in his path. Additionally, there was no reason to question Ultra's identification of the two panzer grenadier divisions. During the drive across France, Ultra correctly placed in Italy certain German divisions that the regular G-2 analysis insisted were opposite Third Army.[92]

The only explanation for Patton's cavalier attitude about what faced him across the river was his dual perception that these identified forces constituted everything the Germans had left and that they were far from first-class fighting formations. A delaying action at the most would be effected at the Moselle while remnants of the shattered Wehrmacht would attempt a more determined but hardly more effective stand at the West Wall.[93] He clearly had lined up with virtually everyone else who believed the German Army in the West to be damaged beyond repair. Here, despite its great contributions, was one of the failings of Ultra intelligence. Its strength was in its accuracy where numbers of troops, tanks, artillery, casualties, many types of supply were concerned, but it oftened failed to say much about vital features such as fighting capabilities, training, morale, and fitness.[94] Patton should have known that any great army is greater than the sum of its material parts.

On September 5 Patton thought, planned, and acted under the erroneous assumption that a pursuit of German forces was not simply possible but actually continuing, though momentarily interrupted by logistical shortfalls. Nothing proved this more than his brief, two page operational directive to Eddy and Walker. Without identifying the numerous hazards waiting to stall his drive, Patton directed Third Army to seize bridgeheads over the Moselle and continue the advance east to secure positions across the Rhine River between Koblenz and Karlsruhe. In so doing, Walker's XX Corps was to seize fortified Metz and advance "rapidly to the northeast" to seize Mainz while being prepared to continue the advance to Frankfurt. Russell Weigley related how Patton "enthusiastically encouraged Walker to drive for Metz."[95] Eddy's XII Corps drew Nancy as its first objective, with the follow-on task of driving northeast to Mannheim on army orders (see Map 4.3).[96] Clearly, Patton felt that he could

Map 4.3
Third Army Plan of Advance/German Dispositions, September 5, 1944

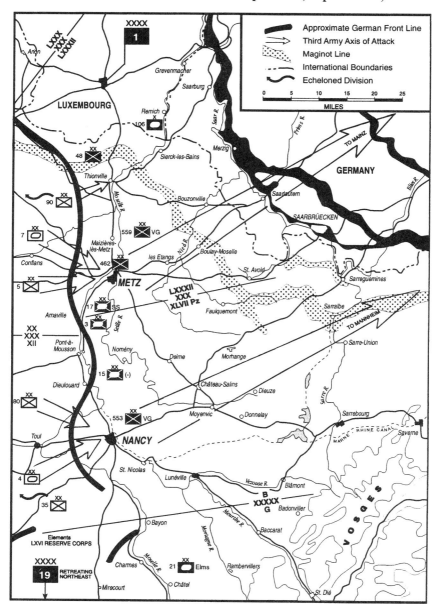

Source: Base map taken from Hugh M. Cole's *The Lorraine Campaign*, U.S. Army in
World War II: European Theater of Operations (Washington, D.C., 1984), Map XXII.
Altered by Eric Drummie and Bill Traer.

seep through the cracks of a weakened enemy line and pour into his rear areas. The great success of this tactic in France had led Blumenson to label Patton a "slasher" and the "master of the *ad hoc* strategy."[97] Starting from a dead stop, Patton was improvising his way across the Moselle.

His initial movement of the Lorraine Campaign was a large reconnaissance in force because he lacked proper intelligence (and failed to heed what was available). Modern U.S. Army doctrine teaches that the primary mission of a reconnaissance in force is to "force the enemy to disclose his strength, dispositions, or intentions" through battle.[98] Patton's chief concern, however, was forestalling enemy concentration ahead of him so that his advance could retain a degree of fluidity. This meant utilizing speed to its fullest extent. Eddy has stated the case for rushing the Moselle in the following manner: "To take the time that would have been consumed in preparing for an organized attack, without being sure that the Germans intended to hold, would have meant either the loss of contact with the main forces if his intentions were to withdraw to the east, or permit him time for further reorganization if he intended to hold."[99]

By holding to the idea that he could throw Third Army across the Moselle in a massive bull rush, Patton violated one of his own firm beliefs. He made a distinction between "haste" and "speed" in offensive operations, noting that the result of haste would be to "get the troops into action early, but to complete the action very slowly."[100] Thus, Eddy's comment that a time factor played a role in the decision to rush the Moselle cannot stand on its own because Patton sat idle for five full days awaiting fuel. This was ample time to coordinate a powerful blow against a portion of Knobelsdorff's line. The failure to do so rests squarely on Patton's misperception of the type of fighting he was about to engage in.

There was no need to concentrate his forces and to discern a decisive point because he thought the entire German line equally flimsy. He was not thinking in terms of a breakthrough, and although his attempt to secure as many crossings as possible was appropriate based on his flawed understanding of circumstances, this strategy rapidly disintegrated in the first days of the advance. For Patton, the litmus test of his generalship in September rested to a very large extent on how quickly he recognized the shift from fluid to static warfare. If in fact he did come to this realization, the next obvious question is how well did he respond to this novel type of battle.

NOTES

1. Quoted in Stephen E. Ambrose, *The Supreme Commander: The War Years of General Dwight D. Eisenhower* (Garden City, N.Y.: Doubleday, 1970), 503.

2. Martin Blumenson, *The Patton Papers* (Boston: Houghton Mifflin, 1974), II: 537.

3. Ronald G. Ruppenthal, *Logistical Support of the Armies*, U.S. Army in World War II: European Theater of Operations (Washington, D.C.: Department of the Army, 1953), I: 491.

4. Dominick Graham and Shelford Bidwell, *Coalitions, Politicians, and Generals: Some Aspects of Command in Two World Wars* (London: Brassey's, 1993), 227.

5. Forrest C. Pogue, *The Supreme Command*, U.S. Army in World War II: European Theater of Operations (Washington, D.C.: Department of the Army, 1954), 249–250.

6. Christopher R. Gabel, *The Lorraine Campaign: An Overview, September–December 1944* (Fort Leavenworth, Kans.: Combat Studies Institute, 1985), 3.

7. Pogue, *The Supreme Command*, 250; Ambrose, *The Supreme Commander*, 505.

8. Graham, *Coalitions, Politicians, and Generals*, 229.

9. Omar N. Bradley and Clay Blair, *A General's Life* (New York: Simon and Schuster, 1983), 218–219.

10. Harry H. Semmes, *Portrait of Patton* (New York: Appleton-Century-Crofts, 1955), 504.

11. Carlo D'Este, *Patton: A Genius for War* (New York: HarperCollins, 1995), 566. Eisenhower wrote to Patton after the slapping episodes, "I must so seriously question your good judgement and your self-discipline as to raise serious doubt in my mind as to your future usefulness." In writing to Marshall in August 1943 Eisenhower recited Patton's brilliant conduct of the Sicilian campaign but continued, "In spite of all this, George Patton continues to exhibit some of those unfortunate personal traits of which you and I have always known." To Marshall again in April 1944 Eisenhower described Patton as "unbalanced." Alfred D. Chandler, ed., *The Papers of Dwight D. Eisenhower: The War Years* (Baltimore: Johns Hopkins University Press, 1970), II: 1340, 1353; III: 1841.

12. Graham, *Coalitions, Politicians, and Generals*, 231, 246.

13. Norman Gelb, *Ike and Monty: Generals at War* (New York: William Morrow, 1994), 353.

14. Blumenson, *Patton Papers*, II: 535.

15. Pogue, *The Supreme Command*, 252.

16. Hugh M. Cole, *The Lorraine Campaign*, U.S. Army in World War II: European Theater of Operations (Washington, D.C.: Center for Military History, 1984), 4.

17. Ibid., 24. The lowest intake of fuel by Third Army occurred on September 2 when a mere 25,390 gallons arrived.

18. Ambrose, *The Supreme Commander*, 508.

19. Ibid., 509.

20. Gelb, *Ike and Monty*, 358.

21. Pogue, *The Supreme Command*, 253.

22. Ambrose, *The Supreme Commander*, 521.

23. Cole, *Lorraine Campaign*, 52.

24. Ronald G. Ruppenthal, *Logistical Support of the Armies*, U.S. Army in World War II: European Theater of Operations (Washington, D.C.: Department of the Army, 1959), II: 193–194. The gasoline rationing continued throughout the campaign with a new level set in late October of 6,500 and 12,500 gallons per day respectively for infantry and armored divisions.

25. Cole, *Lorraine Campaign*, 210. Twelfth Army Group based this figure on the logistical experience of divisions in combat since D-Day. Major General Hobart Gay, Patton's Assistant Chief-of-Staff, pointed out that when Twelfth Army Group removed the 7th Armored Division from Third Army to First Army in late September there was a corresponding decrease and increase in both armies' respective tonnages by four hundred tons thus suggesting that Twelfth Army Group placed the maintenance figure for armored divisions at four hundred tons minimum per day. Hobart R. Gay/Hugh J. Gaffey Diary (Gay/Gaffey Diary), September 23, 1944, Special Collections, United States Military Academy Library, West Point (WP).

26. J. A. Huston, *The Sinews of War* (Washington, D.C.: Office of the Chief of Military History, 1966), 530. Huston cites a higher figure, 650 tons per day for an Allied division engaged in normal fighting.

27. Ruppenthal, *Logistical Support of the Armies*, I: 491.

28. Gay/Gaffey Diary, September 23.

29. Ruppenthal, *Logistical Support of the Armies*, I: 492; Omar N. Bradley, *A Soldier's Story* (New York: Henry Holt and Company, 1951), 412.

30. Anthony Kemp, *The Unknown Battle: Metz, 1944* (New York: Stein and Day, 1981), 4.

31. Blumenson, *Patton Papers*, II: 523.

32. Ibid., 531.

33. Ibid., 537.

34. Cole, *Lorraine Campaign*, 55.

35. Ladislas Farago, *Patton: Ordeal and Triumph* (New York: Ivan Obolensky, 1963), 639.

36. Ibid., 638.

37. Gay/Gaffey Diary, September 4. "Generally west" may not have specifically meant the Moselle River in Gay's mind, however.

38. Ambrose, *The Supreme Commander*, 496.

39. Ibid.

40. Cole, *Lorraine Campaign*, 53. Ambrose stated that "the heady success of the liberation of France had its effect everywhere, even in the mind of the supreme commander." This caused Eisenhower to bet Montgomery that the war would be over by Christmas. Stephen E. Ambrose, *Ike's Spies: Eisenhower and*

the Espionage Establishment (Garden City, N.Y.: Doubleday, 1981), 73. At the time, it appears as though only Omar Bradley engaged in any serious second guessing of future Allied gains. He stated, "While cheered by these reports of enemy chaos, it was to Brest that I looked for a more meaningful clue to the enemy's will to resist. For despite the futility of its position, the garrison at Brest held out under the pounding of three U.S. divisions. If the enemy could command such stubborn resistance in so hopeless a situation as the one at Brest, I was disinclined to believe in any prediction of collapse until we had reached the Rhine." Bradley, *A Soldier's Story*, 409.

41. Ralph Bennett, *Ultra in the West: The Normandy Campaign of 1944–1945* (New York: Charles Scribner's Sons, 1979), 136.

42. Ibid., 137. Bennett continued, "By revealing these anxieties to the Allied commanders, Ultra demonstrated that pressure applied in the Moselle-Saar region might create an opportunity for exploitation as rapid as anything that could be achieved in the north."

43. Cole, *Lorraine Campaign*, 54.

44. Martin Blumenson, *Patton: The Man behind the Legend, 1885–1945* (New York: William Morrow, 1985), 231.

45. Harry C. Butcher, *My Three Years with Eisenhower* (New York: Simon and Schuster, 1946), 47.

46. Blumenson, *Patton: The Man behind the Legend*, 231. Helfers quickly became overwhelmed by Patton's demands for Ultra intelligence and another officer had to be added. Working in twenty-four-hour shifts, the two men were responsible for evaluating an average of ninety intercepts a day, showing their findings on maps and in daily briefings. Harold C. Deutsch, "Commanding Generals and the Uses of Intelligence," *Intelligence and National Security* III, 3 (1988): 230.

47. Deutsch, "Commanding Generals and the Uses of Intelligence," 229.

48. Ibid.

49. Cole, *Lorraine Campaign*, 1.

50. Oscar W. Koch, Manuscript entitled *Intelligence in Combat*, 1955, Fifteen-27 (represents page number), Koch Papers, USAMHI.

51. Deutsch, "Commanding Generals and the Uses of Intelligence," 230.

52. Pogue, *The Supreme Command*, 245.

53. Ibid.

54. Blumenson, *Patton Papers*, II: 530.

55. Pogue, *The Supreme Command*, 245.

56. Blumenson, *Patton Papers*, II: 537. Patton was not alone in his belief that the war could be won quickly. In early September William C. Sylvan, Courtney Hodges' aide, recorded Hodges as saying that if they could get ten days of good weather, the war might be over. William C. Sylvan Papers (USAMHI).

57. Siegfried Westphal, *The German Army in the West* (London: Cassell, 1951), 172, 174.

58. Blumenson, *Patton Papers*, II: 540.

59. Ibid.

60. Farago, *Patton: Ordeal and Triumph*, 548.

61. Gabel, *The Lorraine Campaign: An Overview*, 2.

62. Cole, *Lorraine Campaign*, 26.

63. Ibid.

64. Farago, *Patton: Ordeal and Triumph*, 645.

65. Third Army Terrain Area Analysis No. 10, September 5, 1944, File # 103-2.4 to 103–2.10, Modern Military Reference Branch (MMRB), Suitland, Maryland.

66. Anthony Kemp, *The Maginot Line: Myth and Reality* (New York: Stein and Day, 1982), 101–103.

67. Kemp, *The Unknown Battle*, 29.

68. Terrain Area Analysis No. 10.

69. Cole, *Lorraine Campaign*, 28.

70. George S. Patton, *War as I Knew It* (Boston: Houghton Mifflin, 1947), 89.

71. Cole, *Lorraine Campaign*, 28.

72. Third Army Terrain Area Analysis No. 9, September 1, 1944. File # 103-2.4 to 103-2.10, MMRB.

73. Ibid.

74. Ibid.

75. Farago, *Patton: Ordeal and Triumph*, 561.

76. Blumenson, *Patton Papers*, II: 433.

77. Bennett, *Ultra in the West*, 132.

78. ETHINT 27, "The Siegfried Line, September 12–16, 1944," an Interview with Genmaj der Waffen-SS Fritz Kraemer, Chief of Staff, I SS Panzer Corps, November 29, 1945, Donald S. Detwiler, with Charles B. Burdick and Jurgen Rowher, eds., *World War II German Military Studies* (New York, 1979), II.

79. Gabel, *The Lorraine Campaign: An Overview*, 7.

80. Ibid. See also Ronald Lewin's account in *Ultra Goes to War* (London: Hutchinson, 1989), 345–346.

81. Cole, *Lorraine Campaign*, 119.

82. Patton, *War as I Knew It*, 94. Robert Allen related the same story and suggested that it was the 15th Cavalry Squadron that entered Metz on September 1 and "spent an unmolested night on the Cathedral square." Robert S. Allen, *Lucky Forward: The History of Patton's Third U.S. Army* (New York: Vanguard Press, 1947), 136.

83. Cole, *Lorraine Campaign*, 119.

84. XX Corps Operational Report, "The Reduction of Fortress Metz, 1 September–December 6, 1944," Box 64, Patton Papers (PP), Library of Congress (LC), 3.

85. Cole, *Lorraine Campaign*, 120.

86. Martin Blumenson, *Breakout and Pursuit*, U.S. Army in World War II: European Theater of Operations (Washington, D.C.: Department of the Army, 1961), 350.

87. Cole, *Lorraine Campaign*, 123.

88. Ibid.

89. Ibid., 62, 94.

90. Ibid., 58.

91. Terrain Area Analysis No. 10.

92. Deutsch, "Commanding Generals and the Uses of Intelligence," 231.

93. Cole, *Lorraine Campaign*, 124.

94. Deutsch, "Commanding Generals and the Uses of Intelligence," 198.

95. Russell F. Weigley, *Eisenhower's Lieutenants: The Campaign of France and Germany, 1944–1945* (Bloomington: Indiana University Press, 1981), 482.

96. Third Army Operational Directive, September 5, 1944, File # 103-3.0, MMRB.

97. Martin Blumenson and James L. Stokesbury, *Masters of the Art of Command* (Boston: Houghton Mifflin, 1975), 239.

98. Capt. Andrew F. Demario, "Reconnaissance in Force: To Seize Advantage from the Enemy," *Armor* (November–December 1989), 44. Quoted from FM 100–5.

99. Manton S. Eddy to Harry J. Malony, February 14, 1949, Historical Division Combat Interviews (HDCI), National Archives (NA), Washington, D.C.

100. Patton, *War as I Knew It*, 269.

Chapter 5
_____

Breaching the Line of the Moselle

[H]e can be classed as an army commander that you can use with certainty that the troops will not be stopped by ordinary obstacles.
—Eisenhower to Marshall, August 1943[1]

Patton's strength is that he thinks only in terms of attack as long as there is a single battalion that can keep advancing.
—Eisenhower to Marshall, September 1943[2]

The hastily assembled German forces defending the Moselle River in the first days of Patton's renewed advance wasted no opportunity in displaying their determination to buy time for the reequipping of the West Wall. Defending against a river crossing from hilly features greatly enhanced German defensive capabilities, but Third Army's attack also lacked punch. Logistical shortcomings and faulty perception of the German defenses quickly exacerbated Patton's problems at the Moselle.

   Patton initiated his advance on September 5, ordering his two corps commanders to attack with the "least practical delay."[3] Bradley directed him to advance in two phases: first penetrate the West Wall, and then secure bridgeheads across the Rhine. The quickest route to the West Wall was in XX Corps' sector, and according to Walker, Patton had planned as early as the spring of 1944 to make the main effort with XX Corps, which was to "move east with the utmost speed to cut through the Siegfried Line before it was manned."[4] Yet as Third Army sat on the west bank of the Moselle at the beginning of September with empty gas tanks, both corps were balanced with two infantry divisions and one armored division. There was no "lead" corps, although Eddy would attack on September 5 followed the next day by Walker in a one-two punch.

The intelligence vacuum opposite XII Corps did not weigh heavily on General Eddy as he prepared to test the German defenses along the Moselle. He was convinced as much as Patton was that "if we could obtain the necessary fuel this war might be over in a matter of a few weeks." "None of the Germans in this sector," he added, "have any fight left in them."[5] His optimism may have been fueled in part by the improvement in his gasoline situation. Almost half of the 560,000 gallons requested arrived on the 5th. He was quite confident when he ordered McBride's 80th Infantry Division to secure widely dispersed bridgeheads at Pont-à-Mousson, Marbache, and Toul.

Eddy had originally planned to use armor to grab bridgeheads, but both McBride and John S. Wood, commander of the 4th Armored Division, argued that the corps armor should be conserved for exploiting any bridgeheads won by the infantry. Eddy's initial intention to hurdle the Moselle with armor shocked Wood, who according to Gabel, "understood the difference between snatching an intact bridge on the dead run and forcing a river crossing against an enemy who had had a week to take defensive measures."[6] Both Wood and McBride cited the unknown strength of the enemy and the difficult nature of the Moselle as further reasons not to risk the armor.[7] In his quick understanding of the limitations of armor in Lorraine, Wood displayed a much more realistic perception of the campaign (and would continue to do so) than Eddy and to a certain extent, Patton.

In Eddy's revised plan armored elements were to cross through the Pont-à-Mousson bridgehead and take Nancy from the rear in typical Patton fashion (see Map 5.1). But the categorical failure of the first infantry assaults on September 5 reduced the armor to mere observers on the west bank of the river. The 317th Infantry Regiment of McBride's division suffered an especially bitter repulse at Pont-à-Mousson when it ran into elements of Hans Hecker's 3rd Panzer Grenadier Division. This action resulted in the slender American position on the east bank being annihilated with the loss of nearly three hundred officers and men.

After the disaster at Pont-à-Mousson, Eddy canceled further crossing attempts at this site and lamented that "if the attack had been made the night before, as planned, we would have had the bridgehead today; or if they had used enough smoke . . . we would have made better gains."[8] The attempt by the 318th Regiment to secure a crossing at Marbache was even less successful. It got bogged down simply trying to secure its positions on the western bank. Eddy's only success came at Toul where the 319th Regiment managed to cross the river and secure a small lodgment. The decision to even attack at Toul must be questioned, however. The site lay on the westernmost

Map 5.1
80th Infantry Division's Assault on the Moselle, September 5–10, 1944

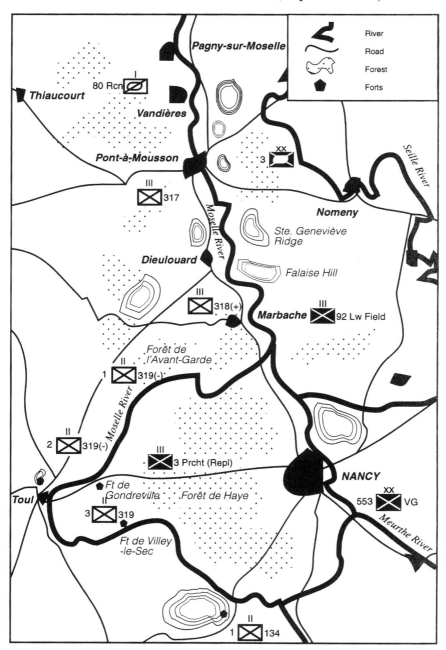

Source: Base map taken from Hugh M. Cole's *The Lorraine Campaign*, U.S. Army in World War II: European Theater of Operations (Washington, D.C., 1984), Map No. 2. Altered by Bill Traer.

point of the salient formed by the Moselle as it looped around Nancy. To expand eastward toward the city, the 319th Regiment had to fight through the dense Forêt de Haye, a natural barrier protecting Nancy on the west. The Germans would prove during the campaign that they were masters of forest fighting. Moreover, two fairly significant forts, de-Villey-le-Sec and de Gondreville, also barred the way. It was little wonder that the 319th made little headway out of its bridgehead because as Eddy stated on the 7th, "Any movement on the part of our troops across the area in the bend of the river at Toul is always met with a withering fire of all types."[9]

Walker's advance on September 6 fared little better than Eddy's. Neither he nor Patton visualized a lengthy siege of Metz and had not prepared for one. Patton's September 5 order to seize the city rested conditionally on its speedy capitulation. Walker reflected Patton's thinking by ordering Major General Lindsay Mcd. Silvester, commander of the 7th Armored Division, to bypass Metz "if it doesn't fall like a ripe plum"[10] and strike straight for the more important objective of bridgeheads over the Saar River. Thionville and Metz, amazingly designated as "intermediate objectives" despite sitting squarely in Walker's immediate path, were assigned to the 90th and 5th Infantry Divisions respectively.[11] Patton's fascination with the West Wall and the Rhine would blind him to the fact that the problems posed by these "intermediate" objectives required immediate attention.

Jumping off on September 6, Walker's advance elements quickly collided with spirited German resistance several miles west of Metz and the Moselle amid the outpost lines manned by the Fahnenjunkerschule (Officer Candidate School) troops of Walther Krause's Division Number 462. Utilizing large-scale Michelin road maps for lack of anything better, Walker possessed only the vaguest idea of the extent of the Metz defensive system. His failure to discern the obstacles in front of him led Anthony Kemp to characterize his initial movements of the campaign as the blind leading the blind.[12] French officials had provided Patton with information concerning the forts of Metz as they stood in 1940, but no one had detailed information concerning whatever improvements the Germans had made since then.[13] Moreover, based on the assumption that the forts were outdated, virtually no information on their layout was passed along to lower units responsible for the fighting, not even to regiments.[14]

Walker's armor, acting in a reconnaissance role, advanced toward the Moselle in four parallel columns searching for all possible crossings of the river. This reflected the normal method of advance for XX Corps armor during the previous operations in France,[15] but Silvester's tanks proved inadequate to break through the German security lines without extensive infantry support. The gasoline shortage had forced Combat Command B (CCB) to attack at 1400 hours on the 6th without the 23rd Armored Infantry Battalion and a company of Armored Engineers in support. Armored divisions were already light in infantry (containing only three battalions of armored infantry) and regularly borrowed an additional battalion from adjacent infantry divisions.[16] But it appears that it was not felt the armor needed assistance at the time. The 5th Infantry Division received enough gasoline to make it fully mobile, but it was not committed to the battle in strength until 0830 on the morning of September 7,[17] which precluded it from giving Silvester maximum support.

Silvester's armor, largely lacking its infantry support, bore the brunt of the initial attacks against emplaced positions, a development that ran completely contrary to American armored doctrine by the fall of 1944, which identified the tank as an exploitive weapon. Wood, for instance, felt that the .50 caliber machine gun was the real tank weapon. Tanks were only being used to their full potential when they could cut into the enemy's "vitals" and rip his equipment and personnel to pieces.[18] In partial disagreement was Major General Robert W. Grow, commander of the 6th Armored Division. In his view, slugging matches were not beyond the capabilities of American armored divisions. Even FM 17-100, the standard field manual on armored divisions, described them as capable of "engaging in most forms of combat."[19] Grow felt that no matter how far ahead of the infantry his armor got, even if they were surrounded, "We've enough fire-power and mobility to punch out of anything the krauts have to offer."[20] Silvester, however, was trying to *break-in* to a complex and carefully prepared system of mutually supporting positions held by excellent troops rather than punch out. Despite its general ability to fight in all types of combat, it is clear that the American armored division was not designed to bludgeon forward an advance against prepared positions.

During the first two days of fighting west of the Moselle, XX Corps did not even attempt to make a crossing, as the various committed elements fought simply to hold their positions. The 23rd Armored Infantry Battalion—finally mobile—and elements of CCB, occupied a weak position near Dornot on the west bank on September 7 but suffered heavily from their exposed position. Most of the casualties sustained here were inflicted by the devastating flanking fire from Battery Moselle, a component of Fort Driant, so situated as to rake the Moselle Valley south of Metz with its three 100-mm guns.[21] While the bridgehead operations faltered, the 2nd Infantry Regiment of Irwin's 5th Infantry Division launched a frontal probing assault against the Metz forts and sustained heavy casualties. With the initial setbacks suffered all along XX Corps's front in the first crossing attempts, Kemp insisted that Walker's advance was "American genius for improvisation at its very worst," highly effective in a fluid situation but inadequate in a static one.[22] Walker was looking for gaps, but few existed.

Patton's opening failures to cross the Moselle were the product of different factors. The most obvious impediment was his failure to concentrate his combat power against a segment of the German defense. He simply did not possess enough striking power in four divisions, two infantry and two armored, to simultaneously engage an enemy on a seventy-mile front and secure several widely separated crossings. Neither corps possessed sufficient resources to penetrate the river line in force.

He knew from terrain and road net studies that the Nancy-Epinal gap offered the best route into and through Lorraine, but he made no move to reinforce Eddy's corps for a decisive advance through this area because he underestimated the German defense. Moreover, taking scarce resources away from XX Corps to reinforce Eddy would have weakened Walker's push for the West Wall and quick bridgeheads over the Saar, which Patton desperately wanted. Ironically, the shortest route to the Rhine, Patton's ultimate objective, ran eastward from Nancy to Strasbourg in Eddy's sector. This was not the first time Patton had mismatched resources with missions. Earlier in Brittany he had sent Grow's 6th Armored Division, lacking good intelligence, on a lone two-hundred-mile sprint to capture the fortified port of Brest. Blumenson labeled this operation as "hardly feasible."[23] In fact, Patton and the Third Army staff had "greatly underestimated" enemy strength at the port of St. Malo as well when VIII Corps began assaulting it on August 6.[24]

Patton lacked numbers because he entered Lorraine without any sort of reserve. Grow's armored division was listed as the army reserve on September 5, but on that date it was strung out between Orleans and Montargis protecting the south flank of the Allied armies along the Loire River. The 83rd Infantry Division, promised to Patton during the five day lull as part of Haislip's XV Corps, was on flank duty as well. Bradley informed Patton on September 5 that these divisions would be made available to him whenever the 94th and 95th Infantry Divisions disembarked on the continent.[25] With these divisions hundreds of miles west and two more of his divisions protecting the flanks of his own army, Patton attacked on September 5 and 6 with all his available strength forward.

On September 8 Patton asked Bradley to release the 6th Armored and 83rd Infantry from their current assignments, but Bradley refused on the basis that a threat still existed to the south flank of the Allied armies. This cautionary measure was excessive but reflected Bradley's natural timidity.[26] Free French Forces were scouting the Loire, and the very capable interdictory power of the XIX TAC was continuously present to discourage major incursions across the river. The bridges spanning the river had been cut to impede any enemy movement northward,[27] and the bulk of Weise's Nineteenth Army in the south of France had already been dislodged by Patch's Seventh Army. The only German armor present south of the Loire was the 11th Panzer Division, and it had been severely mauled protecting Weise's retreat up the Rhone Valley. Ultra revealed that any major threat against the Loire was imaginary, and Alan F. Wilt noted that with the exception of those troops garrisoned in major ports, the Germans were "intent on withdrawing toward eastern France, not launching an attack against Patton's rear."[28]

The impetus of the German retreat and Allied advance was eastward. To waste a powerful armored division guarding against what Patton called "ghosts" was a mismanagement of resources. Grow's division and the 83rd Infantry could have served the much more immediate objective of prying the Germans away from the east bank of the Moselle. The armor would not arrive until mid-month, and the availability of the 83rd rested strictly on Bradley's whim. Patton might also have had the services of the 79th Infantry Division much earlier than he did. The 79th was also a component of Haislip's XV Corps, soon to be reassigned to Third Army. Optimism was so prevalent prior to the start of the Lorraine Campaign, however, that Bradley did not anticipate Patton's need for it until Third Army had actually advanced beyond the West Wall.[29]

Coupled with the lack of extra weight embodied in a good reserve, the diminished presence of the XIX TAC hurt the crossing attempts as well. Air support proved nonexistent for Eddy's attacking regiments on September 5 because Eisenhower diverted Brigadier General O. P. Weyland's entire command to the fortress of Brest four hundred miles from Patton's new front along the Moselle.[30] In fact, between August 26 and September 18, the XIX TAC flew the majority of its sorties against the Brest forts on every day except three.[31] Eisenhower deemed it important to get Patton moving again but apparently did not think Third Army needed any air support.

The heyday of close and continuous air support from XIX TAC was, in fact, over. Due to the increasingly poor weather and the diversion of aircraft to other missions, Third Army received diminishing returns from the XIX TAC from September onward. In August, Weyland's command had flown 12,292 sorties in support of Third Army. During September that figure dropped to 7,791 sorties. In October, November, and December, the monthly sortie totals fell to 4,790, 3,509, and 2,563 respectively.[32] None-theless, the excellent relationship between Patton and Brigadier General Weyland ensured that Third Army's air support was maximized at all times under the circumstances. According to Colonel James Ferguson, Wey-land's A-3, Patton was "completely conscious of the problems, limitations and capabilities of air [power]." Though his corps and divisional command-ers all too often considered air's primary function that of providing constant cover for ground troops,[33] Patton understood its role.

A further reduction in Third Army firepower occurred when a serious deficiency in higher-caliber artillery ammunition developed on September 6. XX Corps possessed a fairly good supply, but XII Corps was short in all types of ammunition and fuses.[34] One explanation for the shortage is short-sightedness on the part of Patton and his G-4, Brigadier General Walter J. Muller. They were so obsessed with gasoline requirements for the pursuit that they failed to requisition sufficient artillery ammunition for sustained fighting.[35] Third Army did not request a large increase in its ammunition stocks to deal with the German resistance at the Moselle until September 7, two days after Eddy's assault began.[36]

It is interesting to note that in the section of his memoirs entitled "Reflec-tions and Suggestions" Patton observed that "a knowledge of the tactical situation will ensure that gasoline and ammunition are asked for in time. The Combat Service and not the Supply Service is responsible for failure to get such things."[37] Yet the problem was deeper than Patton's failure to req-uisition more ammunition. A significant shortage of ammunition arriving in theater, combined with the lack of transportation assets—the root cause of the gasoline shortage—made the delay in ammunition requests a moot point. XX Corps had requested 10,000 tons of ammunition for stockage and estimated that its expenditures would reach 3,000 tons per day as it neared the West Wall. This was a request that could not be met any time in the im-mediate future. As a staff officer reviewing Muller's demands put it, Third Army was asking for the moon.

The depth of the supply and transportation problem was evident by the fact that the total transportation tonnage allotted Third Army for all classes of supply (food, gasoline, ammunition, oil, lubricants, blankets) equaled 3,500 tons per day. Of that total, only 1,280 tons were set aside for ammuni-tion.[38] Furthermore, Twelfth Army Group would announce on September 16 that all theater reserves of 105-mm and heavier caliber artillery ammuni-tion would be exhausted by October 10 at current rates of fire.[39] Third Army was already on reduced rates, and there was little Patton could do.

Patton's logistical competence has been the source of great controversy over the years. Nye labeled him a "superb" logistician, and Blumenson echoed the sentiment, claiming that he was "technically expert" in the field[40] even though he delegated great responsibility in this regard to Muller. General Brehon B. Somervell, essentially the U.S. Army's chief logistician, observed when he visited Third Army in late August that Patton "has no worry about supply."[41] Martin van Creveld actually praised Patton for his logistical touch, noting that "unlike the majority of his fellow commanders . . . he refused to be tied down by the logistician's tables."[42] No better example of this exists than Patton's order to drain gasoline out of as many tanks as possible in order to keep a few advancing towards the Meuse River at the end of August. Bradley, in a rare compliment, noted that "a less aggressive commander than Patton would probably have hoarded the pittance that came his way and halted his line for winter safekeeping behind the Meuse River line. But George plunged boldly on."[43] Ultimately, however, Bradley flatly condemned Patton for his handling of the supply side of war, stating that "logistics were and would remain a mystery to him."[44] In North Africa and Sicily he observed Patton to be indifferent to the fundamentals of supplying an army.[45]

Patton certainly lacked Montgomery's hoarding instincts, but he did possess, according to Eisenhower, "a native shrewdness that operates in such a way that his troops always seem to have ammunition and sufficient food no matter where they are."[46] Part of his shrewdness involved the diversion of First Army fuel trucks to Third Army dumps. Still, Patton should have recognized that if he could not quickly bypass Metz and was forced to tackle the fortifications directly, enormous amounts of ammunition would have been required. It has already been shown that XX Corps anticipated high expenditures at the West Wall. Moreover, the indications coming out of VIII Corps' siege of Brest was that fixed fortifications quickly exhausted normal volumes of ammunition reserves. VIII Corps actually warned Muller on August 10 "of the heavy ammunition demands anticipated for the reduction of Brest."[47] At the very least, Patton had been caught off guard along the Moselle.

Faced with the obvious failure to cross the Moselle rapidly and in strength, Patton's response does not appear to have been overly excited despite Farago's assertion that he was stunned by the reverses.[48] The disaster at Pont-à-Mousson caused him to reflect on Eisenhower's decision to halt Third Army at the end of August, declaring it a "fateful blunder."[49] The logical inference to be made from this statement is that Patton suddenly realized that his window of opportunity had slammed shut. But if he ever admitted this possibility to himself, he never displayed that self-realization in the form of altered tactics for forcing the river.

One is reluctant to afford Patton much latitude when it comes to gauging German intentions and capabilities at the Moselle. Third Army had been so thoroughly repulsed in its first efforts as to indicate a measure of enemy staying power beyond that of a mere rearguard action. Hindsight is of course 20-20, but the observation nevertheless holds its validity. There was at least enough current intelligence available to indicate that the Moselle could not be bounced, and a simple estimation of the natural and man-made obstacles suggested that the race across France was over. The decision to try to bull-rush the river was a bold action that failed.

After the debacle at Pont-à-Mousson, Patton allowed Eddy to spend five precious days regrouping his corps and reconnoitering for a better crossing site.[50] After the war, Eddy stated that his reconnaissance in force on September 5 "left no doubts in our minds that he [Germans] expected to try to hold the line of the Meurthe and the Moselle."[51] A deliberate crossing attempt was now obviously necessary, and he directed McBride to begin preparations for a coordinated assault north of the junction of the Moselle and Meurthe Rivers. A few days later Eddy changed his mind and decided to make the main corps effort south of Nancy. He scheduled this new attack for September 11 but could have prepared another assault with the forces he had. This is what Patton expected him to do.

Patton had anticipated that Eddy would secure a bridgehead with the 80th Infantry and 4th Armored Divisions and expand that bridgehead with the 35th Infantry when it became available.[52] However, the one slender foothold across the Moselle at Toul was not readily expandable because the 3rd Parachute Replacement Regiment stubbornly held against the 319th Regiment until September 10. Eddy's failure to attempt another crossing before the 35th Infantry became available essentially gave the Germans yet another five-day breather in which to prepare defenses. His hesitancy leads one to conclude that he and Patton had widely different concepts of what constituted "speed" of operations. There are numerous other instances of his caution to support this conclusion.

After Eddy assumed command of XII Corps in place of the ill Major General Gilbert R. Cook during mid-August, Patton questioned Eddy's ability to function within his speed-oriented style of fighting on several occasions. On August 20 Patton stated that "he [Eddy] has been thinking [that] a mile a day [was] good going. I told him to go fifty and he turned pale."[53] Similarly, on August 26 Eddy was given an operational jumpoff date, which apparently startled him. "He is not used to our speed yet," declared

Patton, "so [he] was a little surprised."[54] Eddy was likewise startled when Patton told him to simply ignore ninety thousand Germans on his right and eighty thousand on his left during the drive across France.

Retired U.S. Army Lieutenant Colonel Henry G. Phillips, who served in Eddy's 9th Infantry Division in Tunisia, described him as "tactically tidy."[55] Gabel commented that he was "methodical and thorough rather than flashy and daring" and because of this he "did not mix well with Patton and Wood."[56] It is not apparent that Eddy, an infantry general, ever did fully grasp the style of warfare advocated by Patton and executed by Wood. As the campaign wore on, the tension between Eddy and Wood intensified. Wood actually commanded XII Corps for the short space of ten days after Cook's relief until Eddy arrived to take over and felt that he (Wood) deserved the corps command. This was probably the source of some of the tension, yet the major cause was professional. As D'Este noted, "If ever there was an example of the philosophical and personal disparities between the aggressive armor generals and the Fort Benning-trained infantrymen, it was the appalling relations between these two men."[57] There can be little doubt that Patton's fighting style and operational vision in Lorraine would have been better served by having XII Corps commanded by Wood rather than Eddy. A. Harding Ganz, in commenting on Wood's eventual relief from duty on December 3, accurately described the problem arising from Eddy's elevation to command XII Corps. "By keeping Eddy and losing Wood," he stated, "Patton had opted for a style of warfare that was conventional and unimaginative."[58]

Oddly enough, in Sicily Patton had suggested that it was desirable to have different personalities for corps commanders. He pointed to the dash of Major General Geoffrey Keyes, who commanded the Provisional Corps, and the caution of Bradley in command of II Corps as a workable example.[59] This actually reflected the situation in Third Army with Walker and Eddy. The escalating tension between Eddy and Wood, however, proved that major differences in personalities were a great liability when they occurred within the same tactical entity such as a corps. Personalities in war count for at least as much as numbers and quality. Montgomery, in discussing the human element in war, related how "a third of my working hours were spent in the consideration of personalities." He felt that "good senior commanders once chosen must be trusted and 'backed' to the limit," but if a senior commander received full support and still failed, then "he must go."[60] Patton believed in backing his commanders, but he was far less likely to "cut off heads" than his fellow army commanders. Eddy's performance throughout the campaign suggests that Patton probably could have relieved him on several occasions. Yet with this said, Patton must bare some responsibility for Eddy's slowness. His grip on operations on the Moselle was quite loose, in a manner similar to that displayed during the pursuit across France. This was especially evident in his lack of guidance to both Walker and Eddy along the Moselle after their initial setbacks.

While Eddy methodically regrouped for a second effort against the Moselle, Walker continued to batter away at the well-disposed German positions surrounding the environs of Metz with little success. The best results came when the Germans chose to counterattack. On September 8, the flaw in German counterattack doctrine at this stage of the war revealed itself dramatically when Knobelsdorff committed First Army's only available armor, the 106th Panzer Brigade, against elements of Major General Raymond S. McLain's 90th Infantry Division. The advance of the 106th to Briey, well west of Metz, was a clear sign that Knobelsdorff intended to hold XX Corps as far west of the Moselle as possible.

Elements of Generalmajor Kurt Freiherr von Muehlen's 559th Volksgrenadier Division were already giving ground before McLain's advancing infantry when the German armor arrived. The panzer brigade, not fully cognizant of its location, managed to slip between regimental seams and succeeded in taking McLain's Division command post under fire. What ensued was a wild free-for-all in the dark. Though American casualties were numerous, especially among the division's artillery personnel, the panzer brigade suffered most, producing results out of all proportion to its sacrifice.

One American witness to the action recorded that "the rest of the enemy column was ambushed . . . and annihilated. . . . Each time elements of the 106th Brigade tried a new direction, they were stopped cold."[61] By the end of the engagement, the 90th Infantry Division had destroyed thirty tanks, sixty half-tracks, and almost one hundred other vehicles. Much of the German infantry escaped, but over 750 were captured, excluding those killed.[62] German reports indicated that the 106th Panzer Brigade had been reduced to one-quarter of its original combat strength, and some sources reported that the unit returned to its own lines with only nine tanks and assault guns. This was nearer the truth because the brigade hardly constituted more than a name and a number.[63]

Hitler had handicapped Knobelsdorff's use of the 106th, insisting that it could only be used for forty-eight hours. In attempting to get some use out of the unit within the limited time frame, the First Army commander committed the armor too hastily. The result was the near destruction of the only mobile force First Army possessed to plug holes and especially to stop any deep armored penetrations in the short term. Yet even with this setback,

Knobelsdorff still succeeded in thwarting Walker's continuing efforts around Metz. Irwin's infantry managed to establish another small bridgehead near Dornot on September 8 but had to relinquish it on the night of the 10th under the weight of thirty-six separate counterattacks.[64] The effect of the artillery ammunition shortage was acute. Strict rationing in the use of 105-mm ammunition at the crossing meant that German artillery and mortar fire could not be suppressed. German 88s were also positioned to provide direct fire support against the river crossing.[65]

With the abandonment of Dornot, Walker shifted the Corps effort to Arnaville three miles farther south. On September 10, with the timely intervention of a few P-47s from the XIX TAC, Irwin's infantry secured a firm bridgehead there against Ostendorff's 17th SS Panzer Grenadier Division. By September 11, after five days of hard fighting, Arnaville was the only bridgehead Walker had across the Moselle. To exploit the hard-won Arnaville site, he now planned to contain Metz with the 90th Infantry Division and strike east out of the bridgehead with Irwin and Silvester. But the Arnaville site was not readily expandable without grappling with the defenders entrenched in the southern portions of the Metz defensive system. The Verdun group of emplacements, consisting of Forts Sommy and Blaise, situated atop a gently rising hill, obstructed any flanking movement south of the city.

Additional complications arose from the constant fire of Fort Driant's three 150-mm guns, as well as Battery Moselle. These installations proved a considerable nuisance, especially in the construction of a bridge. But by September 12, Walker had solidified his hold on Arnaville despite a coordinated counterattack by various elements of the 17th SS, 3rd and 15th Panzer Grenadier Divisions. Though German attempts to liquidate the bridgehead failed, the hard fight for Arnaville took its toll on Irwin's division, now 1,300 rifleman short of strength.[66]

The problems at the Arnaville bridgehead added to the sense of urgency that filled Patton's operations on September 12. Shortly before, he spoke like a racehorse caught in the starting gate. "I am doing my damdest to get going again," he declared, "but it is hard."[67] Yet in a letter to a friend, he displayed that faulty perception, born of optimism, that continued to guide his actions to a large degree. He divulged that "Due to the necessity of bringing up our tail, we have stopped on the line of the Moselle," but he trusted that he would soon "have a chance to do some broken field running."[68] Patton regularly indulged in slight exaggerations, and this was no exception; he had not stopped on the Moselle of his own volition but had been forcibly repulsed.

Bradley informed Patton on September 12 that if he could not get Third Army established across the Moselle in strength by the evening of the 14th, he would have to assume the defensive.[69] This ultimatum precluded concentration of effort on a narrow sector to a degree because Patton needed to get as much of Third Army across the river as quickly as possible, proving to Bradley that his advance was worth sustaining. Securing several bridgeheads was the only way to rapidly achieve that objective. The possibility of immediately expanding the Arnaville bridgehead dwindled by the 14th, so much so that Irwin deemed Walker's ambitious expansion order impossible.[70] Patton's hopes of gaining the east bank in strength by the 14th thus fell principally on the shoulders of Eddy's XII Corps.

XII Corps' planning for a renewed effort against the Moselle during its five day regrouping was marked by another dispute between Eddy and Wood. Eddy desired to make the main corps effort south of Nancy, basing his plan upon the lack of any apparent large enemy forces in the area, the availability of Baade's Division, and the near approach of Haislip's XV Corps.[71] Most importantly, Eddy felt the succession of streams blocking an advance south of Nancy was more easily negotiable than the single barrier of the Moselle farther north.[72] He assured Wood that the "initial fighting would be done by the doughboys, and not until they had crossed about the 6th stream would he be called into play."[73] Wood was simply "appalled" at Eddy's abysmal grasp of armored warfare. Pushing the entire 4th Armored north of Nancy, where the Moselle offered the only natural impediment to tank maneuver, made more sense. In a compromise (which Eddy took great pains after the war to refute), he divided Wood's division and sent one combat command south and the other north to exploit any foothold gained by McBride's infantry. Subsequent events would prove that Wood's concept had been correct.

On September 11, the 35th Infantry Division and CCB, 4th Armored Division, initiated XII Corps' second attempt on the Moselle and this time succeeded in securing crossings south of Nancy at Crevechamps and Bayon respectively against elements of the 553rd Volksgrenadier and 15th Panzer Grenadier Divisions. CCB had not wasted its valuable bridging equipment at the Moselle but had forded it and improvised a crossing of a canal that flanked the river. After successfully exploiting the gaps in the enemy's overextended line, CCB would have made even better progress had it not been for the poor roads. Three full days after crossing the Moselle the armor crossed the Meurthe River and closed up to the Marne-Rhin Canal, a distance of only seven miles.[74] By the time CCB reached this barrier, its bridging equipment was exhausted, a situation that forced the command to sit idle for two days.[75]

As one of Wood's powerful armored columns crossed one water barrier after another only to run out of bridging equipment, his other column, CCA, displayed the true potential of armor on good terrain. On September 12, the 80th Infantry Division surprised Hecker's 3rd Panzer Grenadier Division south of Pont-à-Mousson at Dieulouard and secured a footing. As Gabel noted, CCA "did not enter the Dieulouard bridgehead to defend it."[76] Wood envisioned a deep attack and achieved it as the command poured through the lodgment won by the infantry. In nine hours CCA had passed through the hard crust of German defenses and quickly covered the twenty miles to Chateau-Salins (see Map 5.2). Wood saw an opportunity and ordered Colonel Bruce C. Clarke, commander of CCA, to exploit weakness rather than attack strength. Conditions were perfect for executing such an order. The "ground was firm, the countryside rolling and open, the road net good," and most importantly, German opposition was minimal.[77]

Clarke's raid was exactly the type of operation Patton always envisioned tanks executing. By the time it reached Chateau-Salins, CCA had taken 354 prisoners and destroyed twelve tanks, 85 vehicles and five guns. Its own losses for September 13 were twelve dead and sixteen wounded. In its next series of raids, which took it to Arracourt, CCA routed a column of the 15th Panzer Grenadier Division and took another 400 prisoners, destroyed 26 armored vehicles, 136 other vehicles, and ten irreplaceable 88-mm guns. CCA casualties in this action amounted to thirty-three and two medium tanks destroyed.[78]

During CCA's subsequent ambushes and raids near Arracourt over the next four days an additional one thousand Germans were captured, eight more tanks, sixteen large-caliber guns, and 232 more vehicles were destroyed at a cost of three killed, fifteen wounded, and four tanks destroyed.[79] Patton's slash-and-run, guerrilla style has been criticized for not inflicting extensive damage on enemy strength,[80] but Clarke's raid proved what could be accomplished with minimal damage to one's own forces if the enemy could be knocked off balance and taken by surprise with armor.

By September 14, CCA and CCB made contact at the Marne-Rhine Canal, a junction that effectively sealed off Nancy from the rear. CCA's bold action prompted the 553rd Volksgrenadier Division to pull out of its defensive positions in and around Nancy. This tactical retreat allowed Baade to take the city without a fight the next day. Nancy possessed neither the extensive fortifications of Metz nor the favorable defensive terrain to facilitate a determined stand in the area. Better terrain existed

Map 5.2
4th Armored's Penetration to Chateau-Salins, September 11–14, 1944

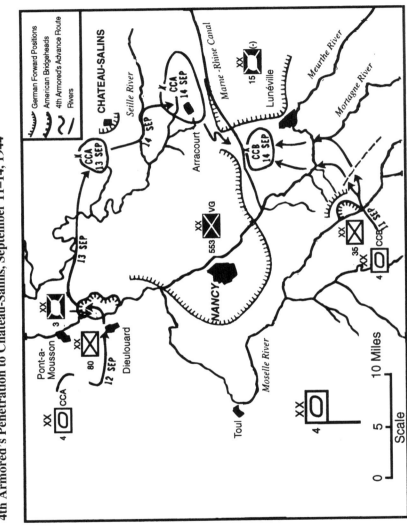

Source: Base map taken from Christopher R. Gabel's *The 4th Armored Division in the Encirclement of Nancy* (Fort Leavenworth, Kansas: Combat Studies Institute, 1986), 13. Altered by Bill Traer.

east of the city. The retreat also reflected the overall strategy Hitler was employing against Patton.

As early as September 3, Hitler planned to launch a powerful counterattack against Third Army's south flank. To facilitate this operation Knobelsdorff's right wing and center were to yield as little ground as possible. No large units were to submit to encirclement so as to provide time for the assembling of an armored force on the left wing. Hitler's strategy was essentially the same as that advocated in the Mortain counterattack, to frustrate the junction of two Allied armies. In this instance, Hitler feared a solid linkup between Third and Seventh Armies.

The arrival of elements of Haislip's XV Corps, newly established in the line to the right of Eddy's corps on September 11, complicated Hitler's ambitious plan. Although Cole indicated that Haislip had no orders to cross the Moselle but simply to close up to it,[81] other evidence suggests that Patton had every intention of getting XV Corps into action across the river as quickly as possible. A memorandum for September 10 and addressed to Haislip clearly indicated that he was to "leave behind only the minimum force necessary" to protect the south flank and "move without delay to seize and secure [a] bridgehead east of [the] Moselle River within [XV Corps] zone."[82] The proposed concentration area for Hitler's counterattack was between Neufchateau, southwest of Nancy, and the Moselle, the exact spot Haislip began to drive into on the 11th.

Another problem confronting Hitler was that to create his mobile force required disengaging his best units from the line. Such a maneuver was difficult to execute at any time, but proportionately more difficult when the intended divisions were hard pressed. Holding the assembly area was the responsibility of the LXVI Corps (essentially a task force under command of Blaskowitz's Army Group G), and its principal element, the 16th Division. Other units included Landesschuetzen (Home Guard) battalions organized as a kampfgruppe and the 19th SS Police Regiment.[83] It was relatively easy for Haislip's forces to press through this motley collection and the overextended German lines.

Wade H. Haislip, an infantryman, was described by Eisenhower as a "Fine Corps C.G.," a "fighter" and "cool" under combat.[84] Patton was equally impressed with his fighting abilities. Haislip originally trained XV Corps in North Ireland as part of Third Army and was committed to battle during the great breakout where the corps performed in excellent fashion. As he prepared to drive into the German front, he commanded two divisions, one armored and one infantry. Major General Ira T. Wyche's 79th Infantry Division had taken heavy casualties since June but had received some 7,500 replacements to bring it near full strength. Cole described the unit as possessing a "good reputation as a veteran division."[85] Wyche was an artilleryman and had been with the 79th since May 1942. The other division under Haislip's command was Major General Jacques Leclerc's 2nd French Armored Division, a unit that had not sustained many casualties since its initial commitment to battle under XV Corps. However, Leclerc was considered to be an aggressive and capable leader by Haislip, and because of their similar experience in attendance at the École Supérieure de Guerre, a high degree of cooperation was achieved between the two.[86]

The ease with which Wyche and Leclerc knifed through the LXVI Corps lines, thus threatening the assembly area, forced Blaskowitz to act. First Army had been transferred to his command on September 8 to facilitate an easier buildup of forces for Hitler's counterattack against Patton. Blaskowitz quickly instructed General der Panzertruppen Hasso von Manteuffel to use elements of his newly reconstituted Fifth Panzer Army (the same army that was forced to surrender in Tunisia) to halt Haislip's advance in its tracks to buy time for the counterattack. In carrying out Blaskowitz's urgent order, Manteuffel subsequently directed Luettwitz, in command of the XLVII Panzer Corps, to launch a counterattack with virtually no reconnaissance and inadequate time for proper coordination. The result was the same kind of useless sacrifice of hard-to-replace men and equipment that the attack of the 106th Panzer Brigade had been a week before. On September 13 Luettwitz's principal armored component, the 112th Panzer Brigade, boasting forty-eight Mark IVs and forty-eight Panthers, engaged a combat command of the 2nd French Armored Division near Dompaire. With the intervention of elements of the XIX TAC, the panzer brigade was decimated. Total German tank losses amounted to sixty, including thirty-four new Panthers and twenty-six Mark IVs. German armor simply could not stand and fight in the face of American air superiority. Moreover, von Mellenthin, commenting on the destruction of the 106th and 112th Panzer Brigades, noted that since this was the first time these units had operated together in combat, it was "no wonder that these panzer brigades did not stand up to conditions and suffered heavy losses in men and material."[87] The 16th Division fared little better fighting against Wyche's infantry. The original strength of the division had been seven thousand, but it sustained four thousand captured and two thousand killed trying to stop the 79th Infantry.[88] By September 15, the 79th reported the German unit as effectively routed.[89]

Haislip's success at blunting another German counterattack and Wood's deep penetration led Patton to conclude that with a little luck he could "keep edging toward the east."[90] But the effect was more significant. The 4th

Armored drive lit a spark in Patton and reinforced the optimism he had displayed from the start. As Cole noted, both Eisenhower and Bradley were optimistic regarding Third Army's continued advance in mid-September, but neither was more optimistic than General Patton, his staff, and his division commanders."[91] At last, Patton had an opening, and he quickly devised a scheme of maneuver to exploit the opportunity.

NOTES

1. Alfred D. Chandler, ed., *The Papers of Dwight D. Eisenhower: The War Years* (Baltimore: Johns Hopkins University Press, 1970), II: 1353.

2. Ibid., III: 1440.

3. Hobart R. Gay/Hugh J. Gaffey Diary, September 5, 1944, Special Collections, United States Military Academy Library, West Point (WP).

4. Walton H. Walker to Hugh M. Cole, October 8, 1947, Historical Division Combat Interviews (HDCI), National Archives (NA), Washington, D.C. Walker stated that "this was General Patton's original plan as conceived in the spring of 1944 in England, and it was finally consummated in its entirety during the period September 1944–March 1945."

5. Manton S. Eddy Diary, September 2, 1944, U.S. Army Infantry School, National Infantry Museum (NIM), Fort Benning, Georgia.

6. Christopher R. Gabel, *The 4th Armored Division in the Encirclement of Nancy* (Fort Leavenworth, Kans.: Combat Studies Institute, 1986), 10.

7. Hugh M. Cole, *The Lorraine Campaign*, U.S. Army in World War II: European Theater of Operations (Washington, D.C.: Center for Military History, 1984), 58.

8. Eddy Diary, September 5. Eddy spoke of the fact that an apparent miscommunication between the infantry and the engineers delayed the building of a bridge across the Moselle.

9. Eddy Diary, September 7.

10. Cole, *Lorraine Campaign*, 121.

11. Ibid., 122.

12. Anthony Kemp, *The Unknown Battle: Metz, 1944* (New York: Stein and Day, 1981), 43.

13. Russell F. Weigley, *Eisenhower's Lieutenants: The Campaign of France and Germany 1944–1945* (Bloomington: Indiana University Press, 1981), 328–329.

14. Charles B. MacDonald and Sidney T. Matthews, *Three Battles: Arnaville, Altuzzo and Schmidt*, U.S. Army in World War II: European Theater of Operations (Washington, D.C.: Department of the Army, 1952), 4.

15. Walker to Cole, October 8, 1947.

16. Gabel, *Encirclement of Nancy*, 2.

17. Cole, *Lorraine Campaign*, 134. On September 6, of the 358,840 gallons of gasoline requested, only 58,605 gallons arrived the next day. Overall receipts for the month were 2,856,000 gallons short. Third Army After Action Report (AAR), Special Collections, WP, I: 67. According to the XX Corps AAR, sufficient gasoline arrived on September 5 to mount both the 7th Armored and 5th Infantry Divisions for the attack. However, both divisions were not committed simultaneously. The armor went into action at 1400 hours, September 6, but the 5th Infantry did not move in strength until 0800 hours the next day. XX Corps AAR, "The Reduction of Fortress Metz, 1 September–6 December, 1944," Box 64, Patton Papers (PP), Library of Congress (LC), Washington, D.C., 2.

18. "Conversation between General Wood and General William A. Borden," January 7, 1945, John S. Wood Papers, Bird Library, Syracuse University (SU), 3. Wood felt strongly that tanks should not be employed against other tanks.

19. Gabel, *Encirclement of Nancy*, 4.

20. Robert W. Grow, *Brest to Bastogne: The Story of the 6th Armored Division* (Paris, 1945), 6.

21. Major Meyer A. Edwards et al., *Armor in the Attack of Fortified Positions* (Armored School, Fort Knox, Kentucky, 1949–1950), 77–78.

22. Kemp, *The Unknown Battle*, 43.

23. Martin Blumenson, *Breakout and Pursuit*, U.S. Army in World War II: European Theater of Operations (Washington, D.C.: Department of the Army, 1961), 370. Blumenson stated that although the mission seemed impossible, Grow never issued any complaints. On the contrary, he wrote that he had "received a cavalry mission from a cavalryman" and that this type of improvisational operation "was what we had spent years studying and training for." Characteristically, Patton wagered Montgomery five pounds that American troops would be in Brest by August 6.

24. Ronald G. Ruppenthal, *Logistical Support of the Armies*, U.S. Army in World War II: European Theater of Operations (Washington, D.C.: Department of the Army, 1953), I: 529.

25. Gay/Gaffey Diary, September 5.

26. Cole, *Lorraine Campaign*, 185; Martin Blumenson, *The Patton Papers* (Boston: Houghton Mifflin, 1974), II: 545.

27. Brigadier General Ralph F. Stearly and Brigadier General Robert M. Lee and Col. James C. McGehee, "The Tactical Air Force in the European Theater of Operations," File R 373/1, Study # 54, OCMH, Washington, D.C.

28. Alan F. Wilt, "Coming of Age: XIX TAC's Roles during the 1944 Dash across France," *Air Force Review* XXXVI (March–April, 1985): 74. Deutsch stated that "among the more reluctant converts to . . . Ultra was Omar Bradley and at no time could one have counted him among its more enthusiastic devotees." Moreover, Bradley "was among the less well served among the Allied commanders from the standpoint of their intelligence staffs." Harold C. Deutsch, "Com-

manding Generals and the Uses of Intelligence," *Intelligence and National Security* III, 3 (1988): 227–228.

29. Cole, *Lorraine Campaign*, 13.

30. Ibid., 63.

31. Weigley, *Eisenhower's Lieutenants*, 285.

32. Cole, *Lorraine Campaign*, 598–599.

33. C. A. Warner to Hugh M. Cole, September 15, 1947, HDCI, NA, Washington, D.C.

34. Charles M. Province, *Patton's Third Army: A Chronology of the Third Army's Advance, August, 1944–May, 1945* (New York: Hippocrene, 1992), 39. This work should be used with caution, for there are numerous factual errors. For example, Province stated that the 319th Infantry Division secured a crossing of the Moselle at Pont-à-Mousson on September 5, when in fact the 317th Infantry Regiment of the 80th Infantry Division failed to cross on that date. The 319th Infantry Regiment fought at Toul. Province no doubt used the Third Army AAR for much of his study, so the reader should cross reference when possible.

35. Kemp, *The Unknown Battle*, 79.

36. Ruppenthal, *Logistical Support of the Armies*, I: 542.

37. George S. Patton, *War as I Knew It* (Boston: Houghton Mifflin, 1947), 271.

38. Ruppenthal, *Logistical Support of the Armies*, I: 542.

39. Ibid., 543. Ruppenthal prepared an excellent chart showing American expenditures of artillery ammunition during July and August. Ammunition was rationed immediately, and the armies "had not been able to fire at desired rates in June or July, or even at the rationed rates later in August." The chart indicated that total daily expenditures for 105-mm howitzers fell from 723,907 during July to 366,952 during August. The average number of rounds fired per gun per day over the same period fell sharply from 40.83 to 27.38. The 155-mm guns went from firing a daily total of 65,484 rounds to 35,140. Average rounds per day for this gun, however, actually rose slightly from 19.7 to 20.6. The heavy gun, the 240-mm howitzer, also had an increase in its average rounds per day, increasing from 6.2 to 7.5 during July and August.

40. Roger H. Nye, *The Patton Mind: The Professional Development of an Extraordinary Leader* (Garden City, N.Y.: Avery Publishing, 1993), 148; Martin Blumenson and James L. Stokesbury, *Masters of the Art of Command* (Boston: Houghton Mifflin, 1975), 232.

41. John Kennedy Ohl, *Supplying the Troops: General Somervell and American Logistics in World War II* (Dekalb, Ill.: Northern Illinois University Press, 1994), 230. Somervell said this in the context of agreeing with Patton's idea about how to finish the war. "The job now," stated Somervell, "is swift pursuit. Patton has the right idea—straight ahead, and let the air forces take care of the flanks."

42. Martin van Creveld, *Supplying War: Logistics from Wallanstein to Patton* (Cambridge: Cambridge University Press, 1977), 214. Van Creveld claimed that

Patton saw Muller only twice, once before he assumed command of Third Army and again in the last week of the war. This was really an irresponsible statement for van Creveld to make. Though Patton did delegate great responsibility to Muller, he would have seen him at daily briefings and other special sessions with the army staff. On October 9, Muller personally accompanied Patton to a meeting at Twelfth Army Group. Omar N. Bradley, *A Soldier's Story* (New York: Henry Holt and Company, 1951), 431.

43. Bradley, *A Soldier's Story*, 412.

44. Omar N. Bradley and Clay Blair, *A General's Life* (New York: Simon and Schuster, 1983), 100.

45. Bradley, *A Soldier's Story*, 51.

46. Chandler, *The Papers of Dwight D. Eisenhower*, III: 1440.

47. Ruppenthal, *Logistical Support of the Armies*, I: 529.

48. Ladislas Farago, *Patton: Ordeal and Triumph* (New York: Ivan Obolensky, 1963), 612.

49. Blumenson, *Patton Papers*, II: 539.

50. Christopher R. Gabel, *The Lorraine Campaign: An Overview, September–December 1944* (Fort Leavenworth, Kans.: Combat Studies Institute, 1985), 15.

51. Manton S. Eddy to Harry J. Malony, February 14, 1949, HDCI, NA, Washington, D.C.

52. Gay/Gaffey Diary, September 5.

53. Blumenson, *Patton Papers*, II: 522.

54. Ibid., 529.

55. Henry G. Phillips, *El Guettar: Crucible of Power, 9th U.S. Infantry Division against the Wehrmacht in Africa, April 1943* (Penn Valley, Calif.: Henry G. Phillips, 1991), 9.

56. Gabel, *Encirclement of Nancy*, 6.

57. Carlo D'Este, *Patton: A Genius for War* (New York: HarperCollins, 1995), 663–664.

58. A. Harding Ganz, "Patton's Relief of General Wood," *The Journal of Military History* LIII, 3 (July 1989): 272.

59. Blumenson, *Patton Papers*, II: 318.

60. B. L. Montgomery, *The Memoirs of Field Marshal the Viscount Montgomery of Alamein* (London: Collins, 1958), 85.

61. John Colby, *War from the Ground Up: The 90th Infantry Division in World War II* (Austin, Tex.: Nortex Press, 1991), 262.

62. Ibid., 263.

63. Cole, *Lorraine Campaign*, 159.

64. Ibid., 145.

65. Ibid., 140–141.

66. Ibid., 151.

67. Blumenson, *Patton Papers*, II: 546.

68. George S. Patton to Major General William Duward Conner, September 10, 1944, Box 26, PP, LC.

69. Bradley, *A Soldier's Story*, 414.

70. Cole, *Lorraine Campaign*, 163.

71. Eddy to Malony, February 14, 1949.

72. Eddy Diary, September 7; Eddy to Malony, February 14, 1949.

73. Eddy Diary, September 7.

74. Gabel, *Encirclement of Nancy*, 12.

75. Ibid.

76. Ibid., 14

77. Ibid., 16.

78. Ibid.

79. Ibid.

80. Farago, *Patton: Ordeal and Triumph*, 550.

81. Cole, *Lorraine Campaign*, 189–190. Cole states, "Unlike the Third Army left and center the XV corps had no orders to cross the Moselle River, but instead operated under instruction to close up to the Moselle between Epinal and Charmes and continue to cover the south flank of the army in the sector of Montargis," 188.

82. Memorandum, September 10, 1944, to Commanding General, XV Corps, MMRB.

83. Cole, *Lorraine Campaign*, 190.

84. Robert H. Berlin, "United States Army World War II Corps Commanders: A Composite Biography," *The Journal of Military History* LIII (April 1989): 166.

85. Cole, *Lorraine Campaign*, 188.

86. Ibid., 187.

87. ETHINT 65, "Comments on Patton and the Third Army," an Interview with Genmaj Friedrich von Mellenthin, May 16, 1946, Donald S. Detwiler, with Charles B. Burdick and Jurgen Rowher, eds., *German World War II Military Studies*, (New York: Garland Publishing, 1979), III.

88. Cole, *Lorraine Campaign*, 204. See footnote 19.

89. Gay/Gaffey Diary, September 15.

90. Patton, *War as I Knew It*, 101.

91. Cole, *Lorraine Campaign*, 214.

Chapter 6

Opportunity and Counterattack

Move swiftly, strike vigorously and secure all the fruits of war.
—Patton, quoting Stonewall Jackson[1]

For the last three days we have had as bitter and protracted fighting as I have ever encountered. The Huns are desperate and are attacking at half a dozen places. Once or twice we gave ground but in all but one case got it back.
—Patton, September 21, 1944[2]

The virtually unopposed penetration by Wood's 4th Armored Division on September 13 and 14 north of Nancy proved Patton's point. Knobelsdorff, who like Patton, had all his available forces well forward, was incapable of defending in depth along the Moselle once his linear defensive system had been ruptured. Patton realized that he had to act quickly with XII Corps to seize the opportunity now open to him east of Nancy. The first priority was convincing Bradley to approve a narrowing of Third Army's front to achieve a greater concentration of forces, the first time in the campaign Patton considered such action.

Bradley approved Patton's request on September 14 with the result that XV Corps' southernmost objective became Mannheim instead of Karls-ruhe.[3] In reality, however, this narrowing of the army's *projected* front link-ing the distant objectives of Koblenz and Mannheim had little effect on the *actual* army front along the Moselle. The Moselle front still extended from north of Grevenmacher to south of Chatel, a distance of almost one hundred miles with the recent insertion of XV Corps on Third Army's right flank. Moreover, Bradley's boundary alteration did not change a fundamental problem with Patton's operational design. Despite the narrowing of the army's projected front, the axis of Third Army's advance remained divergent. XX Corps' axis following Metz-Koblenz and XII Corps' axis following Charmes-Mannheim widened as both corps approached the West Wall. Even after XV Corps was again detached from Third Army late in September, the failure to follow convergent lines meant that mutual support between Patton's two principal maneuver bodies, XII and XX Corps, would not be maximized.

Patton requested the narrowing of Third Army's projected front because he now intended to advance all three of his corps northeast in a column of divisions (one behind the other). XII Corps was to take the lead with armor in the vanguard to exploit Wood's penetration (see Map 6.1). Specifically, Wood's 4th Armored would lead the corps advance from its position around Chateau-Salins and assault the West Wall between Saarguemines and Saarbruecken, a sector roughly nine miles wide.

Following hard on the heels of the armored penetration would be elements of Baade's 35th Infantry Division, charged with the dual responsibility of accompanying Wood through the breach in the West Wall and holding the shoulders of the breech open. McBride's 80th Infantry Division would join in the advance as soon as it could firmly secure the Dieulouard bridgehead area from the 3rd Panzer Grenadier Division.[4] In actuality, on September 14 Patton planned to throw considerably more weight behind the XII Corp' attack. CCB, 6th Armored, en route to Third Army, was also to go to Eddy along with Silvester's 7th Armored Division transferred from XX Corps. This assembly of forces was to achieve a "break-through" all the way to the Rhine.[5]

The exact conditions for 7th Armored's employment with XII Corps, however, are unclear. Cole stated that if Bradley released the 83rd Infantry Division to Third Army in time, Patton intended to give Eddy the 7th Armored from XX Corps and Walker the 83rd Infantry as a replacement.[6] In his own diary for September 15, Patton recorded that Silvester's armor would go to Eddy "if the XII Corps breaks through," suggesting that he expected to give Eddy the division only in the event of XII Corps having penetrated the West Wall.[7] In a following entry for September 16, Patton seems to have changed the conditions, stating that "if he [Walker] could not take it [Metz] in a few days, I would take the 7th Armored Division away from him and give it to the XII Corps leaving him to contain Metz with what he has."[8] This suggested that Patton had not made definite plans to support Wood with Silvester's division. In fact, on September 16, only a day before Patton expected Eddy to launch the operation, Silvester's armor was engaged in a tough battle to expand the Arnaville bridgehead in the XX Corps sector.

Map 6.1
Patton's Plan to Assault the West Wall, September 16, 1944

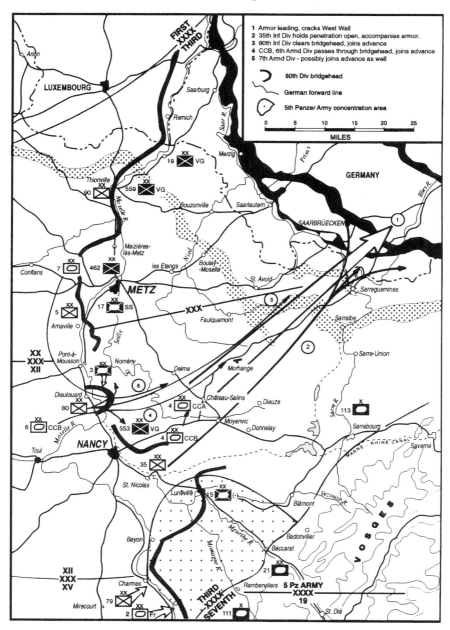

Source: Base map taken from Hugh M. Cole's *The Lorraine Campaign*, U.S. Army in World War II: European Theater of Operations (Washington, D.C., 1984), Map XXII. Altered by Eric Drummie and Bill Traer.

Patton chewed out Walker for slow progress against the maze of fortifications surrounding Metz on the same day proving that he still did not comprehend the harsh reality of assaulting the city directly. Walker, now quite pessimistic about his chances of taking Metz quickly, was given the completely unrealistic mission of continuing his advance to "seize Frankfurt" though he had barely made any progress against Metz at all. While the fortified zone surrounding Metz continued to frustrate XX Corps, Patton nevertheless felt that he and Wood had finally broken the shackles binding Third Army, stating, "I was certainly very full of hopes that day and saw myself crossing the Rhine."[9]

Though Patton's anticipation of quicker movement by Walker was misplaced, his expectation that Eddy would initiate the exploitation as soon as possible was appropriate. But he was to be disappointed. Napoleon had cursed Ney for being "ahead of time by an hour" during a critical moment at Waterloo,[10] but in Eddy's case, he was too slow in executing Patton's plan. On September 16 Patton issued the orders for the XII Corps maneuver, directing Eddy to advance "rapidly" to the northeast.[11] He visited Eddy on the 16th and informed him that his corps was to move the next day. But Eddy's calculations brought XII Corps into position to execute Patton's plan no sooner than the morning of September 19, a date that Patton declared was "too late."[12] As Eddy later stated, "I couldn't let him go giving us that as an order [attacking on September 17] without at least reasoning it out with him, so [I] told him that it would be impossible to do this before the day after tomorrow." Eddy also saw fit to inform Patton that "I was just as anxious to get moving as he and that we would move at the earliest possible time."[13]

On the 17th, Patton sent his Chief of Staff, Major General Hugh J. Gaffey, to hurry Eddy in his preparations. Though Gaffey was a highly capable officer and enjoyed the full confidence of the army commander, it was Patton who needed to be at the front with Eddy, pushing him to make sure that XII Corps attacked on schedule. Patton justified his decision to send Gaffey by stating, "I have been going to the front so much and kicking so much about delay that I have the generals jittery so I am spending a Sunday in the truck with Willie."[14] This may not have been the best time to play with his pet dog.

Eddy again protested when Gaffey arrived, telling him, "All my units were in contact with the enemy and fighting was still going on and that I didn't think that by tomorrow we could either annihilate the enemy or disengage from him."[15] According to Eddy, Gaffey thereupon agreed that XII Corps would need another day to regroup. Interestingly, Gaffey handled Walker in the opposite way. When he visited XX Corps on September 14, he discovered that a scheduled attack had been postponed due to mud. The Chief of Staff thereupon informed Walker in the name of the army commander that the attack would have to be carried out the next day under any circumstances and advised that an alternate plan be formulated so that if the rain continued, the attack could still proceed.[16] No such ultimatum was presented to Eddy. Patton could have ordered the attack to go through without delay had he been present, but he simply recorded with some resignation in his diary that Eddy could "do no better."[17] His failure to get XII Corps moving and his apparent passive acceptance of Eddy's reasons seem out of character.

One cannot help but wonder how Patton would have reacted if Major General Lucian K. Truscott had offered Eddy's excuses in Sicily on the eve of Patton's second amphibious hop. More than likely, Truscott would have been relieved on the spot. Patton said as much when he told Truscott, "If your conscience will not let you conduct this operation, I will relieve you and put someone in command who will."[18] Patton felt that he had earned his pay, that he was a "great leader," for demanding that Truscott carry out the difficult operation immediately.[19] During the battle of El Guettar in Tunisia, Patton had taken Eddy aside at the operations tent of the 47th Regiment, 9th Infantry Division, and "tongue-lashed" him for not being forward with his troops. Eddy noted of the incident, "In all my career I've never been talked to as Patton talked to me this morning. I may be relieved of command."[20]

There is no evidence that Patton was ever as forceful with Eddy in Lorraine as he had been with him and Truscott earlier, and it is difficult to explain why. Patton recorded his desire to accompany the 4th Armored in their attack on the 19th "as a little personal influence may be helpful,"[21] but he missed an opportunity to have a decisive influence on the operation when he allowed Gaffey to confront Eddy in his place. Patton chose not to directly interfere when he knew that Eddy was naturally cautious. On the 16th he had taken keen note of his state of mind. He observed him to be "quite tense" over the situation at the new Dieulouard bridgehead and around Nancy but was still "doing a good job." The 3rd Panzer Grenadier Division and the 553rd Volksgrenadier Division had not disintegrated when CCA cut in behind them. On the contrary, they had dug in on the high ground east of the Moselle.[22] In this situation they were vulnerable to being encircled and cut off. Eddy's caution prevented him from seeing this, and he took excessive steps to protect his rear.

Wood's 4th Armored stood ready to lead the advance, but Eddy ordered CCB back to help McBride's infantry consolidate the bridgehead. This was unnecessary because the pressure against McBride's division was not unbearable. Eddy's decision to clear out pockets behind the vanguard of the corps gave the Germans three full days to bring reinforcements into the area. The decision also certainly violated Patton's belief, expressed on September 19, that "it is always best to attack, especially against the Germans, because if you defend against them, they get a chance to get set and make plans to attack you."[23] In North Africa he insisted that he had to "hit Rommel before he hits us."[24]

In regards to the difficulty in the Dieulouard bridgehead area and east of Nancy, it is difficult not to conclude that Eddy panicked. Haislip wrote after the war that "a corps commander must be flexible; he must be able to adjust himself to any situation without worry, fuss or bother. No matter what happens, it must be considered entirely normal."[25] Patton expected Eddy to adjust to the new operational scheme he had devised, but Eddy could not operate in Patton's improvisational world. According to Cole, by September 16 all the key terrain features covering the bridgehead at Dieulouard, including Mousson Hill and the Ste. Genevieve Ridge, were in Third Army hands.[26] Eddy himself declared on the same day that "the 80th [Infantry Division] . . . were expanding their bridgehead okay."[27] The next day, he again recorded a favorable situation, stating that "with proper dispositions of their units, they [80th Infantry Division] certainly should be able to hold their bridgehead." Moreover, Eddy thought it possible that McBride's division might "even advance."[28]

Diverting the 4th Armored Division to help McBride was unnecessary. CCB, 6th Armored Division had come within range of the bridgehead by September 17 and could have assisted the 80th Infantry Division. In this way the forward momentum of Wood's division would not have had to be interrupted. In fact, if Patton had wanted to alleviate Eddy's nervousness, he could have passed a combat command of Silvester's division through the Dieulouard bridgehead to reinforce McBride. It is unfortunate that this was not done because prospects for a successful, deep penetration by XII Corps on September 17 were excellent. The entire 35th Infantry Division had crossed the Marne-Rhine Canal the day before and was in a position to "wheel into column behind the 4th Armored."[29] According to Eddy, CCA was "right where we want them," and on the 16th CCB was closing up for the advance as well.[30]

Von Mellenthin, the Chief of Staff to General der Panzertruppen Herman Balck (who would replace Blaskowitz in command of Army Group G on September 21), was not overly sympathetic with Eddy's hesitancy. He applauded Patton's bold maneuver as the product of a commander who could "think on big lines" and who "thoroughly understood the character of armored warfare." He felt that Patton's order to advance rapidly "could not possibly be misunderstood or misconstrued."[31] Yet for Eddy, functioning at the pace of the infantry, the thought of plunging onward with intact German units in his rear was more than his infantry-trained mind could handle. He was not temperamentally inclined to go for the jugular.

Had Eddy advanced promptly at the speed Patton desired, a great gap would have been torn in the German defense. As Gabel noted, "Eddy's decision to consolidate before pressing on toward Germany may have strengthened the XII Corps' foothold across the Moselle, but it also proved to be a godsend to the Germans."[32] There were no reserves to block an eastward armored advance from Arracourt, and the Germans had not had time to prepare the entire area with extensive road blocks in depth as they would during October. The combination of these factors meant that Wood could have used the main hard-surfaced roads. Von Mellenthin stated that Wood's penetration had created a fifteen- to twenty-mile gap between the First and Fifth Panzer Armies in the Chateau-Salins sector. He suggested that if Patton had been able to throw in "one or two additional divisions, the weak German formations would not have been able to stop a breakthrough; the road to the Saar would have been open. There were no troops in appreciable strength behind Lorraine."[33] In fact, the only German armor in a position to interfere with the XII Corps' spearhead was the 113th Panzer Brigade, which was still off-loading its Panther battalion at the time.

The failure of Third Army to exploit the success achieved by Wood's division in mid-September represented the greatest missed opportunity of the campaign. Indeed, opportunities for such armored action were rare. Eddy must take the blame for his obvious failures, but Patton cannot escape unscathed. The master motivator and prodigious ass-kicker failed to display his ruthless driving power at a critical moment. Such an opportunity would not present itself again.

The counterattack launched by General der Panzertruppen Hasso von Manteuffel's Fifth Panzer Army against Patton's right flank was the largest counterattack mounted by German forces in the West since crossing the Seine in August and Hitler's only attempt to take the initiative against Third Army on a large scale (see Map 6.2). Manteuffel was the right man for the assignment. A small man, not over five feet two inches, he had started the war in command of Panzer School II in Potsdam-Krampnitz and had missed both the Polish and French campaigns. As the school's instructor, however, he developed his views on armored warfare, principally from his friend, Heinz Guderian.[34] Manteuffel finally got into combat on the Russian front with the 7th Panzer Division and ultimately led a battle group of the di-

Map 6.2
Fifth Panzer Army Counterattack, September 18, 1944

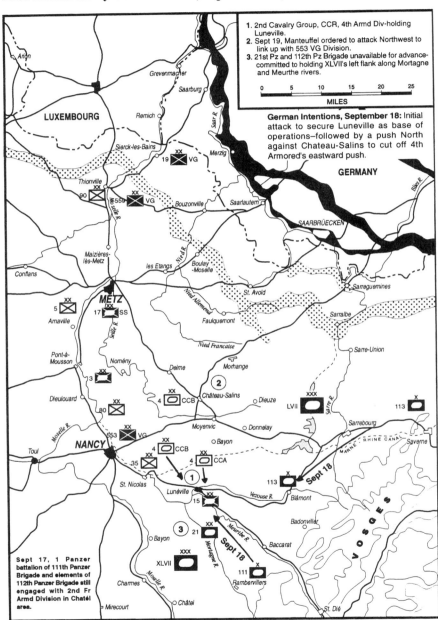

Source: Base map taken from Hugh M. Cole's *The Lorraine Campaign* U.S., Army in World War II: European Theater of Operations (Washington, D.C., 1984), Map XXII. Altered by Eric Drummie and Bill Traer.

vision to the gates of Moscow before it was ordered to retreat. For a short time, he found himself in Tunisia, fighting to preserve the escape routes for the Fifth Panzer Army from Patton's II Corps. In August 1943 he was given command of the 7th Panzer Division and performed brilliantly in the defensive battles on the Dneiper and in the Kiev salient. In January 1944 he took command of the massive 27,000-man Grossdeutschland Division and fought a series of defensive battles against superior Russian forces in East Prussia and Lithuania.[35] He was continually cited in OKW operational reports for his tactical brilliance, and von Mellenthin described him as an officer who possessed the qualities of adaptability and energy in abundance and had the "personal dash and courage required to inspire his men."[36] On September 2 Manteuffel was summoned to Hitler's headquarters where he was promoted to General der Panzertruppen over nine senior ranking officers, even though he had never commanded a corps in battle, and was given Fifth Panzer Army.

The original plan Manteuffel was to execute involved striking Wood's 4th Armored Division in flank near Luneville and wiping out Patton's bridgeheads across the Moselle. Thereupon, he was to press his attack as far west as possible.[37] It was based on a rigid timetable and required extensive alterations. Most notably, Blaskowitz informed von Rundstedt that the original assembly area for Manteuffel's forces had already been wiped out by Haislip's XV Corps. In one of his few instances of common sense, Hitler permitted the Nineteenth Army to shorten its lines by a withdrawal on its right flank so as to allow General Heinrich Freiherr von Luettwitz's XLVII Panzer Corps to take part in the operation.[38]

Blaskowitz then proposed a smaller attack than that proposed by Hitler, and remarkably for this stage of the war, the Führer agreed. The initial scheme of maneuver for Manteuffel's forces was as follows: Luettwitz's XLVII Panzer Corps, built around the new 111th and 112th Panzer Brigades and the 21st Panzer Division, was to hold the left flank of Fifth Panzer Army with minimal forces and push its main armored force across the Marne-Rhine Canal in coordination with General Walter Krueger's LVIII Panzer Corps positioned around Saarebourg. Krueger, who was to have the new 113th Panzer Brigade, was also to take command of Rodt's 15th Panzer Grenadier Division, already positioned just east of Luneville, as his corps pushed west. The objective was to cut off Wood's division moving east by occupying the road junction at Chateau-Salins.[39]

All the German field commanders involved felt their strength insufficient to successfully carry out even this scaled-down operation. As Manteuffel noted, Hitler was "juggling with divisions that are divisions no more."[40] The paper strength of Manteuffel's army was quite impressive, consisting of the 15th Panzer Grenadier Division; 111th, 112th, and 113th Panzer Brigades; and the 11th and 21st Panzer Divisions,[41] but the actual striking power of the army was much less. Many of the assigned units had been decimated in previous fighting and had not been fully rebuilt before committed to battle under Manteuffel. General Edgar Feuchtinger's once elite 21st Panzer Division hardly deserved the label as an armored unit. It had just received twenty-four tanks, but such meager forces did not inspire confidence. In actuality, Feuchtinger's division was now only a "second-rate infantry formation." Wietersheim's 11th Panzer Division was also sorely depleted of armor and was still moving from Nineteenth Army at the time of the counterattack. His Panthers needed major overhauls after covering nearly eight hundred kilometers since mid-August.[42] Of the assigned panzer brigades, the 112th had been almost annihilated by Leclerc's 2nd French Armored Division, and the 113th was still moving to its start lines from the Saarebourg area.[43] Even the 111th Panzer Brigade, the only German unit to attack on September 18 with any strength, still had a panzer battalion engaged against Leclerc's armor near Chatel the day before. Elements of Rodt's division were already fighting in Luneville, and Krueger's LVIII Panzer Corps was widely dispersed.

Despite the lack of coordination, Manteuffel still achieved a good degree of surprise in his opening attacks, which Hitler demanded start no later than the 18th. Third Army intelligence had picked up the assembly of armored forces on the 12th but assumed that it would be thrown in against Seventh Army. Patton initially viewed the assaults by the 111th Panzer Brigade against Combat Combat Reserve (CCR), 4th Armored Division at Luneville on September 18 as a local counterattack. At first there was no reason to suspect otherwise, for the scale of the attack resembled the previous unsuccessful attacks by the 106th and 112th Panzer Brigades. For this reason, Patton felt confident that XII Corps' planned advance could still be executed the next morning, "German counterattack or not."[44] Eddy prepared to carry out Patton's orders but was worried about the situation. While Wood rushed a task force from CCA to Luneville to help out, Eddy ordered CCB of Grow's 6th Armored Division, finally positioned east of Nancy, into the fray as well. Manteuffel's first attack was beat off with the loss of almost fifty tanks,[45] and during the night he received new orders to change the direction of the advance away from Chateau-Salins to Nancy so as to link up with the hard pressed 553rd Volksgrenadier Division, threatened with encirclement by XII Corps. Blaskowitz ordered him to press his attack "without regard to the losses already suffered or the crippled condition of the 113th Panzer Brigade."[46]

Manteuffel quickly recognized the absurdity of this plan in the face of XV Corp's continued advances into the rear of Luettwitz's thinly stretched line and ordered a general regrouping. Rodt's division was given to Luettwitz to help defend the flank of XLVII Panzer Corps. Krueger took command of the 111th Panzer Brigade, and with the substantial armor force of the 113th Panzer Brigade, drove for Arracourt northeast of Luneville the next morning to strike Wood's exposed flank. The resulting clash at Arracourt represented one of the biggest armored battles fought in the West since Normandy.

On September 19, Panthers from the 113th Panzer Brigade succeeded in penetrating CCA's defensive screen. Only by employing a battalion of self-propelled 105-mm howitzers in a direct fire capacity were the Panthers driven back. In the foggy conditions, the Panther's greater gun range was nullified, and the American tanks, relying on their great mobility, succeeded in continually outmaneuvering them.[47] As Cole described one action, after some Panthers had retreated, American tanks "raced the enemy some three thousand yards to a commanding ridge. . . . Arriving on the position about three minutes before eight Panthers appeared, [the] . . . tanks got set and knocked out four of the German tanks before they could return the fire; then they withdrew over the crest of the ridge, moved south a short distance, reappeared, and finished off the remaining Panthers."[48]

By the end of the day CCA had inflicted grievous casualties on the Panther battalion of the 113th Panzer Brigade, destroying forty-three factory-new tanks for a trade-off of only four Shermans, three tank destroyers, and less than twenty killed or wounded.[49] Patton's optimism remained intact even though he noted that the Germans were "really putting on a show." He realized that Wood's division was "pretty thinly extended" by the disjointed fighting with the piecemeal commitment of German armor but felt that the "risk of continuing the attack is justified, owing to the effect it will have on the Germans if we break through the Siegfried Line."[50]

Patton still had his eyes fixed squarely on the Rhine in the midst of the counterattack. He took solace in the fact that at least 80 percent of the German armor in the West was opposed to the Third Army and believed that "the Germans fighting us now are all the Germans there are, and that they have no depth."[51] Only slowly did he begin to sense that his plan to exploit the gap in the German lines was faltering. On September 20, when Wood's armor and the 111th Panzer Brigade traded fairly equal tank losses, Patton had a rare moment of pessimism. According to Eddy, Patton told him that "it may be impossible to complete the mission which we started out on, but we could kill a lot of Germans trying."[52] The German resolve to hold the line was evident by September 21, for Manteuffel was ordered to continue his attacks regardless of casualties or tank losses.

Had not Manteuffel's offensive succeeded in blunting Patton's drive east, Eisenhower's decision of the 23rd would have. It was "one of those bad days" of Patton's military career because Eisenhower gave Montgomery's Twenty-First Army Group first call on all supplies as the British made another attempt to cross the lower Rhine. By the 25th, Patton's divisions were consolidating their positions in the face of continuing attacks by Manteuffel's battered army. Patton had once again seen his momentum stopped cold.

Manteuffel continued to throw everything he had at Wood's division including the 11th Panzer Division on September 25, but it was impossible to continue the attacks beyond September 29 because he had virtually nothing left to fight with by that time. Even when Weitersheim took command of the remnants of the 111th Panzer Brigade, he could dispose of no more than sixteen tanks.[53] The kill ratio had been overwhelmingly in favor of the American tanks. Wood's division claimed 285 Mark IVs and Panthers and other armored vehicles destroyed during the fighting around Arracourt. CCA, which bore the brunt of the armored battles, recorded only twenty-five Shermans and seven tank destroyers lost in the actions. Most of Wood's tank losses were attributed to frontal attacks against emplaced German armor or on level ground where the Panther gun's greater range proved decisive.[54]

The counterattack by Manteuffel's Fifth Panzer Army could have been of enormous operational benefit to the hard pressed German forces responsible for defending Lorraine. Von Mellenthin felt, "From our point of view there was much to be said for counterattacking the spearheads of the XIIth Corps to discourage the Americans from advancing farther."[55] In this sense, the German counterattack doctrine functioned properly in demanding action against the 4th Armored because the real German fear was that Wood's division could crack the still, as yet, unmanned West Wall. Von Mellenthin did not think that any effective defense could be manned there if Wood succeeded in getting any momentum eastward.[56]

Hitler's unyielding insistence, however, that Manteuffel attack on September 18 meant that carefully accumulated assets of armor once again were wasted in piecemeal commitments without proper support. Manteuffel could have struck with a greater degree of concentration in the opening stages if Hitler had given him only one more day to prepare. The offensive failed to inflict proportionate damage on Patton's armor for a host of reasons, not the least of which was poor coordination that threw the armor in piecemeal. A. Harding Ganz implied that such coordination would have been little help. The real reason for the exceptionally high German tank losses was the poorly trained crews manning the new panzer brigades. He pointed out that the brigades had no organic artillery or maintenance and were not "balanced combined arms teams." Moreover, flak assets were "weak" and American air power was decisive.[57] One can readily see the real reasons for the crushing defeat.

In twelve days of fighting, Third Army managed to destroy the greater part of the new tanks sent to the West by Hitler in the fall of 1944. Patton did not seek the battle. He wanted crossings over the Saar and a penetration of the West Wall, but his aggressiveness in this direction nonetheless paid dividends. Manteuffel's counteroffensive might have posed a significant threat to the Allies had not Patton repeatedly sucked in German reserves by persisting in his own offensive.[58] His philosophy of constant offensive action would continue even as he sat on the defensive during October.

NOTES

1. Patton's index cards containing his distilled thinking, Patton Papers (PP), Library of Congress (LC), Washington, D.C.

2. Martin Blumenson, *The Patton Papers* (Boston: Houghton Mifflin, 1974), II: 552.

3. Hobart R. Gay/Hugh J. Gaffey Diary, September 14, 1944, Special Collections, United States Military Academy Library, West Point (WP). The actual boundary between Third and Seventh Armies was not conclusively set at the time of Patton's planned advance, but Bradley had indicated that it would be Mannheim.

4. Hugh M. Cole, *The Lorraine Campaign*, U.S. Army in World War II: European Theater of Operations (Washington, D.C.: Center for Military History, 1984), 215. The plan envisaged McBride taking Saarbruecken and then continuing on to the Rhine.

5. Ibid., 215.

6. Ibid.

7. George S. Patton Diary, September 15, 1944, Special Collections, WP.

8. Blumenson, *Patton Papers*, II: 549. Patton noted that this threat "may get him [Walker] going."

9. George S. Patton, *War as I Knew It* (Boston: Houghton Mifflin, 1947), 102.

10. Octave Aubry, *Napoleon: Soldier and Emperor* (London, 1938), 424.

11. Third Army Operational Directive, September 16, 1944, File # 103–3.0, Modern Military Reference Branch (MMRB), National Archives (NA), Washington, D.C.

12. Blumenson, *Patton Papers*, II: 550.

13. Manton S. Eddy Diary, September 16, 1944, U.S. Army Infantry School, National Infantry Museum (NIM), Fort Benning, Georgia.

14. Blumenson, *Patton Papers*, II: 550.

15. Eddy Diary, September 17.

16. Gay/Gaffey Diary, September 14.

17. Blumenson, *Patton Papers*, II: 550.

18. Ibid., 319.

19. Ibid. Truscott was to execute the amphibious assault with an understrength battalion while operating in "inconceivably difficult terrain." This force was hard pressed for many hours until Truscott's infantry managed to break through to the battalion. The operation was touch and go all the way, and the 650-man battalion suffered 167 casualties. Truscott concluded, however, that "had we delayed a day, we might have captured most of the German force. Nevertheless, we had gained important time." Lucian K. Truscott, *Command Missions: A Personal Story* (New York: Arno Press, 1979), 240.

20. Carlo D'Este, *Patton: A Genius for War* (New York: HarperCollins, 1995), 478.

21. Blumenson, *Patton Papers*, II: 550.

22. Christopher R. Gabel, *The 4th Armored Division in the Encirclement of Nancy* (Fort Leavenworth, Kans.: Combat Studies Institute, 1986), 18.

23. Patton Diary, September 19.

24. Blumenson, *Patton Papers*, II: 194. Patton's faith in his speed-oriented battle philosophy was reinforced by events in Sicily. He noted, "My policy of continuous attack is correct. The farther we progress, the more stuff we find abandoned that should not be abandoned."

25. Wade H. Haislip, "Corps Command in World War II," *Military Review*, (May 1990): 32.

26. Cole, *Lorraine Campaign*, 104.

27. Eddy Diary, September 16.

28. Eddy Diary, September 17.

29. Cole, *Lorraine Campaign*, 107.

30. Eddy Diary, September 16.

31. Major General F. W. von Mellenthin, *Panzer Battles: A Study of the Employment of Armour in the Second World War* (Norman, Okla.: Oklahoma University Press, 1971), 314.

32. Gabel, *Encirclement of Nancy*, 18–19.

33. ETHINT 65 "Comments on Patton and the Third Army," an Interview with Genmaj Friedrich von Mellenthin, May 16, 1946, Donald S. Detwiler, with Charles B. Burdick and Jurgen Rowher, eds., *World War II German Military Studies* (New York: Garland Publishing, 1979), III.

34. Donald G. Brownlow, *Panzer Baron: The Military Exploits of General Hasso von Manteuffel* (North Quincy, Mass.: The Christopher Publishing House, 1975), 63.

35. Ibid., 99, 116.

36. Mellenthin, *Panzer Battles*, 259.

37. Brownlow, *Panzer Baron*, 123.

38. Cole, *Lorraine Campaign*, 217.

39. Richard Giziowski, *The Enigma of General Blaskowitz* (London: Leo Cooper, 1997), 360.

40. Hans von Luck, *Panzer Commander: The Memoirs of Colonel Hans von Luck* (New York: Praeger, 1989), 168–169.

41. Mellenthin, *Panzer Battles*, 316.

42. A. Harding Ganz, "The 11th Panzers in the Defense, 1944," *Armor* (March–April 1994): 31.

43. Mellenthin, *Panzer Battles*, 316.

44. Blumenson, *Patton Papers*, II: 551. Patton wrote that "Eddy still thinks my attack is premature—I hope the Germans agree with him."

45. Brownlow, *Panzer Baron*, 123.

46. Giziowski, *The Enigma of General Blaskowitz*, 360.

47. Gabel, *Encirclement of Nancy*, 21.

48. Cole, *Lorraine Campaign*, 225.

49. Ibid., 225.

50. Patton Diary, September 19.

51. Ibid., September 20.

52. Eddy Diary, September 20. When Patton visited Eddy the day before, he found him to be "quite down and in a defeated state of mind." Patton thereupon told him what Grant had once said, "In every battle there comes a time when both sides consider themselves beaten; then he who continues the attack wins." Patton Diary, September 19.

53. Ganz, "11th Panzers in the Defense," 31.

54. Cole, *Lorraine Campaign*, 243.

55. Mellenthin, *Panzer Battles*, 320.

56. Ibid.

57. Ganz, "11th Panzers in the Defense," 31.

58. Russell F. Weigley, *Eisenhower's Lieutenants: The Campaign of France and Germany, 1944–1945* (Bloomington: Indiana University Press, 1981), 344.

Chapter 7

The Problem of Metz

[B]esieging a fortress increases the problems of the attacker. Clearly, there is nothing that will diminish his strength so much and is therefore so likely temporarily to rob him of his superiority. Still, there are times when a siege is unavoidable if the attack is to progress at all.

— Clausewitz[1]

The October pause in Patton's operations in Lorraine resembled halftime of a football game. He had commenced operations in the first half of the campaign with a game plan that failed to yield the results he had anticipated. Resembling a coach adapting to the opposition, Patton made on-the-spot adjustments, though not as quickly or as successfully as he might have. His one major adjustment in September, his intention to exploit 4th Armored's success east of Nancy, had great potential, but errors in execution stalled the drive and time ran out in the first half before further options could be identified and developed. In October, with the front relatively quiet, his resources exhausted, and the necessity of rapid decision-making reduced, Patton could take a hard look at his situation and prepare for the "second half." Colonel Harkins has said of Patton that he was principally "a student of other's mistakes."[2] If so, and because he must be held ultimately responsible for the failings of his command, Patton now needed to be his own best critic.

There were positive aspects to the fighting in September despite the various setbacks. The nature of the combat all along the Lorraine front in the first phase caused Patton to declare on October 3 that the fighting thus far had been "severe" and "vicious . . . not exactly on World War I principles but more analogous to it than anything we have had yet so far."[3] Although such slugging was not supposed to be Patton's style, Third Army nevertheless inflicted far greater damage on the enemy during the September battles than it suffered. Despite a less-than-favorable attacker-to-defender ratio, Patton's 18,647 battle and nonbattle casualties compared favorably with an estimated 55,000 Germans killed, wounded, or captured on Third Army's front. In equipment destroyed, Third Army had a definite edge with an almost 4:1 ratio in tanks, a 16:1 ratio in artillery, and a 5:1 ratio in vehicles of all types (see Appendix D). It goes without saying that Patton would have readily traded these impressive numbers for greater distance gained, yet even in this category he enjoyed a measure of success in September.

The shift to a defensive posture on September 25 left Patton's battle line resembling a door swinging on a hinge. The center and right wing of the army, XII and XV Corps, had achieved a relatively high degree of success, advancing the army line some fifteen to twenty miles beyond the Moselle in twenty days of combat (see Map 7.1). With this fact in mind, Kemp's criticism of Patton's progress at this stage loses its veracity. Kemp argued that the bitter fighting in early September clearly indicated that for Patton "to make a serious dent in the enemy along the Moselle, a massive injection of fresh manpower was needed" as well as unlimited air support,[4] but Wood's great raid had done more than dent Knobelsdorff's line, it had actually ruptured it. Moreover, Haislip's XV Corps had also performed exceptionally well in its sector and had gained significant ground. In contrast to these achievements Third Army's left wing was thoroughly impaled on the sturdy fortifications of Metz where only two-thirds of XX Corps had managed to gain the opposite bank. Even then, the elements that had crossed, the 5th Infantry Division and the 7th Armored Division, were confined to a limited bridgehead with scant opportunity for rapid expansion.

Metz thus continued to act precisely as the Germans had always intended, as an anchor position for their defense along the line of the Moselle. Hitler never had any intention of allowing German forces in the Metz-Thionville area to withdraw to the West Wall. Even if adjacent units along the Moselle were forced to give ground, every attempt would be made to hold a bridgehead west of the Moselle at Metz.[5] According to Blaskowitz, the principal benefit of holding Metz was that it provided a point where the retreating German army could "check backward movement . . . where your troops can rally and have some additional means to continue a delaying action."[6] As long as Metz held out against assault, or was not displaced, men and material could be diverted to counter the progress of XII Corps. This was successfully done on September 13 when Knobelsdorff was able to move two battalions of the 17th SS Panzer Grenadier Division from Metz to help in the counterattack against the Dieulouard bridgehead. Similarly, on

Map 7.1
Third Army's Front, September 25, 1944

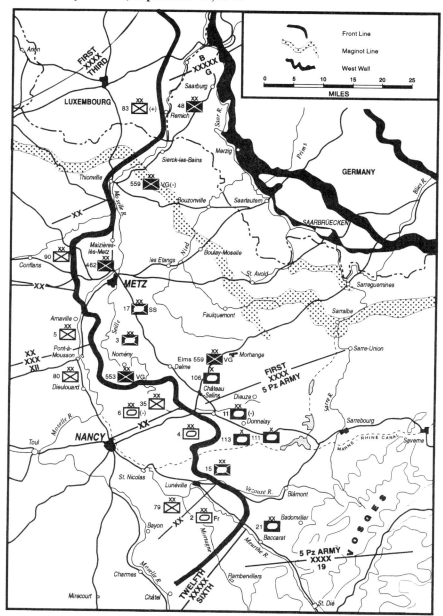

Source: Base map taken from Hugh M. Cole's *The Lorraine Campaign*, U.S. Army in World
War II: European Theater of Operations (Washington, D.C., 1984), Map XXII. Altered
by Eric Drummie and Bill Traer.

September 22, Rundstedt moved the entire 559th Volksgrenadier Division from the sector north of Metz to use in a strike against Wood's 4th Armored.[7] While the ability to hold Metz freed up much needed German forces for fire brigade duties elsewhere, Patton's operations against the city's defenses had the opposite effect of tying down limited Third Army resources. Though he would eventually be reinforced to ten divisions for the November offensive, Patton now found his army once again reduced to four infantry and two armored divisions.

Third Army had been hit hard by the priority given Montgomery's northern operations. On September 23 Bradley ordered the 7th Armored Division north to join Major General Charles H. Corlett's XIX Corps of First Army. Six days later, Haislip departed Patton's command for a second time after Devers had assured Eisenhower that Sixth Army Group could sustain XV Corps in an advance better than Third Army.[8] The loss of XV Corps prompted Patton to think that higher command was intentionally hindering his operations. He stated that "I am not usually inclined to grumble or to think that the cards are stacked against me, but sometimes I wish that someone would get committed to do something for me." He informed Bradley that if Devers could supply XV Corps in Patch's Seventh Army then he could supply it in the Third Army because the "truck haul from Dijon to Luneville is less than a hundred miles."[9] The reinforcement later in October and November would be a godsend to Third Army, but more divisions present on an order of battle did not guarantee success. They had to be used properly. The key to the Lorraine Campaign rested in how Patton handled the deteriorating situation at Metz, the most heavily fortified city in Europe.

The Metz defensive system that confronted Patton and Third Army in the fall of 1944 was based on forty-three various types of forts divided into two distinct belts, an inner and an outer belt, around the city (see Map 7.2). The inner belt consisted of fifteen forts designed and constructed in the eighteenth century under the supervision of the famous French engineer Vauban. Eventually completed by Napoleon III in 1866, the forts of the inner belt were designed to withstand all types of ordnance and infantry assaults of the era. Originally, and even as late as 1940, these forts possessed no artillery, and French Army engineers did not think it possible to add the heavy concrete structures necessary to accommodate heavy guns.[10] The Germans, however, after taking possession of Metz in 1940, began to upgrade the inner belt, and although the allure of successive victories dampened their enthusiasm for fortified works, much improvement took place in the forts before Patton arrived. Fort St. Quentin received the most improvement, with the installation of a radio station for use as a military signal center. In

Map 7.2
The Metz Defensive System

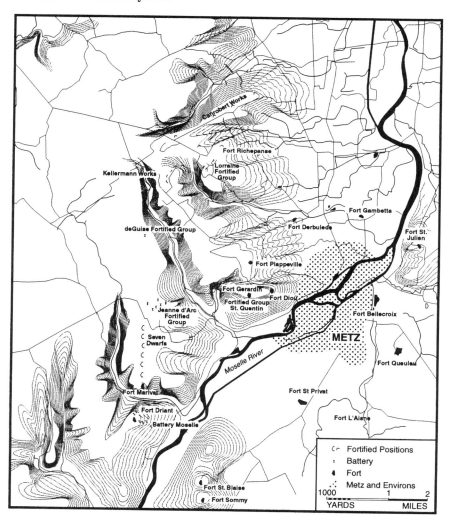

Source: Base map taken from Hugh M. Cole's *The Lorraine Campaign*, U.S. Army in
World War II: European Theater of Operations (Washington, D.C., 11984), Map XXIII.
Altered by Eric Drummie and Bill Traer.

the German tradition of incorporating forts into a defensive group, or *Feste*, St. Quentin was linked to its supporting forts, Giradin and Diou, through a series of supporting bunkers, pillboxes, armored observation posts, heavily reinforced casements, mine fields, and a trench system that extended around the entire circumference of the hill. For firepower, the Germans installed two 210-mm guns in protective, modern, revolving steel observation posts. Additional guns of 105-mm caliber were also installed at the site while considerable and deliberate field fortifications were erected at the remaining twelve forts of the inner belt.[11]

The outer belt of fortifications, began after the German annexation in 1871, and completed by them in 1912, formed a salient approximately six miles west of the Moselle and extended perhaps three to four miles east of the Moselle. Compared to the forts of the inner belt, which were essentially infantry strong points, the outer belt was specifically designed to house artillery. To defend against attacking infantry, each fort or fortified group employed interlocking fields of automatic fire to protect deep moats surrounding the position. The gun emplacements themselves were generally underground, their large-caliber guns mounted in rounded, revolving steel turrets that barely protruded above ground. Each of the forts was built around a main central emplacement supported by two or three smaller reserve forts, batteries, or casements.

The whole Metz system was designed to hold an entire field army. Each fort or group could accommodate 2,000–3,000 men and the 150–200 men needed to properly operate each battery. All forts had direct communication with other positions through a central exchange in Metz. The two largest fortified groups of the outer belt, known in 1944 by their French names Jeanne D'Arc and Driant, were connected by a string of seven minor forts known to XX Corps as "The Seven Dwarfs." The French felt the Seven Dwarfs useful only as infantry positions but the Germans installed one 150-mm howitzer in Fort Marival and numerous 88-mm antitank batteries in and around the remaining forts. Altogether, by 1944 the inner and outer belts boasted 128 artillery pieces of differing caliber.[12] However, many of the forts, particularly in the northern section, lacked usable guns, ammunition, and fire control apparatus by the time Third Army closed with them in September.[13]

Twenty to twenty-five miles north of Metz around Thionville stood forts Koenigsmacker and D'Illange, the final components in what the Germans called the Metz-Thionville *Stellung* (position). Each of these forts had a battery of four 100-mm guns. Fort Yutz, on the eastern bank of the Moselle in Thionville itself, was in poor shape and had no artillery but did command the road network leading east from Thionville.[14] One strength of the entire Metz system was that the most-modern parts of the defenses faced west. However, von Mellethin, in discussing the strength of Metz during postwar interviews with American historians, stated that "The individual works were not integrated into a defensive system. Metz was not a fortress capable of holding out against a strong force for a protracted period."[15] Yet this is precisely what did happen. It is quite clear that Metz was a formidable position both in terms of firepower and the extent of area it covered, but Patton's contempt for the defensive form of warfare and especially defensive positions was too engrained for him to be overawed by Metz.

Patton's views on fixed fortifications had been enunciated quite clearly by the time he entered Lorraine. In discussing the effectiveness of the Maginot Line, he once commented to Harkins, "This is man's monument to stupidity. The enemy knows where you are and will just leave you there."[16] The Germans had proven the value of this strategy during the battle of France in May 1940. The real punch of the German offensive, von Rundstedt's center army group consisting of seven panzer divisions, outflanked the western edge of the line and drove deep into France. As Kemp observed, "The Maginot Line garrisons were left to wither on the vine, becoming known as the forgotten army."[17]

Similarly, on the first day of Operation "Barbarossa," German forces isolated the Russian frontier fortress of Brest-Litovsk. The axis of advance for Guderian's armor, as part of Field Marshal Gunther von Kluge's 4th Army, was along the road to Minsk, which was obstructed by the presence of Brest-Litovsk. The fortress was protected by the River Bug in much the same fashion as Metz was covered by the Moselle. To save time, infantry divisions were used to reduce the fortress while the panzer divisions flanked it. After crossing the river, the panzer group, to use Liddell Hart's phraseology, "sped forward independently—like a shell from a gun."[18] By the time it fell a week later, an irrelevant development, the panzer divisions of Herman Hoth and Guderian were ranging far to the east in search of more lucrative objectives. Patton's comments about the fortifications used in Sicily mirrored his belief about the value of the West Wall. "The Italians and Germans spent tremendous effort in time, labor, and money, building defensive positions," he stated, and "I am sure that just as in the case of the walls of Troy and the Roman walls across Europe, the fact that they trusted to defensive positions reduced their power to fight."[19]

In mid-September 1944 Patton visited the smashed remains of Fort Douaumont as part of a trip to the old Verdun battlefields of World War I. After calling the fort a great monument to heroism, he noted, "To me Douaumont epitomizes the folly of defensive warfare."[20] His grasp of military history told him that all defensive positions had eventually succumbed to assault. He was apparently prepared to overlook the fact that throughout history strong defensive positions had also exacted a high toll on the ultimate victors. Metz, as it turned out, had not been taken by storm since A.D. 451.

Despite a strong sense of the place of sieges in history, Patton's practical experience with fortresses was nil. He had quickly taken the walled city of Enna in Sicily, and his distance from the scene in Brittany meant that he could not really direct the fighting against the fortifications of Brest. To supplement his own knowledge of fortifications, Patton did have access to FM 31-50, a U.S. army manual prepared in 1944 to disseminate Allied erudition on the attack of fortified positions, but it is not clear whether he ever read it. Chief among the concerns reflected in FM 31-50 was the possible inability of the American infantry division to generate sufficient combat power to single-handedly reduce fortifications. In a fairly accurate prediction of the situation at Metz, it also concluded that only elite assault formations using special weapons and tactics could prevail against heavy defensive positions.[21] Patton had no units such as the German *Sturmpioniere* ("assault engineers"), which had successfully seized the Belgian Fort Eben-Emael and captured La Ferte, the only portion of the Maginot Line to succumb in battle in 1940.[22] Michael Doubler complained that "one of the army's greatest shortfalls was its neglect in developing doctrine and equipment to support mobile operations against heavy fortifications" when the "maneuvers of 1940–1941 and British operations in North Africa confirmed the need for additional resources to support infantry attacks against prepared positions."[23]

The obvious lesson that Patton should have been able to perceive quite well for himself after the first phase of the Lorraine Campaign was that operations against the Metz fortifications would be slow, tedious, and deadly. Rommel had quickly come to this conclusion after being repulsed in the initial attacks against Tobruk. "Clearly," he wrote, "it can be seen that the casualty curve rises steeply when one goes from mobile to static warfare" and added that "it follows that static warfare is always a struggle to destroy men, as opposed to mobile warfare, where destruction of the enemy's material is the key."[24] Such bloodletting was totally out of sync with Patton's fighting style. It is equally apparent from the fighting in September that if Patton had no experience in battling fortresses, neither did the infantry of Third Army. From mid-September his growing disenchantment with his infantry's performance at Metz, and elsewhere along the front, was frequently in evidence.

On September 18 Patton deemed it highly unlikely that the Metz forts could be taken by conventional infantry assault. Whether out of pure frustration or a genuine professional observation, he declared that "there is no use in making poor infantry worse by batting their heads against forts they won't take."[25] Part of the problem seems to have been plain fatigue. Patton's men had burned their candles at both ends during the August pursuit, and though nobody would have admitted it, Third Army was tired at the beginning of the Lorraine Campaign.[26] Eddy verified this observation. On the last day of August he passed elements of the 80th Infantry Division and noted that they were "straggling very badly, definitely confirming the fact that physical conditioning of troops is a thing that must be attained, then maintained. They had marched about 25 miles and scores of them had fallen out along the road to have their feet cared for."[27] This begs the question of who suffers more from a pursuit battle, the pursued or the pursuer.

Patton's derogatory statement about his infantry stands in stark contrast to his earlier comment to General Alphonse-Pierre Juin, Chief of Staff of the reborn French Army in late August. Then, in discussing the strength of the West Wall, he had proudly declared, "I believe that American troops can break any [defensive] line."[28] During the war, he fluctuated between an intense adoration and outright condemnation of the American infantryman. For instance, in Sicily he gave the lion's share of the credit for the success there to "the superior fighting ability of the American soldier."[29] Yet during the Battle of the Bulge he would bitterly note that though the Germans were "colder and hungrier than we are . . . they fight better. I can never get over the stupidity of our green troops."[30] Indicative of Patton's constant change of opinion concerning American troops, only a few days previous he wrote that "the Bosch is fighting all out and so are we and doing it better."[31]

The truth was that Patton seriously questioned whether or not American training truly prepared men for battle.[32] In this regard he was on solid ground, but the problem went beyond training into the area of the infantry selection process itself. Of all the armed services, the fact that the Army Ground Forces received the least-promising recruits is one of the more important factors in explaining problems with infantry quality. After the air force, navy, marines, airborne, and technical services had taken the cream of the available manpower in terms of intelligence and physical ability, the ground forces had to develop fighting power with the remainder.[33] But fighting power was a distant second in priority next to the doctrine of confronting the Germans with the greatest possible firepower.[34]

This is why the Germans held American artillery in such high regard while paying much less respect to American infantrymen, who, they concluded, depended upon tremendous material support to bring a battle to a successful conclusion.[35] Patton, recalling the comment of French General Koechlin-Schwartz during World War I that "the poorer the infantry, the more artillery it needs; the American infantry needs all it can get," concluded, "He was right then, and still is."[36] Allan R. Millet has pointed out that professional evaluations by both the Allies and the Germans concluded that American divisions required "overwhelming artillery barrages on front-line units and air strikes on German reserves unless they enjoyed a local superiority of around 4:1."[37] Max Hastings put the numerical ratio in proper perspective when he observed, "Throughout the Second World War, wherever British or American troops met the Germans in anything like equal strength, the Germans prevailed."[38] This is an important thought to consider if truly accurate.

Given the U.S. Army's reliance on artillery, it is sobering to reflect on Millet's assertion that the Metz defensive works often defied indirect weapons. In the case of the sunken casements around Metz this was certainly the case. They required direct infantry assaults assisted by tanks, self-propelled artillery, and antitank guns. Utilizing these weapons required the infantry to close with the field work using sophisticated fire and maneuver, and most infantry units did not possess the "requisite skill or ardor to do so."[39] This does not mean of course that American infantry did not fight hard at Metz in September 1944. So grueling was the fighting around the perimeter that Irwin's division alone sustained 380 men killed, 2,097 wounded, and 569 missing since early September. This represented the equivalent of the division's entire strength of riflemen, the thin, fragile edge of any infantry division.[40] Yet even the best and most highly motivated infantry would have had an extremely difficult time dealing with the Metz forts if they had had no previous training whatsoever in fortress warfare.

Patton has been described by D'Este as an outstanding trainer of men for war, this being perhaps his greatest talent. That said, Patton should not have criticized his infantry for failing to excel in a style of fighting for which they were not trained. Knowing the weaknesses of the cutting edge of his army, he should have avoided Metz at all costs and sought to help his infantry by placing them in the most favorable environment possible. Instead, the infantry of XX Corps found themselves testing their mettle against reinforced concrete, and withering—indeed impenetrable—firepower, a development difficult to explain satisfactorily. One possible explanation for Patton's ill-conceived assault on Metz is the simple magnetism of the fortress itself. Grow indicated that prestige played a prominent part in Patton's gravitation towards Metz, an opinion shared by Weigley, who stated that, "to assault a famous and legendarily impregnable fortified city was a challenge scarcely to be resisted by a soldier with Patton's sense of his military destiny."[41]

One sees in the operations at Metz shades of Patton's obsession with Palermo in Sicily. Moreover, in his stubborn refusal to allow military logic to control ambition, his tackling of Metz also resembled the futile siege of Brest by VIII Corps. He and Bradley both readily admitted that by September 9 the capture of Brest had become pointless because of its distance from the front and the extensive damage to the port facilities. Nevertheless, Patton concluded, "On the other hand, we agreed that, when the American Army had once put its hand to the plough, it should not let go. Therefore, it was necessary to take Brest."[42] At least a portion of this mentality was directly attributable to the fact that Patton and other American commanders were still trying to exercise the defeat at Kasserine Pass.

It is more than likely that had Walker managed to quickly bypass Metz during the first days of the offensive, the city would have been left alone and simply contained. But when resistance stiffened and it became apparent that the American Army was being rebuked, one cannot help but think that Patton invoked his "hand to the plough" philosophy and simply refused to abandon Metz until he had completely reduced it. The question of the tactical importance of this measure requires some treatment in greater depth.

Grow, in his postwar studies, cut to the chase when he declared that "since Metz was an intermediate or secondary objective the first question that arises is whether or not its capture was a compelling requirement."[43] If the fighting in the first phase had proven anything, it was that First Army was not critically vulnerable in the area around Metz. Rather, its weak spot lay in the area that Liddell Hart would have referred to as a "joint," east of Nancy. It was also quite apparent that Third Army's advance had progressed independent of Walker's operations at Metz. Manteuffel's disruptive counterattack of late September against Eddy aside, the potential for sustainable success by Third Army remained squarely on its southern flank in the area of Chateau-Salins. Patton appeared to have come to this conclusion on September 29 when he stated that "they will put all their efforts, which are not excessive, to recapturing Nancy because they realize, as I did when I captured it, that Nancy, and particularly Chateau-Salins, is the doorway to . . . Germany."[44]

In his diary at the time Patton put conditions on his drive to the West Wall, stating, "Before I start east I must either take, or contain, Metz,"[45] but in his memoirs he set out a specific course. "It was on this day [September 20]," he declared, "that I definitely decided not to waste time capturing Metz, but to contain it with as few troops as possible and drive for the

Rhine."[46] It was on September 20 that Patton second-guessed XII Corps' ability to attack the West Wall because of the strenuous resistance put up by Manteuffel's forces.

A Leavenworth study, after suggesting that Metz was "not simply a pocket of resistance that could be simply bypassed," went on to conclude that the "bridge and road network that ran through Metz had to be secured if the Third Army was to continue its drive [east]."[47] Grow admitted that the road and rail nets around Metz were important for Patton's "strategical, tactical and logistical operations," but were not vital.[48] Even the Leavenworth study conceded that the road net adjacent the city was poorly developed and concluded that it "probably could not support the traffic associated with an army or corps line of communication."[49] Grow argued that the road and rail facilities to the north of Metz, at Thionville, could have facilitated XX Corps' crossing, thus giving Walker a better chance to use his mobility.

Ultimately, Patton had no clear conception of what he wanted to do with Metz after Walker found himself stuck on the outer defenses. His grip on the situation at Metz had been unsure during September and remained so into the October lull. Despite explicit declarations to the contrary, Patton would persist in his attack on Metz throughout October, certainly his single most questionable decision of the entire campaign. The reality of the tactical situation at Metz was that it posed a threat to Third Army's advance only if he chose to assault it. Therein lies the true liability of fixed fortifications susceptible to complete envelopment: Their defensive power rests almost exclusively on the decision of the aggressor to attack. Their value in a static defense is forfeited once enemy forces manage to flank or encircle the position.

Nominally, a displaced fortified position may interfere with the enemy's supply lines, but such ability is proportional to the size and capabilities of the occupying garrison. Rommel had to attack the British position at Tobruk because that fortress was reinforceable from sea and the garrison (9th Australian Division) possessed an offensive capacity in the form of substantial raids. Tobruk represented a real threat to Rommel's supply lines stretching from Egypt back to Tripoli.[50] Yet General der Infanterie Kurt von Tippelskirch, who would take over command of the Metz garrison on October 30, believed that "it was quite sufficient to observe them [Metz forts] or encircle them with small forces, for they did not dispose of a main reserve in the classical sense of the word with which they might operate outside of the fortress area, or stop the enemy supply."[51]

The threat of offensive action on the part of the Metz garrison, although numbering fourteen thousand men, was minimal. Despite the high quality of the Officer Candidate School and Non-Commisioned Officers (NCO) School troops that constituted roughly a third of Division Number 462, the unit charged with the defense of the city, the garrison possessed limited artillery (most of it fixed in the main casements), no tanks, no air cover, and little transport. Most importantly, the garrison could be effectively cut off from resupply or reinforcement. Raids may have been initiated by the school troops based on their thorough understanding of the terrain, but the possibility of seriously disrupting Third Army supply lines protected by a screening force was remote in the face of American mobility and firepower. Moreover, to venture forth beyond the protection of the Metz forts played into American hands. In the open the garrison could be destroyed in detail.

Some historians have taken the size of the Metz defensive system to be the most serious impediment to a quick flanking operation like that conducted by Guderian at Brest-Litovsk. Ronald Andidora states that the network of forts and bunkers was "Too large to be ignored" and would require "too many troops to be satisfactorily contained." Therefore, Metz "would have to be taken before any major attempt could be made to pierce the West Wall."[52] Weigley agreed that Metz had to be captured, claiming that "the Metz fortress system was too big to leave as a thorn in the line of communication."[53] This estimate can withstand some additional examination.

Patton himself determined that three full infantry divisions—the 5th, 83rd, and 90th—would be necessary to contain the system of forts,[54] but this seems excessive. In September this force constituted half of Third Army. Though he underestimated the defensive power of Metz against assault, he seems to have overestimated its ability to interfere with his lines of communication. Although Patton did not state specific numbers, Grow felt that a "very thin screening force would have sufficed" to keep Metz and its garrison in check.[55] Far from Patton's three full division figure, the force required to realistically mask Metz need not have exceeded one infantry division. More likely, six battalions of infantry, a separate tank battalion, a few field artillery battalions and some cavalry could have decisively dealt with any mixture of forces venturing forth from the forts. Metz could have been effectively masked by Third Army, a belief shared by Major General Gunther Blumentritt, von Rundstedt's Chief of Staff.[56]

Masking Metz would have offered Patton the ability to accomplish what he had so far in the campaign been unable to do: achieve a marked numerical superiority over the enemy at a given point elsewhere along the front. Moltke wrote, "One must be as strong as possible where one intends to seek the decision. If one lacks a general superiority, the only means of attaining superiority at the decisive point of the battlefield is to employ economy of force at other less important points."[57] Moltke referred to the *decisive point*, a term that has various related meanings. The term *Schwerpunkt*, first applied to war by Clausewitz, has been translated over the years as "center of gravity," "main effort," or "focus of efforts."[58] If one reads into Moltke's observation above, it is apparent that the identification of the decisive point on the battlefield was of paramount importance, followed by the identification of those areas where success is less likely in the short term. The modern American definition of the decisive point is helpful here: "Decisive points provide commanders with a marked advantage over the enemy and greatly influence the outcome of an action."[59] From the beginning, the decisive point should be readily apparent or at the very least prove itself to be the best expedient of the available options.

There is no question but that Metz represented the strongest position in the German defense along the Moselle, and Clausewitz was insistent that the defensive form of warfare was inherently stronger than the offensive.[60] There is sufficient evidence to suggest, however, that Patton would not have fully agreed with Clausewitz on this point because his contempt for fortified positions blinded him to this concept. There was no "marked advantage over the enemy" at Metz. In contrast, the enemy's vulnerability east of Nancy had been proven again and again. Patton at one time took careful note of Sun Tzu's warning not to besiege towns or walled cities. And yet—despite this and all the obvious signs—in late September 1944, he prepared for a full-scale assault on the area. He now focused his attention on a key section of the Metz defensive system known as Fort Driant. This would be the site of his greatest defeat, one that brings into question his generalship at this stage of the campaign.

NOTES

1. Carl von Clausewitz, *On War* edited and translated by Michael Howard and Peter Paret (Princeton, N.J.: Princeton University Press, 1976), 551.

2. Conversation Between Gen. Paul D. Harkins and Major Jacob B. Couch, Jr., Senior Officers Debriefing Program, Harkins Papers, United States Army Military History Institute (USAMHI), Carlisle Barracks, Pa., 35.

3. Martin Blumenson, *The Patton Papers* (Boston: Houghton Mifflin, 1974), II: 561.

4. Anthony Kemp, *The Unknown Battle: Metz, 1944* (New York: Stein and Day, 1981), 84.

5. Hugh M. Cole, *The Lorraine Campaign*, U.S. Army in World War II: European Theater of Operations (Washington, D.C.: Center for Military History, 1984), 124.

6. ETHINT 32, "The Defence of Metz," an Interview with Genobst Johannes Blaskowitz, July 20, 1945, Donald S. Detwiler, with Charles B. Burdick and Jurgen Rowher, eds., *World War II German Military Studies* (New York: Garland Publishing, 1979), II.

7. Cole, *Lorraine Campaign*, 96, 236.

8. Blumenson, *Patton Papers*, II: 553.

9. George S. Patton Diary, September 23, 1944, Special Collections, United States Military Academy Library, West Point (WP).

10. XX Corps AAR, "The Reduction of Fortress Metz, 1 September–6 December, 1944," Box 64, Patton Papers (PP), Library of Congress (LC), Washington, D.C., 7.

11. Ibid.

12. Ibid.

13. Charles B. MacDonald and Sidney T. Matthews, *Three Battles: Arnaville, Altuzzo and Schmidt*, U.S. Army in World War II: European Theater of Operations (Washington, D.C.: Department of the Army, 1952), 5.

14. "Reduction of Fortress Metz," 9.

15. MS A-999, Foreign Military Studies, NA, Washington, D.C.

16. Conversation between Harkins and Couch, 35.

17. Anthony Kemp, *The Maginot Line: Myth and Reality* (New York: Stein and Day, 1982), 83.

18. B. H. Liddell Hart, *History of the Second World War* (New York: G. P. Putnam, 1970), 161.

19. Blumenson, *Patton Papers*, II: 291.

20. George S. Patton, *War as I Knew It* (Boston: Houghton Mifflin, 1947), 102.

21. Michael D. Doubler, *Closing with the Enemy: How GIs Fought the War in Europe, 1944–1945* (Lawrence, Kans.: University Press of Kansas, 1994), 112.

22. John A. English and Bruce I. Gudmundsson, *On Infantry*, revised edition (Westport, Conn.: Praeger, 1994), 61.

23. Doubler, *Closing with the Enemy*, 113.

24. John Pimlott, ed., *Rommel in His Own Words* (London: Greenhill, 1994), 69.

25. Patton Diary, September 18.

26. Kemp, *The Unknown Battle*, 25.

27. Manton S. Eddy Diary, August 31, 1944, U.S. Army Infantry School, National Infantry Museum (NIM), Fort Benning, Georgia.

28. Blumenson, *Patton Papers*, II: 526.

29. Ibid., 317. He also noted the "wonderful efficiency of our mechanical transport."

30. Ibid., 615.

31. Ibid., 614.

32. Paul D. Harkins, *When the Third Cracked Europe: The Story of Patton's Incredible Army* (Harrisburg, Pa.: Army Times Publishing, 1969), 16.

33. Robert R. Palmer, Bell I. Wiley, and William R. Keast, *The Procurement and Training of Ground Combat Troops*, U.S. Army in World War II: European Theater of Operations (Washington, D.C.: Government Printing Office, 1948), 3.

34. Martin van Creveld, *Fighting Power: German and U.S. Army Performance, 1939–1945* (Westport, Conn.: Greenwood Press, 1982), 167.

35. Cole, *Lorraine Campaign*, 590–592. In addition to the artillery support, the infantry divisions found it necessary to have a separate tank battalion present at all times.

36. Blumenson, *Patton Papers*, II: 521.

37. Alan Millet and Williamson Murray, eds., *Military Effectiveness*, III: *The Second World War* (Boston: Allen and Unwin, 1988), 61.

38. Max Hastings, *Overlord: D-Day, June 6, 1944* (New York: Simon and Schuster, 1984), 24. "They possessed an historic reputation as formidable soldiers," stated Hastings, and "under Hitler their army attained it's zenith. Weapon for weapon and tank for tank, even in 1944, its equipment decisively outclassed that of the Allies in every category save artillery and transport."

39. Millet and Murray, *Military Effectiveness*, III: 79.

40. Cole, *Lorraine Campaign*, 269. Losses did not include sick and combat exhaustion cases, which reached such a rate that Patton sent Gay to 5th Infantry headquarters to investigate. Gay concluded that morale remained high despite the casualties and the fact that the division had been "fighting hard for a long time." Hobart R. Gay/ Hugh J. Gaffey Diary, September 26, 1944, Special Collections, WP.

41. Russell F. Weigley, *Eisenhower's Lieutenants: The Campaign of France and Germany 1944–1945* (Bloomington: Indiana University Press, 1981), 329.

42. Patton, *War as I Knew It*, 99.

43. Robert W. Grow, "Mobility Unused," Hist 314.7, Box: "General Grow, Special Studies on World War II," USAMHI.

44. Blumenson, *Patton Papers*, II: 559. In late August, General Juin visited Patton and told him that the soft place in the West Wall was through the Nancy Gap.

45. Patton Diary, September 20.

46. Patton, *War as I Knew It*, 104.

47. R. Stephenson et al., "The Battle of Metz," Combat Studies Institute Battlebook 13–A (Fort Leavenworth, Kans., 1985), 65.

48. Grow, "Mobility Unused," 4.

49. Stephenson, "The Battle of Metz," 65.

50. Pimlott, *Rommel in His Own Words*, 69.

51. MS B-491, "First Army, 1–11 November, 1944," by Gen der Infanterie Kurt von Tippelskirch, March 1, 1947, Foreign Military Studies, NA, Washington, D.C.

52. Ronald Andidora, "The Autumn of 1944: Boldness Is Not Enough," *Parameters: US Army War College Quarterly* XVII, 4 (1987): 73.

53. Weigley, *Eisenhower's Lieutenants*, 329.

54. Patton Diary, September 15; Patton, *War as I Knew It*, 102.

55. Grow, "Mobility Unused," 5.

56. B. H. Liddell Hart, *The Other Side of the Hill* (London: Cassell, 1951), 428.

57. Daniel J. Hughes, ed., *Moltke on the Art of War: Selected Writings* (Novato, Calif.: Presidio, 1993), 56.

58. English and Gudmundsson, *On Infantry*, 61.

59. Captain David J. Lemalin, "The Decisive Point," *Armor* (July–August 1994), 38.

60. Clausewitz, *On War*, 357.

From center right: Patton, Brigadier General O. P. Weyland, Major General Walton "Bulldog" Walker, and members of the Third Army Staff await the green light to assault the Moselle. Photo courtesy of the Special Collections, United States Military Academy Library, West Point

Patton visited by Army Chief of Staff George Marshall, and Omar Bradley during the fighting at Fort Driant. Photo courtesy of the Special Collections, United States Military Academy Library, West Point

GIs of Twaddle's 95th Infantry Division close in on the center of Metz. Photo courtesy of the Special Collections, United States Military Academy Library, West Point

Patton escorts U.S. Ambassador to Russia, Averill Harriman (center) around Third Army in November. Photo courtesy of the Special Collections, United States Military Academy Library, West Point

Patton (right), and Major General John Shirley Wood (left), on a bridge over the Saar River two days before Patton was forced to relieve Wood from command of the 4th Armored Division. Photo courtesy of the Special Collections, United States Military Academy Library, West Point

GIs of Van Fleet's 90th Infantry Division pass evidence of German delaying tactics on their way to new positions on the Saar River in early December. Photo courtesy of the Special Collections, United States Military Academy Library, West Point

Patton inspecting a bridge across the Saar River. Manton Eddy is probably the third individual from the left. Photo courtesy of the Special Collections, United States Military Academy Library, West Point

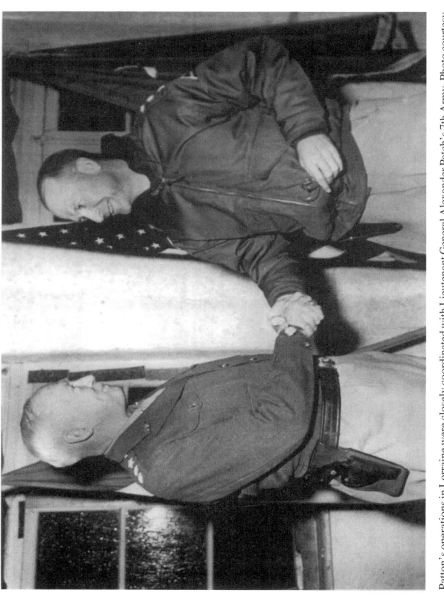

Patton's operations in Lorraine were closely coordinated with Lieutenant General Alexander Patch's 7th Army. Photo courtesy of the Special Collections, United States Military Academy Library, West Point

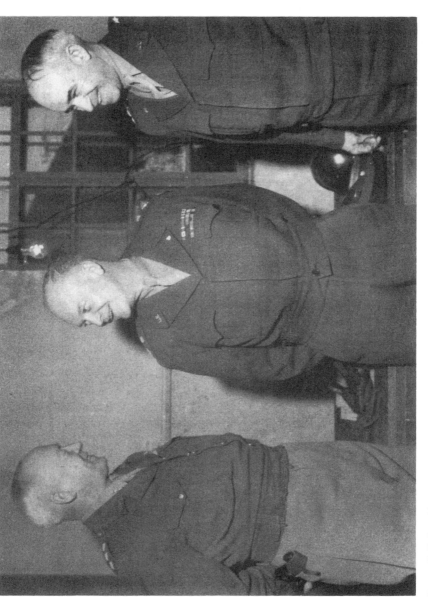

Patton (left) found it exceedingly difficult to understand Eisenhower's strategy and could never reconcile himself to Bradley's (right) natural timidity. Photo courtesy of the Special Collections, United States Military Academy Library, West Point

View looking due south from atop Fort St. Quentin.

The view from Pont-à-Mousson looking east across the Moselle River. Mousson Hill is in the background.

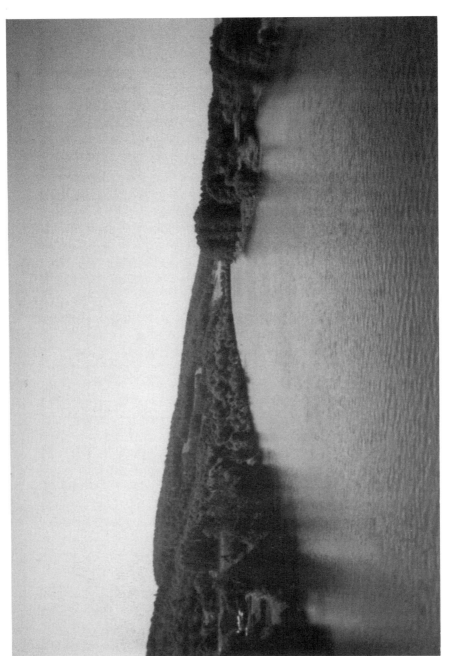

View of the Moselle River looking due south from below Arnaville.

View looking due south from atop Fort Sommy.

View looking due east from atop Fort Sommy.

Chapter 8

Correcting the Army Line

> Things are going very badly at Fort Driant. We may have to abandon the attack, since it is not worth the cost.
>
> —Patton, October 6, 1944[1]

Patton's failure to see the benefits in avoiding a direct assault against Metz and his distaste for playing a defensive role paved the way for his "pecking" campaign against the perimeter forts in late September and early October. His obsession with the offensive was not merely calculated to gain publicity, as Bradley has suggested,[2] but reflected the Clausewitzian conception that decisions on the battlefield could only be achieved through offensive action. His belief in the tactical benefits of constant action manifested itself at a press conference on September 23 when he declared that "the best way to defend is to attack, and the best way to attack is to attack."[3] The chances of Third Army standing idle for over a month, even though caught in the clutches of a logistical drought, were remote.

Halting Third Army completely required a direct and unequivocal order from Eisenhower or Bradley for Patton to "dig in."[4] As no such order was likely to be forthcoming, Patton forbade such action and instead directed Walker and Eddy to maintain the initiative by executing limited objective attacks to "correct" the army line in an "active defense."[5] Specifically, Third Army would not "dig in, wire, or mine, but will utilize a thin outpost zone backed at suitable places by powerful mobile reserves. We will further insure that all possible avenues of tank attacks are registered in by all batteries—Division, Corps, and Armies—whose guns can bear. . . . Counterattacks by our mobile reserves should be planned and executed to secure a double envelopment of the hostile effort with the purpose of not only defeating it but destroying it."[6] The purpose of this aggressive defensive posture was simple. Patton sought a favorable departure line from which to move rapidly when Eisenhower once again gave the green light.[7] Limited in objective though Patton's various line-correcting operations may have been, sizable forces would nonetheless be committed in the process, all based on available logistical support.

The only problem with this course of action was that various forts around Metz now became objectives for XX Corps. Securing better ground in XII Corps' sector farther south near Chateau-Salins, the area that Patton had determined was the gateway through Lorraine, made more sense and in retrospect proved highly beneficial to Third Army operations later in November. Needlessly butting one's head against the Metz forts, however, simply for the purpose of "keeping our troops alert,"[8] as Walker suggested, was a poor decision.

Nonetheless, it is clear that by September 25, the complete reduction of Metz had become a key component in Patton's future operational plans. In establishing a number of different priorities for the lull, XX Corps was given the job of driving a wedge into the concentric fortifications of Metz by reducing forts west and southwest of the city. XV Corps had originally been given first priority on resources to reduce the Foret de Parroy, but when it left the army, XX Corps's mission became first priority.[9] Walker's principal effort was to be against Fort Driant, a mysterious fortress complex located on the southwestern perimeter five miles from Metz. This fort was considered to be the key to the Metz fortified area from the west. Its capture would permit a tank drive up the Moselle valley into the heart of Metz.[10]

Walker had been thinking of Metz and how to reduce the various peripheral bastions since mid-September. On the 15th Patton accused him of having lead in his pants for failing to take Metz quicker, a personal rebuke that inspired him to devise a new stratagem. By September 17, he had drawn up Operation "Thunderbolt," a combined air and ground effort to take Metz with Fort Driant as the first objective. The air support was to consist of close ground coordination from the XIX TAC as well as massed bomber support from the 9th Air Division (Medium Bombers).[11] He was impatient with this ambitious plan because as Farago has pointed out, he "did not cherish the prospect of twiddling his thumbs at Metz while Eddy was running for the end zone."[12] Once the lull had started on September 25, Walker still insisted that the operation against Fort Driant be carried out because it was now an official part of Patton's overall plan.

Walker's initial interest in attacking Fort Driant had been raised when Colonel Charles W. Yuill, commanding officer of the 11th Infantry Regiment in Irwin's 5th Infantry Division, suggested that the fort could be taken by storm. Cole stated that Yuill "seems to have been instrumental in selling this idea to the corps and army staffs."[13] Whatever the source of inspiration for the operation, the actions contemplated against Fort Driant were not "of minor importance initiated for training purposes" as Walker later recorded in response to reading Cole's original draft of the campaign history.[14] In fact, Walker had taken great exception to Cole's draft, believing that he had been dealt with in a "very unfriendly, unsympathetic manner," and that Cole possessed a "definite personal antipathy or antagonism toward me." He felt that the Fort Driant operation had been "magnified into a major and discreditable operation."[15] It is apparent, however, that the operations against Driant were poorly conceived and executed, and Walker, as the corps commander, must bare some responsibility.

The key component in "Thunderbolt" was the presence of the medium bombers, an asset whose capabilities against reinforced concrete Patton overestimated. He possessed a strong conviction that air power could provide the necessary catalyst to carry Metz. His diary is full of references to air power, and as early as September 15 he was hoping to "bomb hell" out of the various forts on the perimeter.[16] On the 21st he announced that "Metz, the strongest fortress in the world, is sticky but we will get it as soon as we can get the air [force]."[17] He continually reiterated his belief that if he could get eleven groups of medium bombers for three consecutive days, he could take Metz.[18] Such hopes quickly vanished, for after September 25, Twelfth Army Group allocated bomber support on a day-to-day basis.[19] Finding three consecutive days of good weather was also a serious impediment to this plan.

This notion that air power was the cure-all for the tactical stalemate at Metz brings into question Patton's vaunted understanding of that important component in the Allied arsenal. He needed only to analyze VIII Corps' use of heavy aerial bombardment at Brest, the Anglo-Canadian experience at Caen, or the "Cobra" operation to test his "bomb hell" hypothesis. The day after Walker began planning "Thunderbolt," the German garrison at Brest finally surrendered following three weeks of siege. During that protracted battle the heavy and medium bomber effort "had been less effective than expected because the planes were sometimes assigned tasks beyond their capabilities."[20] The Ninth Air Force would later record that there was "no authenticated report of one [reinforced concrete emplacement] being destroyed."[21] There is no evidence to indicate that Patton ever scrutinized the lessons derivable from the use of air power at Brest for his subsequent actions at Metz. He was to be disappointed in the effectiveness of air power at Metz. On September 25 he examined firsthand the effects of aerial bombardment against reinforced concrete forts. On inspecting Fort Vaux, he concluded that the fort "certainly is a monument to concrete, because it was pounded to pieces and is still a defensible locality."[22] These results were not encouraging for the infantry who had to make the assault later against Driant.

Patton's misunderstanding of the strength of Metz, and especially its virtual invulnerability to anything but massive air power, was significant. Though he vowed on September 23 to keep the campaign from becoming static, "because that is a poor way of fighting,"[23] he quickly allowed Walker to execute the first phase of "Thunderbolt" with the intention of capturing Fort Driant, a position described as "probably the most formidable and well-prepared heavy fortification that the American army attempted to reduce in all of World War II."[24] Again, Patton was going against enemy strength.

Located atop a 360-m hill, Fort Driant faced southwest and had a frontage of 1,000 yards and a depth of 700 yards.[25] The main complex contained four artillery casements and five bunkers capable of holding three hundred men each. Just off the southeast corner of the main complex sat the fifth artillery casement, Battery Moselle, the position that had wreaked havoc with Walker's crossing attempts in early September (see Map 8.1). These casements stood flush with the ground, and only the gun turrets, four concrete bunkers, and some armored observation posts and pillboxes sat above ground. Surrounded by a dry moat sixty feet wide and thirty feet deep, the central fort was a daunting position to assault. Getting there was an even greater task, for the garrison deployed infantry up to 1,000–1,500 yards out from the fort, and barbed wire, reaching a depth of sixty feet in places, covered the entire perimeter. Finally, all the fort's various components, bunkers, casements, and OPs were accessible through an underground network of tunnels.[26] Patton and Walker did not know all this at the time but quickly found out.

On September 27, the failure of a full regimental effort by McLain's 90th Infantry Division in attacking Fort Jeanne d'Arc indicated the inherent strength of the various fortified positions blocking entry into the heart of Metz. Moreover, the XIX TAC dropped twenty-one 1,000-lb bombs on the position during the day with minimal results. Weyland commenced strikes against Driant, Jeanne d'Arc, and other forts with fighter bombers on the 15th and continued this action well into October (see Table 8.1). Despite highly accurate strikes with napalm and 1,000-lb bombs against Fort Driant, it retained its defensive potential virtually intact.[27] By September 28 Weyland himself had become discouraged and admitted that the forts were

Map 8.1
The Fort Driant Complex

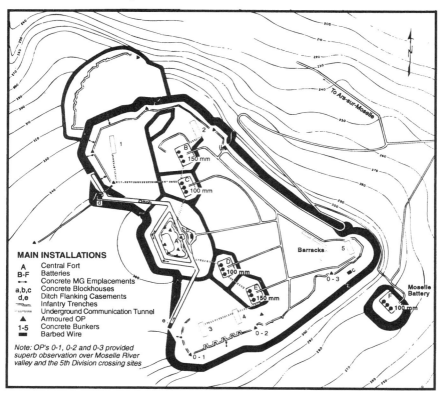

MAIN INSTALLATIONS

A	Central Fort
B-F	Batteries
↔	Concrete MG Emplacements
a,b,c	Concrete Blockhouses
d,e	Ditch Flanking Casements
	Infantry Trenches
	Underground Communication Tunnel
▲	Armoured OP
1-5	Concrete Bunkers
▬	Barbed Wire

Note: OP's 0-1, 0-2 and 0-3 provided
superb observation over Moselle River
valley and the 5th Division crossing sites

Source: Base map taken from Hugh M. Cole's *The Lorraine Campaign*, U.S. Army in
World War II: European Theater of Operations (Washington, D.C., 1984), Map XXIII.
Altered by Bill Traer.

"not a proper target for fighter bombers."[28] Even the 240-mm artillery, though scoring several direct hits, had simply "slipped off" the fort without causing any extensive structural damage.[29]

Table 8.1
Air Attack Data, September 10–October 13, 1944

Date	Target	Bomb Load
September 10	Fortified Area	12 x 500 lb.
September 10	Fort Verdun	23 x 500 lb.
September 10	Fortified Area	24 x 500 lb.
September 20	Fort L'Aisne	6 Napalm
		4 x 500 lb.
September 22	Fort Driant	8 Napalm
		8 x 500 lb.
September 26	Fort Driant	8 x 1,000 lb.
		8 Napalm
		7 x 1,000 lb.
		7 Napalm
		6 x 1,000 lb.
		6 Napalm
September 27	Fort Driant	5 x 1,000 lb.
		8 Napalm
		8 x 1,000 lb.
		8 Napalm
		8 x 1,000 lb.
		4 Napalm
September 27	Fort Verdun	15 x 1,000 lb.
		7 Napalm
		8 x 1,000 lb.
		8 Naplam
		8 x 1,000 lb.
		8 Napalm
September 27	Fort Jeanne d'Arc	21 x 1,000 lb.
		24 Napalm
October 3	Fort Verdun	22 x 1,000 lb.
		22 x 1,000 lb.
		4 x 500 lb.
		24 x 1,000 lb.
October 3	Fort Driant	33 Napalm
October 6	Fort Driant	24 x 500 lb.
October 8	Fort Verdun	8 x 1,000 lb.
October 13	Fort Driant	16 x 500 lb.

Source: "The Effect of Air Power in the Battle of Metz," USAFHRC, A1174, 8–9.

On the 27th, probing infantry assaults also began against Fort Driant, as part of a dress rehearsal for a later attack, by elements of Irwin's 5th Infantry Division. The results were meager because initial intelligence was nil. The only information available about the fort was that received from a prisoner captured by the 11th Infantry Regiment on September 20. According to the prisoner, Fort Driant was garrisoned by 100–120 straggler personnel from various units, 45 Naval Marine personnel manning the guns, and 40–50 first-rate troops from the Officer Candidate School.[30] Despite only minor losses in the initial assault against Driant, Irwin correctly surmised that the fort was a far more complex and deadly stronghold than previously anticipated. On September 28 the French provided fairly comprehensive plans for the fort that proved his assertion. Walker, however, considered the initial failure to be indicative of a deficiency in aggressiveness rather than the strength of reinforced concrete.

Cole's original draft of the official history contended that Walker accused Irwin's infantry of "quitting" at Fort Driant, a comment that quickly brought a heated response from Irwin, who pointed out that intelligence gave no indication of the strength of the position. Walker, defending himself after the war, denied Cole's accusation but "did insist on more aggressive action on the part of the forces attacking Fort Driant."[31] Irwin had made it clear to Walker over the telephone on the 28th that his infantry were confronted with great difficulties, not the least of which was the fact that air photos completely failed to reveal the intricate wire patterns or the pillboxes surrounding the fort's perimeter.[32] Irwin may very well have been the only senior officer who fully appreciated the difficulty of assaulting Driant directly.

On the same day, both Walker and Irwin conferred with Patton concerning the situation at the fort, and it is more than likely that Irwin reiterated to Patton what he had told Walker. Patton may have agreed with Irwin's assessment, for according to Cole, he did not press Irwin to persist at Fort Driant but rather instructed him to rest and rotate his battered division.[33] Indicative of the general fatigue of the entire army, even the ever aggressive Wood informed Patton a few days later that the 4th Armored needed "a little time out for maintenance and regrouping."[34] Patton, however, was not quite ready to give up on Driant and Metz. In his memoirs he stated on or around October 3 that he had been contemplating "trying out the defensive qualities" of the western forts for quite some time.[35] Irwin's observations should have given Patton a fairly good idea of Fort Driant's defensive qualities, but he nevertheless permitted Walker to continue assaulting the position. Walker remembered Patton saying at the time, "We have put our hands to the plow, we must finish the job."[36] Here was Patton's reasoning for continuing the siege at Brest.

Patton's decision to persist with the assault on Driant went against the advice furnished by two of his most trusted aides, General Gay and Colonel Halley Maddox, Third Army's Operations officer (G-3). Both men supported Irwin's reservations and informed Patton that, in their opinion, neither Fort Driant nor Metz could be taken by frontal assault.[37] After having personally reconnoitered the Metz area at Patton's insistence, they advised a double envelopment with no less than five divisions.[38]

Walker's enthusiasm for the operation and Patton's inability to sit still explain much of the decision to continue at Fort Driant. Indeed, Stephen Ambrose has recently suggested that Patton "lusted for Metz" and to get it, "he had to take Fort Driant."[39] Patton certainly deserved his reputation as the most aggressive Allied commander of the war, and Eisenhower once commented that his "strength is that he thinks only in terms of attack as long as there is a single battalion that can keep advancing."[40] But Liddell Hart observed that Patton was so attack-minded that he failed to recognize the inherent advantages of defense,[41] a statement that is not wholly accurate but does go a long way in explaining Patton's underestimation of the defenses around Metz.

On September 28 Patton tentatively authorized the systematic reduction of Fort Driant and issued a new operational directive giving priority to reducing various Metz forts instead of rectifying the army line in the Chateau-Salins area.[42] By doing this, he committed Irwin's division to another infantry-intense operation after once again voicing strong displeasure at the quality of his infantry the day before. Concerning the repulse of a battalion of Baade's 35th Infantry Division in the Chateau-Salins sector, Patton declared, "Our infantry is certainly not up to the rest of our troops."[43]

There was a more compelling reason not to throw unprepared troops against Driant, for on September 29 during a meeting with his corps commanders and key staff, Patton presented a perfect reason to avoid Metz altogether. The Germans were "content" at Metz, he declared, and "will stay quiet there."[44] Furthermore, he stated that he intended to encircle Metz rather than assault it directly. But previously established priorities were still in effect. XX Corps had to take Fort Driant.[45]

The 5th Infantry Division renewed its attack on Fort Driant at noon on October 3 without the anticipated air support from the IX Bombardment Division due to poor weather. Though artillery had been allocated in great quantity for the attack, the failure of eight direct hits on one of the fort's turrets the day before reinforced the evidence from September 27 that massed artillery did not guarantee success against reinforced concrete.[46] Indicative of the siege mentality surrounding the assault on Driant, the guns of the 588th Field Artillery Battalion were dug in and parapeted with earth and sandbags. Moreover, an attempt to rectify the paucity of training in the reduction of fortresses was also attempted between September 28 and October 3, although five days could hardly take the place of extensive and lengthy training.

Unlike the initial assault on September 27, the new effort was a combined arms operation including tanks. Phones were attached to the rear of the tanks to provide communication between them and the infantry. High-explosive (HE) 76-mm ammunition was converted to concrete-piercing ammunition by changing the fuses. New demolition equipment had to be constructed because much of the original equipment had been left at the fort during the initial assault. This equipment consisted of satchel charges, pole charges, bangalore torpedoes, and snakes. The snakes were explosives fitted in long pipes. Attached to tanks, they were dragged up to a wire obstacle where they were pushed through the obstacle and electrically detonated from within the tank. Special handling crews spent October 1 and 2 practicing the use of the snakes.

Incredibly, despite knowing that Fort Driant was held by some elite troops, higher headquarters sent the assault teams into the complex on October 3 with the guarantee that the fort was "manned by about 100 old men and boys, whose morale is low. They will probably not make a determined effort to hold the fort."[47] It is debatable whether troops fight better when convinced they are fighting an enemy of poor quality, but it quickly became apparent that the Driant defenders were motivated.

The effort of the first day's fighting, personally viewed by both Patton and Weyland, has been described as "badly disorganized."[48] The various platoons could not keep the enemy from continually infiltrating their lines. The initial attacks did not produce the results Walker anticipated, and the next day Patton responded forcibly, ordering him to "completely occupy Fort Driant if it took every man in the corps."[49] This was pure frustration on his part. He could not allow an attack by Third Army to fail, especially when as D'Este suggests, he wanted to present Driant as a present to Marshall, who would visit Patton on the 7th.[50]

The fighting at Driant quickly moved underground, and by the 4th the armor played no role. Irwin decided to reinforce his attack on the 5th. This decision was apparently influenced by the report of the commander of the 2nd Battalion, 11th Infantry Regiment containing the views of infantry Captain Jack Gerrie at the fort. "The situation is critical," declared Captain Gerrie, and "a couple more barrages and another counterattack and we are sunk. We have no men, our equipment is shot and we just can't go. The trs [troops] in G Company are done. . . . [The] Enemy has infiltrated and pinned what is here down. . . . We cannot delay any longer on replacement. . . . The enemy arty [artillery] is butchering these trs [troops] until we have nothing left to hold with." As Gerrie saw it,

There is only one answer the way things stand. First either to withdraw and saturate it with hvy [heavy] bombers or reinforce with a hell of a strong force. This strong force might hold here but eventually they'll get it by arty too. . . . All our charges have been useless against this stuff. The few leaders are trying to keep what is left intact and that's all they can do. . . . Everything is committed and we cannot follow attack plan. . . . If we want this dammed fort let's get the stuff required to take it and then go. Right now you haven't got it.[51]

In summing up his report the battalion commander added, "All agree this can't be held tonight by these troops."[52]

The effectiveness of the German artillery was paramount in their ability to hold Driant against Irwin's infantry. It was not the strongest position in the defensive system by accident. The nearby forts—Jeanne d'Arc, Blaise, Sommy, and Marival—could all rake the surface of Driant with artillery fire, dramatically enhancing the defensive quality of the fort. Still, Irwin proceeded with the reinforcement. He formed Task Force Driant (later designated Task Force Warnock) under the command of Brigadier General A. D. Warnock, the Assistant Division Commander. On the nights of October 5 and 6, additional infantry troops went into the Driant battle. The key to successfully storming Driant, however, was extensive fortress warfare training not sheer numbers, but training at this point was sadly lacking.

Captain Gerrie commented on training at the time he submitted his gloomy report of the fighting at Driant noting that the troops were "just not sufficiently trained and what is more they have no training in even basic infantry."[53] Even Major General Horace L. McBride, commander of the 80th Infantry Division, had noticed the deplorable nature of the training his own replacements were given. Eddy recorded on October 2 that McBride "complained about the replacements that he had been receiving in that they were not infantrymen, but coast artillerymen . . . and that some of the men he received had not been given basic training."[54] As one student of siege warfare has pointed out, "No operation requires such perfection of teamwork down to the last individual as that of dislodging a determined enemy from a well fortified position" and that "green, unacquainted replacements, just arrived in a unit are of little or no value in such an operation."[55]

Far from "old men with low morale," the Officer Candidate School troops were an exceptional complement to the naturally strong defensive features of Driant. Brigadier General Warnock, in describing them, stated that "it's a sight to see these OCS men . . . come charging in shooting from the hip with both hands, screaming 'Heil Hitler.' They're fanatics. They fight to the end, very few surrender. They've been charging us ever since we hit here."[56] By October 6 Patton seriously considered abandoning the operation. He admitted at this point that he had been "overoptimistic" in permitting the assault, but one of his concerns in canceling the operation was his contention that good initiative was not something to be readily stifled. Moreover, he still firmly believed that "it is desirable to inculcate in the German mind that when the Third Army attacks, it always succeeds."[57] But the efforts of Irwin, the exhortings of Walker and Patton, and the riflemen of the 5th Infantry Division could not overcome Fort Driant, at least not without suffering a pyrrhic victory. Indeed, Patton was not far from this situation, for the troops "both above and below the ground were living a rat-like existence in shallow holes or choking tunnels" and the casualty rate was "climbing."[58]

By October 9 Patton admitted that the "show is going sour. We will have to pull out."[59] Four days later Irwin's infantry withdrew from the fort after having sustained 64 men killed, 547 wounded, and 187 missing. Farago has claimed that Patton was "badly shaken" by the defeat at Driant and suggested that general fatigue of both the commanding general and the troops played a major role in the stinging reverse.[60] Connecting troop performance with fatigue is plausible, for Patton himself declared on October 8, after watching a XII Corps attack, that "the whole tempo of our infantry attack is too slow."[61] Referring specifically to Irwin's division during mid-September, Cole stated that the infantry had "begun to slow down" and that there was "little drive left in the battalions."[62] However, suggesting that Patton himself made poor decisions regarding Driant because of fatigue is not supportable. Even when he knew that the situation at Driant had deteriorated badly and chances for success were not great, he still had enough enthusiasm for war to declare on October 8 that "peace is going to be a hell of a let down."[63] Additionally, Weigley noticed a "considerable measure of good sense" beneath Patton's outwardly defiant attitude at Driant, stating that Patton was still "enough surer of himself than Bradley had been at Brest to concede at least tacit admission of a mistake."[64] It was good for Irwin's infantry that he did. While the exhausted 5th Infantry was failing at Fort Driant, other line-correcting operations were taking place with much better prospects of success (see Map 8.2).

Map 8.2
Third Army Line Correcting Operations, September 27–October 31, 1944

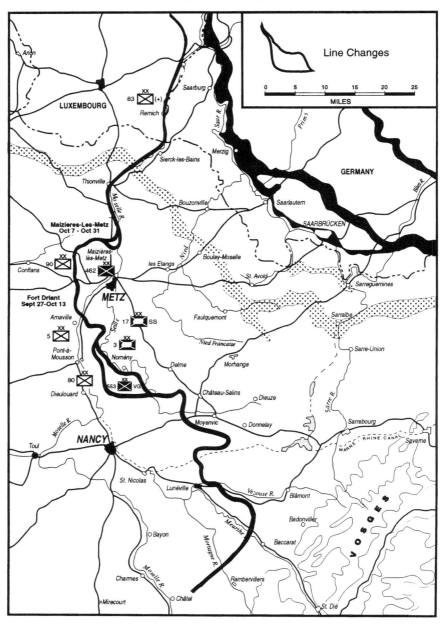

Source: Base map taken from Hugh M. Cole's *The Lorraine Campaign*, U.S. Army in World
War II: European Theater of Operations (Washington, D.C., 1984), Map XXII. Altered
by Eric Drummie and Bill Traer.

On October 8, Eddy launched a three-division effort—80th Infantry, 35th Infantry, and 6th Armored Divisions, almost ninety thousand men—to clear the enemy from south and west of the Seille River. The operation was tactically sound, but as at Driant, Patton wanted to prove that "we were still in the ring."[65] With Grow's armor leading and supported by all Corps and divisional guns, XII Corps inflicted heavy damage on the 553rd Volks-grenadier Division on its push to the river.[66] The 553rd's supporting division, the 3rd Panzer Grenadier Division, had been pulled out of the line and sent to reinforce the Aachen sector leaving the 553rd badly stretched and outnumbered. The mass of the division's infantry was destroyed by October 9th.[67] A single day's fighting brought a portion of the corps across the Seille where a solid jumpoff point for the November offensive was secured. It also proved the correctness of a strategy aimed at concentrating in the Nancy area.

Walker may not have taken Driant, but he did have success in his zone at the industrial town of Maizieres-les-Metz five miles north of Metz. With plenty of large stone buildings, the town was ideally suited for defense against Major General McLain's 90th Infantry Division, which began an assault on October 3. McLain had been the spark behind the attack for the purposes of fixing XX Corp's line and getting his infantry some experience in battling fortifications. Walker, as eager as Patton to attack, needed little convincing to authorize the operation.[68]

In many ways, the month-long fight to clear Maizieres-les-Metz was just as grueling as the battle for Driant. The Germans quickly reinforced the town with a regiment of the 19th Volksgrenadier Division because they understood the problems of holding Metz against encirclement if the town fell. The fighting turned into a "house-to-house affair. The Germans . . . had orders to defend each house to the last man and this, precisely, is what they did during the next 23 days. Mines and booby traps were in every house, and artillery and mortar fire literally poured down day and night. Every weapon in the arsenal, including satchel charges and 105-mm and 155-mm self-propelled guns, was used against the stubborn defenders."[69] Yet with alternating success and failure, General McLain, and from October 15th onward, Major General James A. Van Fleet, managed to capture the town by October 30. The significance of the success at Maizieres-les-Metz was that one of the important Metz peripheral anchors had been unlocked.

The cost to the 90th Infantry was 51 dead and 552 wounded.[70] In total, Third Army suffered some 9,000 casualties during the "lull," a result of Patton's staunch refusal to relinquish the initiative and offensive spirit to the Germans. The criticism that limited operations merely cost American lives downplayed the benefits accrued to Third Army by remaining active. In contrast, the Germans sustained an estimated 43,200 casualties during the lull. Moreover, at a cost of 51 light and medium tanks, 6 artillery pieces, and 120 vehicles of all types, Third Army destroyed 176 (hard to replace) German tanks, 55 artillery pieces, and 432 other vehicles. Indeed, with the exception of the attack on Fort Driant, Third Army's limited objective attacks throughout October were a success and would further Patton's plans for the new offensive.

NOTES

1. George S. Patton Diary, October 6, 1944, Special Collections, United States Military Academy Library, West Point (WP).

2. Bradley, in referring to Patton's pecking campaign against the Metz forts in October, declared that "George couldn't sit still—he wanted movement for his headlines." Bradley Commentary as Recorded by Chester Hansen, Bradley Papers, United States Army Military History Institute (USAMHI), Carlisle Barracks, Pa.

3. Martin Blumenson, *The Patton Papers* (Boston: Houghton Mifflin, 1974), II: 555.

4. Dominick Graham and Shelford Bidwell, *Coalitions, Politicians, and Generals: Some Aspects of Command in Two World Wars* (London: Brassey's, 1993), 246.

5. Walton H. Walker to Hugh M. Cole, October 8, 1947, Historical Division Combat Interviews (HDCI), National Achives (NA), Washington, D.C.

6. George S. Patton, *War as I Knew It* (Boston: Houghton Mifflin, 1947), 322.

7. Hugh M. Cole, *The Lorraine Campaign*, U.S. Army in World War II: European Theater of Operations (Washington, D.C.: Center for Military History, 1984), 259. He also wanted to maintain the offensive spirit in the troops "so that when we attack we will not be pacifists." Patton Diary, September 25.

8. Walker to Cole, October 8, 1947.

9. Cole, *Lorraine Campaign*, 259; XX Corps After Action Report (AAR), "The Reduction of Fortress Metz, 1 September–6 December, 1944," Box 64, Patton Papers (PP), Library of Congress (LC), Washington, D.C., 10.

10. "The Reduction of Fortress Metz," 10.

11. Brigadier General Ralph F. Stearly, Brigadier General Robert M. Lee, and Colonel James C. McGehee, "The Tactical Air Force in the European Theater of Operations," File R 373/1, Study #54, Washington, D.C., Office of the Chief of Military History (OCMH), 3. The 9th Air Division was a component of the IX Air Force.

12. Ladislas Farago, *Patton: Ordeal and Triumph* (New York: Ivan Obolensky, 1963), 651.

13. Cole, *Lorraine Campaign*, 262.

14. Walton H. Walker to Harry J. Malony, January 6, 1949, HDCI, NA, Washington, D.C.

15. Ibid.

16. Blumenson, *Patton Papers*, II: 548.

17. Ibid., 552.

18. Patton Diary, September 20.

19. Cole, *Lorraine Campaign*, 266, footnote 21.

20. Martin Blumenson, *Breakout and Pursuit*, U.S. Army in World War II: European Theater of Operations (Washington, D.C.: Department of the Army, 1961), 653.

21. Cole, *Lorraine Campaign*, 260.

22. Patton Diary, September 25.

23. Blumenson, *Patton Papers*, II: 555.

24. Michael D. Doubler, *Closing with the Enemy: How GIs Fought the War in Europe, 1944–1945* (Lawrence, Kans.: University Press of Kansas, 1994), 144.

25. Major Meyer A. Edwards et al., "Armor in the Attack of Fortified Positions" (Fort Knox, Ky., 1949–1950), 75.

26. Cole, *Lorraine Campaign*, 264–265.

27. "The Effect of Air Power in the Battle of Metz," United States Air Force Historical Records Center (USAFHRC), microfilm A1174, 12. A German prisoner stated that the napalm and 500-lb bombs caused no damage and only minor casualties and that the garrison felt confident that they could hold out against assault after the ineffectual air strikes.

28. David N. Spires, *Air Power for Patton's Army: The XIX Tactical Air Command in the Second World War*, Draft Manuscript, 468.

29. Edwards, "Armor in the Attack of Fortified Positions," 95.

30. Ibid., 83.

31. Walker to Malony, January 6, 1949.

32. Cole, *Lorraine Campaign*, 269.

33. Ibid.

34. John S. Wood to George S. Patton, October 2, 1944, Box 3, Wood Papers, Syracuse University (SU).

35. Patton, *War as I Knew It*, 114.

36. Walker to Malony, January 6, 1949.

37. Farago, *Patton: Ordeal and Triumph*, 654.

38. Harry H. Semmes, *Portrait of Patton* (New York: Appleton-Century-Crofts, 1955), 217.

39. Stephen E. Ambrose, *Citizen Soldiers: The U.S. Army from the Normandy Beaches to the Bulge to the Surrender of Germany* (New York: Simon and Schuster, 1997), 136.

40. Alfred D. Chandler, ed., *The Papers of Dwight D. Eisenhower: The War Years* (Baltimore: Johns Hopkins University Press, 1970), III: 1440.

41. B. H. Liddell Hart, *History of the Second World War* (New York: G. P. Putnam, 1970), 415. Liddell Hart continued, "even against much superior numbers, especially when conducted by highly skilled troops against inexperienced attackers." He is here referring to Patton's insistence that Orlando Ward storm the heights around Maknassy against an emplaced enemy.

42. Third Army Operational Directive, September 28, 1944, File #103–3.0, Modern Military Reference Branch (MMRB), Suitland, Maryland.

43. Patton Diary, September 27.

44. Blumenson, *Patton Papers*, II: 559.

45. Hobart R. Gay/Hugh J. Gaffey Diary, September 29, 1944, Special Collections, WP.

46. Cole, *Lorraine Campaign*, 270.

47. Edwards, "Armor in the Attack of Fortified Positions," 91.

48. Cole, *Lorraine Campaign*, 271–272.

49. Blumenson, *Patton Papers*, II: 562–563.

50. Carlo D'Este, *Patton: A Genius for War* (New York: HarperCollins, 1995), 666.

51. Cole, *Lorraine Campaign*, 271–272, footnote 38.

52. Edwards, "Armor in the Attack of Fortified Positions," 101.

53. Cole, *Lorraine Campaign*, 272, footnote 38.

54. Eddy Diary, October 2.

55. Lieutenant Colonel Fred L. Walker, Jr., "Seige Methods: 1945 Part I," *Infantry Journal* (January, 1945): 13.

56. Edwards, "Armor in the Attack of Fortified Positions," 103.

57. Blumenson, *Patton Papers*, II: 562.

58. Edwards, "Armor in the Attack of Fortified Positions," 104.

59. Blumenson, *Patton Papers*, II: 564.

60. Farago, *Patton: Ordeal and Triumph*, 657.

61. Blumenson, *Patton Papers*, II: 564.

62. Cole, *Lorraine Campaign*, 170.

63. Blumenson, *Patton Papers*, II: 563.

64. Russell F. Weigley, *Eisenhower's Lieutenants: The Campaign of France and Germany, 1944–1945* (Bloomington: Indiana University Press, 1981), 387.

65. Blumenson, *Patton Papers*, II: 563.

66. Cole, *Lorraine Campaign*, 285–289.

67. Ibid., 288, footnote 73.

68. Ibid., 276–277.

69. John Colby, *War from the Ground Up: The 90th Infantry Division in World War II* (Austin, Tex.: Nortex Press, 1991), 267.

70. Ibid., 268.

Chapter 9

Planning for the November Offensive

> Plans must be simple and flexible. Actually they only form a datum plane from which you build as necessity directs or opportunity offers. They should be made by the people who are going to execute them.
> —Patton, Letter of Instruction, March, 1944[1]

When Eisenhower sat down with his chief subordinates to plan his renewal of the broad front advance on October 18, he still viewed Third Army's axis of advance as a secondary thrust. Montgomery had priority on supplies and was assigned the mission of opening the vital port of Antwerp, which he had failed to accomplish in September, opting instead for "Market Garden," the airborne assault on the Rhine. Bradley's First and Ninth Armies were responsible for encircling the Rhur industrial region, and it was decided that Third Army would move only when logistics allowed.[2]

On October 21, the day that Aachen finally fell to Hodges' First Army, Bradley tentatively set the date for Third Army's renewed advance around November 10. This was approximately five days after First and Ninth Army were to launch their own fresh offensives. However, Bradley insisted upon awaiting the return of the 104th Infantry and 7th Armored Divisions from Montgomery before committing First and Ninth Armies. Eager to get going nonetheless, Bradley turned to Patton on November 2, inquiring when Third Army could advance, and as Weigley noted "The answer was not surprising."[3] Patton informed his superior that Third Army would attack no later than November 8 regardless of weather conditions. With that simple declaration, Third Army now became Twelfth Army Group's vanguard in an offensive that Patton had been preparing for with considerable effort, a dramatic change from his free-wheeling days of August and September.

A few short days after Irwin pulled the remnants of the 5th Infantry Division back from Fort Driant on October 14, Patton and his principal staff officers gathered to put the finishing touches on alternate plans for the resumption of the offensive. The alternate plans are important because they reveal the lessons Patton had learned, or failed to learn, from the fighting in September and early October. They were "outlines" to guide more-specific planning at a later date. Patton's basic premise for the renewed offensive, as manifested in plans "A" and "B," was the envelopment of Metz from north and south. This course of action reflected the advice furnished earlier in the campaign by Hobart Gay and Halley Maddox and the bitter experience of the fighting at Fort Driant. The heavy casualties sustained there convinced virtually all the commanders, including Patton, that Third Army needed additional training in fortress warfare and that it was necessary to encircle and isolate Metz rather than assault the forts directly.[4] The assumptions and general plan of "A" and "B" were identical but offered different schemes of maneuver and corps missions. The principal assumption was that Third Army's strength would be boosted to six infantry and three armored divisions (5th, 26th, 35th, 80th, 90th, 95th Infantry and 4th, 6th, and 10th Armored Divisions) for the November offensive. Another corps headquarters, Major General John Millikin's III Corps, was also to be added to handle the increased number of divisions. This reinforcement was vital in order to execute Patton's conception.

In Plan "A" Metz was to be contained on the west, probably by the new 95th Infantry Division, while a minimum of one armored and one infantry division (10th Armored, 90th Infantry), crossed the Moselle north of Metz near Thionville and drove for Boulay-Moselle to seize road and rail facilities. The 5th Infantry Division was to advance northeast out of its Arnaville bridgehead south of Metz and link up with these elements circling the city from the north. Enemy forces withdrawing from Metz were to be destroyed with the help of Eddy's XII Corps, which would push a minimum of one infantry and one armored division northeast from the vicinity of Pont-à-Mousson to seize road and rail facilities at Faulquemont a day before the XX Corps attack commenced (see Map 9.1).

In his memoirs, Patton spelled out the specifics of XII Corps' role and what he referred to simply as "the plan" in a little more detail. The three infantry divisions of XII Corps—26th, 35th, and 80th—were to launch the initial attacks to gain bridgeheads over the Seille River. Following up would be the 4th and 6th Armored Divisions. Grow was to secure the high ground east of Metz around Faulquemont while Wood struck directly for a crossing of the Saar River south of Saargemung.[5] Once both corps had

Map 9.1
Outline Plan "A," October 18, 1944

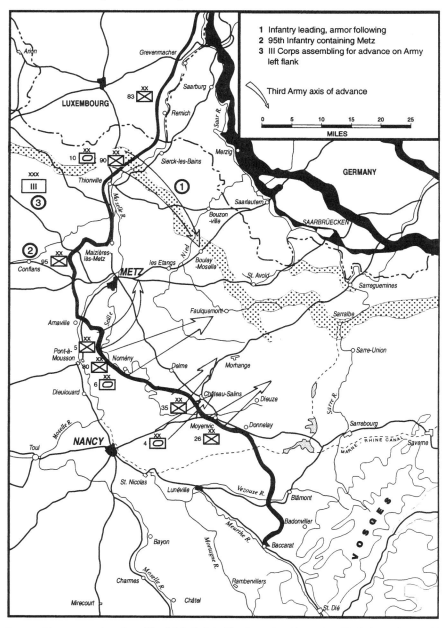

Source: Base map taken from Hugh M. Cole's *The Lorraine Campaign*, U.S. Army in World
War II: European Theater of Operations (Washington, D.C., 1984), Map XXII. Altered
by Eric Drummie and Bill Traer.

linked up, a general reorientation would take place with Morris's 10th Armored driving for a crossing of the Saar at Saarburg. Millikin's III Corps was to assemble on Walker's left rear flank near Briey and advance on Army order to the northeast. The axis of advance for all three corps was northeast with the ultimate objective being the Rhine in the area from Mainz to Mannheim.[6] Patton further stipulated that in the advance all corps would be disposed in column of divisions with armor leading, reinforced with motorized infantry. These leading elements would bypass resistance and make a hard push for the Rhine.[7] Once Metz had been encircled and escape routes cut off, the 95th Infantry Division would cross the Moselle in strength and take the city. Thus, Plan "A" intended to encircle and bypass Metz as a prerequisite to storming the Rhine with XX and XII Corps abreast.

Plan "B" called for advancing the bulk of XX and XII Corps, some seven divisions, south of Metz, a scheme that would have provided Patton with a greater degree of concentration. XX Corps would push the 10th Armored and two infantry divisions northeast from Pont-à-Mousson to seize road and rail facilities at both Boulay-Moselle and Faulquemont. XII Corps would simultaneously advance northeast with the 4th and 6th Armored Divisions and two unspecified infantry divisions from Nancy to help secure Faulquemont, destroy enemy forces on its front, and protect the right flank of the army. III Corps, which for plan "B" would have two infantry divisions, one tank group, and one tank destroyer group, was charged with a number of tasks. First, it would contain Metz on the west with no less than one division. With the remainder of its assets, the corps would seize and secure crossings at Thionville and attack southeast to help XX Corps secure Boulay-Moselle. It would then stay echeloned to the left rear and protect the left flank of the army (see Map 9.2).[8] The chief difference between Plans "A" and "B" is the element of concentration, especially of Third Army's powerful complement of armor.

It is evident from even a cursory glimpse at both plans that Metz was the center of gravity for the entire November offensive. The proposed envelopment in Plan "A" was really a concentric tightening to isolate and reduce the city's garrison. Utilizing the 10th Armored Division on the far northern flank suggested elements of a classic slash-and-run flanking operation, but a significant portion of Van Fleet's 90th Infantry Division was earmarked for the encirclement operation instead of exploitation. No less than four divisions (5th, 90th, 95th Inf and 10th Armd) were directly assigned for the Metz operation, and despite Walker's November 3 directive that XX Corps's mission was the "destruction or capture of the Metz garrison, with-

Map 9.2
Outline Plan "B," October 18, 1944

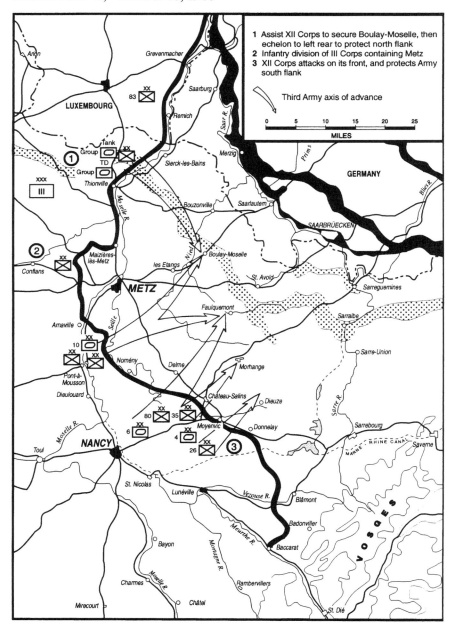

Source: Base map taken from Hugh M. Cole's *The Lorraine Campaign*, U.S. Army in World
  War II: European Theater of Operations (Washington, D.C., 1984), Map XXII. Altered
  by Eric Drummie and Bill Traer.

out the investiture or siege of the Metz forts,"[9] significant elements of the corps would be drawn into bitter fighting. Though the main forts were to be bypassed, infiltration tactics were to be used to capture the heart of the city.[10] Indicative of the firm intention to reduce Metz, all of XX Corps' divisions rotated out of the line to train in the reduction of fortifications during October.[11] Once relieved by the 95th Infantry Division on October 16, Irwin conducted ten days of fortress training on old pillboxes and bunkers of the Maginot Line, and Van Fleet organized the same training for his division.

Roy E. Appleman set the problem of gravitating towards Metz in proper context when he stated, "It is not clear why Patton chose to butt his head against the Metz fortifications when he had the opportunity of penetrating the German line much more easily around an open flank [Chateau-Salins]."[12] This sector did possess its own natural barriers such as the Delme Ridge, which offered observation of the entire area encompassed by both the Seille and Nied Rivers. Additionally, west of the Saar and directly in the path of Eddy's projected advance extended two long, narrow plateaus that threatened to canalize his advance.[13] But in comparison to the heavily fortified area around Metz, these various obstacles must have appeared quite insignificant even to Patton.

The only physical benefit provided by a Metz axis of attack was the closer proximity to the Saar River and West Wall. Robert Allen suggested that this axis of advance would "uncover a direct corridor (Trier-Koblenz) to the Rhine."[14] Yet to shift the weight of his renewed advance to Metz, where an important portion of XX Corps (10th Armored Division) stood on the wrong side of the Moselle, was essentially reinforcing failure instead of success. Patton may not have recognized Metz for what it was, as the anchor upon which the entire German defense of Lorraine rested, but this seems doubtful. Koch's intelligence estimate for November 1 suggested that the "Germans could pivot on Metz to establish a general defensive line paralleling the Siegfried Line and take advantage of favorable terrain in the Third Army zone of advance to construct new organized defensive positions."[15] The importance of Metz to the German defense was quite obvious.

The Germans had had over a month to bolster frontline positions and prepare secondary ones during the lull. Their quickly improvised defense in early September had been staunch despite a far less lengthy preparatory period. Though Patton showed concern for German ability to quickly improvise defense, it was not an overriding consideration with him prior to the November offensive. He confided to Bradley on October 19 that he could reach the West Wall in a period "not to exceed D plus two days,"[16] an operational forecast described by Kemp as unfeasible because Third Army held an eighty-five mile front with nine divisions at the time.[17] This ambitious schedule could obviously only be met in XX Corps's sector if Metz was bypassed quickly. To facilitate this, virtually the entire air effort in the November offensive was designed to coordinate with XX Corps for the capture of Metz.

On October 23 Weyland unveiled his air plan designated Operation "Madison." The main attacks, consisting of heavy bombardment from the Eighth and Ninth Air Forces, would seek to "kill and stun enemy troops in exposed or semi-exposed positions in the zone of the attacking infantry and to damage the major forts in the area thus rendering them untenable."[18] The 5th Infantry's passage south of Metz was to be facilitated by heavy bomber strikes against seven key forts dominating the roads south and southeast of the city.[19] While the bombers offered a powerful punch, the XIX TAC was slowly losing its striking power. On November 2 Weyland told Patton what could be realistically expected from the XIX TAC in the coming offensive. His forces had been reduced to only four groups of fighter-bombers to give General "Pete" Quesada's IX TAC, supporting First Army, more weight. When this fact was added to the bad weather and shorter flying days, Weyland estimated that XIX TAC could give Third Army ground forces only 25 percent of its former effort.[20]

Patton's attitude toward air power changed as frequently as the weather in Lorraine. Though he welcomed what would amount to the "greatest air support ever" from the bombers, he noted on November 6, after a bombing strike against the forts was canceled due to rain, that "it is useless to put any confidence in the air at this time of year."[21] But he clearly was putting confidence in the air. As Cole suggested, as it became increasingly apparent to the ground commanders around Metz in September that the infantry-artillery team could not penetrate the Metz defensive system alone, air support became an "overriding consideration in all thinking and planning."[22] The detailed planning of October rested to a large extent on the blunt use of air power.

One conclusion readily discernible from the two outline plans and the design of the offensive as a whole was that Patton proved capable of a measure of detailed set-piece battle planning. One author would not agree, claiming that "Patton could not and probably would not have liked to have been forced to sit down and plan for several weeks a set-piece type of battle such as Montgomery's El Alamein."[23] But there was nothing haphazard about his planning for taking Metz in November. Throughout October he spent more time with Gaffey, Gay, and the rest of his special staff minutely planning each portion of his maneuvers.[24] Bradley had little faith in Patton's principal staff officers, claiming that they were not "outstanding individual performers" like those who made up the staffs of First and Ninth Armies. The truth was that Patton cared little for "outstanding individual performers" but believed exclusively in the team concept. Bradley ultimately agreed with another senior commander who stated that Patton could "get more good work out of a mediocre bunch of staff officers than anyone I ever saw."[25]

From Patton downward, more attention was paid to the finer points of the upcoming operations. Walker's plan identified every building in Metz known to be occupied by the enemy. Weigley commented that this attention to detail was "a remarkable change from the free-wheeling style of the Third Army in August [and September]."[26] Patton's reasoning for more-involved preparation at this stage is interesting. In his memoirs he stated that "it will be noted that both the plans for the operation for the capture of Metz and the Saar campaign were worked out with much greater detail than were our operations while going across France. The reason for this is evident. Touring France was a catch-as-catch-can performance where we had to keep going to maintain our initial advantage. In this operation [November offensive] we had to start moving from an initial disadvantage."[27]

Patton seemed to forget that his position on September 5 was also less than advantageous, because he advanced from a dead stop against an enemy of unknown strength and disposition. If he had finally recognized that his static position necessitated more-involved preparation, his perception of both the difficulties and opportunities posed by the German defense of Lorraine remained faulty. Of particular significance was the fact that the specifics of the two plans lost much of their focus as Third Army's operations neared the West Wall. After Metz the operations were referred to in the sweeping terminology that characterized the advance in September. Patton himself continued to ignore the tactical significance of the West Wall and Rhine. In both outlines, the army, after "neutralizing" Metz, was to "continue [the] advance *rapidly*" [emphasis added], not to deal with the West Wall, but to establish bridgeheads across the Rhine.[28]

The emphasis on encircling Metz broke the advance into two distinct stages and made a rapid strike into the depths of the German defenses unlikely. Because of less-than-ideal terrain and, more importantly, deteriorating weather, any degree of fluid operations could only be facilitated by helping the armored formations as much as possible in regards to jumpoff points, avenues of attack, and objectives. The plans provided for only one armored division, Wood's 4th, to strike opportunistically for the Saar and

Rhine. The 10th Armored Division, if committed under plan "A," would have its striking potential contingent on the ability of Van Fleet's infantry to quickly win bridgeheads over the river. The fighting in September had clearly proven that gaining the east bank of the Moselle was a difficult operation. Plan "B" at least positioned the 10th Armored to begin from the east side of the river in the already established Arnaville bridgehead. Yet Walker made it clear, "I never gave serious consideration to putting the Armor in south of Metz," although he was prepared to do so "in case I could get no bridge across the river to the north."[29]

There were legitimate reasons to think twice about putting the 10th Armored Division in south of Metz. When the final boundary between XII and XX Corps was settled, Walker got the main and only west-east road anywhere near the boundary between the two corps. The road was well defiladed from the forts south and southeast of Metz. As Walker pointed out to Cole, "All terrain to the north of this road was enfiladed by the Metz forts and was practically impregnable."[30] Because this road was the best route east available anywhere near the corps boundary, Eddy requested and received permission to put Grow's 6th Armored Division on it to open the XII Corps offensive with the added catch that Grow would quickly reenter the XII Corps sector.

Facilitating this move required Walker holding back Irwin's division for a full day until the 6th Armored had vacated the road. Thus, pushing the 10th Armored out of the Arnaville bridgehead from the outset of the offensive might have resulted in a major traffic jam on the main road. Walker was insistent that the 5th Infantry should not have to attack north of the road because this would have forced Irwin to "make frontal attacks over open ground on the Metz forts" and "these could not possibly have succeeded."[31] Apparently, Eddy had discussed with McBride the possibility of moving the corps boundary south to allow for a coordinated attack by both corps, but "McBride did not like this at all" because his sector would have been narrowed considerably leaving him with little "room to maneuver."[32] The inability to coordinate the advance of the two corps would create serious problems during the November offensive.

Another problem with Patton's plans was that even though the army front would be reduced to some sixty miles, from Sierck-les-Bains to the Marne-Rhine Canal, neither of them positioned Third Army's substantial forces to achieve an overwhelming degree of concentration. Patton had been prepared to concentrate his forces to quite a degree when Wood drove through German lines to Chateau-Salins, but this had been a case of rare opportunity. Whether or not Patton was temperamentally suited to concentration in situations other than opportunistic ones is questionable. Perhaps a partial answer can be found in the lessons derivable from his experience in the various training maneuvers of 1941. At that time, Patton operated in Walter Krueger's Third Army, and Gabel has commented that of the various field armies taking part in the extensive 1941 maneuvers, only Krueger's "clearly anticipated the operational art that would characterize American operations in World War II."[33] He fought on a broad front but retained a high degree of responsiveness because of his dexterous use of motorized vehicles and the wide latitude given to subordinates.

Gabel's general conclusion was that Krueger's "powerful operations were clear and straightforward, and they produced maximum results at minimum risk."[34] Patton's operations in Normandy had been waged over an enormous front, and whereas Troy Middleton, the VIII Corps commander, for example, often found himself left out of the equation, Patton retained a high degree of flexibility due to the freedom afforded his divisional commanders. One may also characterize Third Army's operations in Lorraine, like Krueger's in 1941, as straightforward. There is enough of a similarity between the two to suggest that Krueger may have influenced Patton's broad operational style. Yet though Patton, like virtually all other American commanders in Europe, tended to favor a wide deployment of forces, one must seek to uncover additional motives for his broad front advance in November.

Patton stormed the Moselle on a broad front in September because he perceived the enemy to be weak, unable to defend in depth, and susceptible to a quick bull rush across the river. Faulty intelligence and a faulty instinct told him this was possible. By mid-October the intelligence picture had cleared considerably. Thanks to Ultra and additional sources, Patton had a fairly clear picture of the German order of battle.[35] Though he desired to get moving as quickly as possible, because "the enemy continues to dig and mine ahead of us,"[36] he did not anticipate meeting large German reinforcements once the advance had begun. Accumulating reserves from frontline units would be almost impossible for the Germans because their forces were spread out to one battalion per each mile of front.[37] The new commander of Army Group G, Balck, had ordered each division under his command to establish a reserve of one infantry regiment, one antitank company, and two battalions of light howitzers. According to Cole, however, "most divisional commanders were fortunate if they had so much as a battalion in reserve when the Americans attacked on 8 and 9 November."[38] Patton informed Bradley on the 19th that the enemy "has disposed his entire strength in his front line and that he is not disposed in depth" and that he wanted to use "penetrations and quick envelopments" to capture or destroy all the enemy on his immediate front.[39]

Patton also knew through Ultra that the Germans had instituted fuel rationing like Third Army and that the panzer divisions were partially dependent upon horse-drawn transport.[40] He also appreciated the effect the rain was having on the ground, announcing on October 21 that "the country is about as muddy as I have ever seen it."[41] This dual hindrance—poor weather and lack of fuel—no doubt led him to conclude that German reaction to Third Army's advance would be quite sluggish. It was a logical assumption.

For Patton to achieve quick envelopments required the active and early participation of the armored divisions. He intended to punch several holes in the enemy line with his armor to effect these quick envelopments, but to expect the armor to make deep penetrations under soggy conditions against a defense in depth prepared over an entire month was probably asking too much, although Grow concluded that the plan was sound based on Patton's estimate of the enemy's capabilities at the time.[42] The best explanation for Patton's reliance on a broad advance in November is that he probably felt confident with his substantial reinforcements, which were all in place by November 8.

As his plans were further developed during late October and early November, Plan "A" became dominant. Both Patton and Walker hoped that once German forces had been siphoned into defending the Metz area, opportunities would present themselves for quick exploitation elsewhere. Ironically, they felt that such opportunities would open up north of Metz, not in Eddy's sector. Specifically, Patton and Walker intended to send the regimental combat teams of the 83rd Infantry Division, promised to Patton during October, through the 90th Infantry bridgehead at Thionville once Morris had crossed all his armor. The 83rd Infantry Division was to proceed rapidly over the base of the Saar-Moselle triangle and seize a bridgehead over the Saar River at Saarburg.[43]

The 83rd Infantry Division had figured in Patton's plan for forcing the Moselle line earlier in September when he had attempted to push the division across the river at Remich after its arrival in Third Army's zone on September 21, but the subsequent lull forced the cancellation of the operation.[44] Beyond the 83rd's assigned task, Patton also wanted to send a task force of combat command size (CCB, 10th Armored Division) to make a surprise attack upon Merzig in hopes of securing yet another bridgehead over the Saar.[45] The proposed operations by the 83rd Infantry Division and CCB,

10th Armored Division were subsidiary, however, to the main effort of XX Corps's attack, which followed a Metz-Saarlautern axis.[46]

Patton's two-phase plan was devised with the assumption that the speed of the first phase would facilitate the rapid execution of the second. Ultimately, however, neither the outline plans nor the final scheme of maneuver for the November offensive properly aligned assets and objectives with terrain and weather. Yet if Patton still did not realize that Metz could be masked, he at least took measures to ensure that the city would fall in short order if vigorously pressed. Indeed, from the standpoint of dealing with Metz on a tactical level, Patton had learned the hard lesson that cracking such a defensive system required extensive preparation, not on-the-spot improvisation. Of equal importance was the fact that prior to the November offensive, many of the problems that had plagued his operations in September had been solved, particularly the shortage of infantry.

Third Army received substantial armored and infantry reinforcements during the lull. The first addition, III Corps, commanded by Major General John Millikin, had been assigned to Patton's command on October 10 but as yet possessed corps troops only. Blumenson has suggested that there was a "coolness between them, perhaps dating from some inconsequential yet lasting disagreement at West Point."[47] Indeed, Patton was not entirely pleased to have Millikin as one of his corps commanders. He felt that it was "wrong to put an officer in command of a corps who had never commanded a division in battle, while all the Division Commanders were veterans." This was a serious concern on Patton's part, but he still considered Millikin an "excellent general."[48] He would speak well of him for his actions in the Bulge, but in March 1945 Courtney Hodges relieved Millikin of command at the Remagen Bridge.[49]

The newly arrived 26th Infantry Division, under Major General Williard S. Paul, relieved Wood's 4th Armored on October 12, and elements of the new 95th Infantry Division, commanded by Major General Harry L. Twaddle, replaced Irwin's weary infantry in front of Fort Driant six days later. Neither division had combat experience to date, and to rectify this situation a limited objective attack was set up east of Arracourt for the 26th Infantry on October 22. In this baptism of fire, the division performed quite well in "very hard fighting," an effort that drew Patton's attention and praise.[50] Eddy told General Paul on the 25th, "I thought they were going to be a first class outfit in the future."[51] As for the division's commander, General Paul was well known to Patton, having been at Schofield Barracks with him during 1925–1926. Patton recorded, "I had formed a very high opinion of him" during the interwar period, an opinion "which was subsequently amply justified" in Lorraine.[52] General Twaddle had activated and trained the 95th Infantry Division and been in command since March 1942. Patton met Twaddle on October 16 at XX Corps headquarters and noted that he was "not impressive," but that the "general appearance of the officers and men of the Division is satisfactory."[53]

To replace the loss of Silvester's 7th Armored Division, Major General William H. H. Morris, Jr.'s 10th Armored Division arrived in XX Corps' sector on November 2. It came directly from the United States, disembarking on the continent on September 23; had trained at Teurtheville, France, until October 25; and then began moving into Third Army's zone. The third of Patton's new divisions without any combat experience, the 10th Armored would nonetheless be ably led by General Morris. Although originally an infantryman by training, he had commanded an armored infantry regiment before transferring to the 10th Armored in July 1944. In November he would instill great pride and confidence in his division and command it with considerable skill.

A further augmentation in Walker's strength was to be the "operational control" of Major General R. C. Macon's 83rd Infantry Division. This formation had been placed on the extreme northern boundary of XX Corps on September 21 to protect the army's flank. On October 29 Patton secured the use of two regimental combat teams of the 83rd for use across the Moselle from Bradley.[54] Employment of the 83rd would become a serious point of difference between Patton and Bradley shortly after the November offensive started. The loss of this division would adversely affect operations on Walker's north flank as envisioned by Patton's finalized scheme of maneuver.

While Patton's army was bolstered by divisional reinforcements throughout the lull, German forces in Lorraine underwent a drastic downsizing in order to free divisions for the Ardennes offensive. Everything had now become subsidiary to the preparations for Hitler's last great gamble. Besides losing the valuable headquarters staffs of the Fifth Panzer Army, XLVII Panzer Corps and LVIII Panzer Corps, Balck also gave up the veteran 3rd and 15th Panzer Grenadier Divisions, both of which were still rated as limited attack units.[55] As well, the 553rd Volksgrenadier Division, hardly an elite unit but still a solid infantry formation, was transferred to Nineteenth Army. With the loss of these dependable formations and the arrival of "untrained infantry divisions of dubious quality,"[56] Balck possessed nine paper divisions to halt Patton's November offensive. Of these nine divisions, five were designated as ordinary defensive units. Only two were sufficiently organized, equipped, and trained for limited assaults.

None of the three replacement divisions Balck received for the loss of the panzer grenadier divisions was of even relatively good quality.

Generalleutenant Kurt Pflieger had brought his 416th Division into First Army's sector around Sierck-les-Bains north of Thionville after reorganizing in Denmark. This formation, containing a total strength of perhaps 8,500 men, averaging nearly forty years of age with no combat experience, was capable of "very limited use as a defensive formation." Its artillery assets were virtually nonexistent, consisting mainly of fortress guns and captured Russian pieces.[57] Colonel Karl Britzelmayr's 19th Volksgrenadier Division was also weak in all respects. It had about the same number of men as the 416th and was not capable of sustained offensive action. It did have combat experience, however, and possessed the modest artillery complement of three field battalions and eleven new assault guns.[58] The last of the replacement formations was Colonel Alfred Philippi's new and inexperienced 361st Volksgrenadier Division that relieved the 11th Panzer Division on October 23. It possessed a two-battalion-per-regiment table of organization, horse-drawn artillery, one battery of assault guns, and an estimated strength of 7,000 men consisting of a mixture of veterans, sailors, and Luftwaffe personnel.[59] It too was far from a frontline division even though it would be called upon to act in such a manner in November.

As for the original divisions of First Army, Balck still had the 559th Volksgrenadier Division, the 17th SS Panzer Grenadier Division, the 462nd Volksgrenadier Division (upgraded from the Division Number 462), and the 48th Division. Casper's 48th Division relieved the wrecked 553rd Volksgrenadier Division on October 13, and although rebuilt somewhat with overaged replacements, higher command considered the 48th to be the poorest division in First Army.[60] Its weakness was readily apparent in the opening stages of Eddy's attack. XII Corps intelligence placed the strength of Generalmajor Kurt Freiherr von Muehlen's 559th Volksgrenadier Division at only 4,000,[61] and the 17th SS Panzer Grenadier and 462nd Volksgrenadier Divisions were down to 6,000 and 9,000 men respectively.[62] For all intents and purposes the 462nd lost the backbone of its strength when the officer candidates were graduated on October 9 and sent to other sectors. Overaged and poorly trained replacements filled the gap.[63]

Balck's sole army reserve was Wietersheim's 11th Panzer Division positioned west of St. Avold. Pulled out of the line at the end of October, the division's tank strength had been brought up to forty panthers, twenty Mark IVs, and ten Jagdpanzer IV assault guns by November 8,[64] but as with all German panzer divisions at this time, it was more of an infantry division than an armored one. Feuchtinger's 21st Panzer Division had also been intended for use as an additional operational reserve for Balck, but difficulty in locating and transporting a relieving infantry division kept his armor in the Nineteenth Army sector when Patton attacked on November 8.

In absolute terms, Third Army now outnumbered First Army 250,000 to 86,000. Third Army's cutting edge was improved at the outset of the new offensive because replacements exceeded losses from September 26 to November 7 by 1,864 men, but the shortage of replacements would once again rise dramatically during the final phase of the campaign. From November 8 to December 2, Third Army would find itself short over 10,000 riflemen (see Appendix C). Like Third Army, there were few replacements behind First Army lines, but the divisional augmentation, however, which brought Third Army up to seven infantry divisions (5th, 26th, 35th, 80th, 90th, 95th, and provisional use of the 83rd) and three armored divisions (4th, 6th, and 10th), gave Patton for the first time in the campaign a marked numerical superiority over his opponent in all categories—armor, artillery, and all importantly, infantry. The November battles would prove to be the principal domain of the foot slogging infantry.

Additional support was given Third Army when by November 8 most of its supply problems had been corrected, at least in the short term. Logistical shortfalls had undermined Patton's operations in September at least as much as the manpower shortage, and as late as October 29 it looked as if supply difficulties might persist into the new offensive. He was still anxious over his logistical support when he stated on October 17 that the entire plan now "hinges on ammunition, and apparently there is none."[65] Gay recorded that "The situation at present is summed up to the effect that until the supply situation improves, a large offensive on the part of Third Army is out of the question."[66] Only one hundred tons of ammunition arrived on the 29th, representing the first delivery in seven days, and gasoline receipts continued to barely match expenditures.[67] But this situation changed dramatically by November 7. By then Third Army had accumulated a five-day reserve of fuel, an absolute necessity if any quick advance was to be achieved. The ammunition problem in the last week of October, where 80 percent of the shells fired by Third Army were actually German, had also been rectified to the point where only white phosphorous shells for the 105-mm and 155-mm guns continued in short supply.[68] The army's daily maintenance requirements, calculated at one thousand tons of rations, two thousand tons of fuel, two thousand tons of ammunition, and one thousand tons of other items, had become assured.

The revamped logistical system permitted Patton to accumulate a ten-thousand-ton stock of engineer supplies, items that would become invaluable as the rivers and streams of Lorraine flooded during November.[69] He owed this logistical buildup to the fact that during the lull large portions of the devastated French railway system were repaired for military purposes, bringing Third Army railheads all the way to Nancy.[70] The only marked deficiency in Patton's logistical base was a serious shortage of replacement medium tanks in the army's ordnance depots,[71] but compared to the supply situation in September, Third Army was now capable of an all-out attack for an extended period of time.

NOTES

1. George S. Patton, *War as I Knew It* (Boston: Houghton Mifflin, 1947), 308.

2. Hugh M. Cole, *The Lorraine Campaign*, U.S. Army in World War II: European Theater of Operations (Washington, D.C.: Center for Military History, 1984), 299. Patton's chief role at the time was to drive in a northeasterly direction covering the right flank of Hodges' First Army.

3. Russell F. Weigley, *Eisenhower's Lieutenants: The Campaign of France and Germany, 1944–1945* (Bloomington: Indiana University Press, 1981), 385.

4. Michael D. Doubler, *Closing with the Enemy: How GIs Fought the War in Europe, 1944–1945* (Lawrence, Kans.: University Press of Kansas, 1994), 149.

5. Patton, *War as I Knew It*, 119.

6. Third Army "Outline Plan 'A' for the Resumption of the Offensive," October 18, 1944, Modern Military Reference Branch (MMRB), Suitland, Maryland.

7. Ibid.

8. Third Army "Outline Plan 'B' for the Resumption of the Offensive," October 18, 1944, MMRB.

9. Cole, Lorraine Campaign, 373.

10. Third Army After Action Report (AAR), I: October 18, 1944, Special Collections, United States Military Academy Library, West Point (WP).

11. Christopher R. Gabel, *The Lorraine Campaign: An Overview, September–December 1944* (Fort Leavenworth, Kans.: Combat Studies Institute, 1985), 23.

12. Major Roy E. Appleman, "Comments on Grow's Broad Front vs Narrow Front," October 15, 1952, Hist 314.7, Box: "General Grow, Special Studies on World War II," United States Army Military History Institute (USAMHI), Carlisle Barracks, Pa.

13. Cole, *Lorraine Campaign*, 314.

14. Robert S. Allen, *Lucky Forward: The History of Patton's Third U.S. Army* (New York: Vanguard Press, 1947), 162.

15. Charles M. Province, *Patton's Third Army: A Chronology of the Third Army's Advance, August, 1944 to May, 1945* (New York: Hippocrene, 1992), 80.

16. Cole, *Lorraine Campaign*, 300.

17. Anthony Kemp, *The Unknown Battle: Metz, 1944* (New York: Stein and Day, 1981), 143. Patton told Bradley that he could reach the West Wall in two days if he was given the Daily Maintenance Requirement of 6,000 tons plus the Additional Pre-D-Day Requirement of 2,123 tons. Hobart R. Gay/Hugh J. Gaffey Diary, October 18, 1944, Special Collections, WP.

18. "The Effectiveness of Third Phase Tactical Air Operations in the European Theater, May 5, 1944–May 8, 1945," United States Air Force Historical Records Center (USAFHRC), microfilm A1175, 156.

19. Ibid., 156–158.

20. David N. Spires, *Air Power for Patton's Third Army: The XIX Tactical Air Command in the Second World War*, Draft Manuscript, 188.

21. Martin Blumenson, *The Patton Papers* (Boston: Houghton Mifflin, 1974), II: 569. Three hundred bombers were scheduled to hit the Metz forts as part of a softening-up program. Though Patton realized that the weather would be a serious impediment to large-scale air support, he also had complete confidence in not only Weyland but others whom he considered close friends. On November 9 he commented, "I think that all the bombers we had today were really an expression of friendship to me from Spaatz and Doolittle—personality plays a tremendous part in war," 572.

22. Cole, *Lorraine Campaign*, 261.

23. Charles Whiting, *Patton* (New York: Ballantine, 1970), 150.

24. Ladislas Farago, *Patton: Ordeal and Triumph* (New York: Ivan Obolensky, 1963), 661.

25. Omar N. Bradley, *A Soldier's Story* (New York: Henry Holt and Company, 1951), 473.

26. Weigley, *Eisenhower's Lieutenants*, 387.

27. Patton, *War as I Knew It*, 119.

28. Outline Plan "A."

29. Walton H. Walker to Hugh M. Cole, October 8, 1947, Historical Division Combat Interviews (HDCI), National Archives (NA), Washington, D.C.

30. Ibid.

31. Ibid.

32. Manton S. Eddy Diary, October 31, 1944, U.S. Army Infantry School, National Infantry Museum (NIM), Fort Benning, Ga.

33. Christopher R. Gabel, *The U.S. Army GHQ Maneuvers of 1941* (Washington, D.C.: Office of the Chief of Military History, 1991), 188.

34. Ibid.

35. Gabel, *The Lorraine Campaign: An Overview*, 23.

36. Blumenson, *Patton Papers*, II: 565.

37. Gabel, *The Lorraine Campaign: An Overview*, 30.

38. Cole, *Lorraine Campaign*, 308.

39. Gay/Gaffey Diary, October 18–19.

40. Gabel, *The Lorraine Campaign: An Overview*, 23.

41. George S. Patton Diary, October 21, 1944, Special Collections, WP.

42. Robert W. Grow, "Broad Front vs Narrow Front," Hist 314.7, Box: "General Grow, Special Studies on World War II," USAMHI.

43. XX Corps AAR, "The Reduction of Fortress Metz, 1 September–6 December, 1944," Box 64, Patton Papers (PP), Library of Congress (LC), Washington, D.C., 12.

44. Cole, *Lorraine Campaign*, 281.

45. "Reduction of Fortress Metz," 13.

46. Walker to Cole, October 8, 1947.

47. Martin Blumenson, *Patton: The Man behind the Legend, 1885–1945* (New York: William Morrow, 1985), 246.

48. Patton, *War as I Knew It*, 120.

49. Robert H. Berlin, "United States Army World War II Corps Commanders: A Composite Biography," *The Journal of Military History* LIII (April 1989): 166.

50. Cole, *Lorraine Campaign*, 290.

51. Eddy Diary, October 25.

52. Patton, *War as I Knew It*, 115–116.

53. Patton Diary, October 16.

54. Patton, *War as I Knew It*, 123.

55. Cole, *Lorraine Campaign*, 305.

56. Ibid.

57. Ibid., 388.

58. Ibid., 308.

59. John S. Wood, "Writings: Forward to Study on 4th Armored Division," Box 4, Wood Papers, Syracuse University (SU); Cole, *Lorraine Campaign*, 312.

60. Cole, *Lorraine Campaign*, 312.

61. Wood, "Writings," Annex II, "Intelligence."

62. "Reduction of Fortress Metz," 14.

63. Cole, *Lorraine Campaign*, 417.

64. A. Harding Ganz, "The 11th Panzers in the Defense, 1944," *Armor* (March–April, 1994): 34. Cole stated that the division had been reequipped with nineteen Mark IVs and fifty new panthers and not more than one or two tank destroyers. Cole, *Lorraine Campaign*, 313.

65. Patton Diary, October 17.

66. Gay/Gaffey Diary, October 28.

67. Ibid., October 29.

68. Ronald G. Ruppenthal, *Logistical Support of the Armies*, U.S Army in World War II: European Theater of Operations (Washington, D.C.: Department of the Army, 1959), II: 256; Cole, *Lorraine Campaign*, 302. The artillery ammunition situation had been so bad in mid-October that Third Army rationed its various calibers as follows: 1.1 rounds per 105-mm gun, 0.4 rounds per 155-mm gun, and 0.3 rounds per 240-mm guns per day.

69. Cole, *Lorraine Campaign*, 302.

70. Gabel, *The Lorraine Campaign: An Overview*, 22. In addition, the French civilian sector provided rolling stock along with trained personnel to assist Third Army quartermasters.

71. Cole, *Lorraine Campaign*, 302.

Chapter 10

The Fall of Metz

The plans for the show are good and the men are keen and we have
plenty of ammunition and enough gas. I think we will get to the Rhine.
— Patton, November 7, 1944[1]

We have completely surrounded Metz and are fighting in the
streets. . . . I think that only Attila and the Third Army have ever taken
Metz by assault.
— Patton, November 19, 1944[2]

In picking out the one factor primarily responsible for Patton's slow advance in Lorraine during November and December 1944, historians have with few exceptions pointed to the poor weather. Most accounts of this portion of the campaign conclude that Napoleon's "fifth element of war," mud, threw Patton's plans askew. Indeed, the weather did play a role. Seven inches of rain, about twice the normal amount, fell during November giving Lorraine its worst flood in thirty-five years (see Table 10.1).[3] As a result of this unforeseeable development, Third Army engineers would construct 121 Bailey bridges, 111 treadway bridges, eighty-four timber spans, and five heavy pontoon bridges during the month to keep the army moving.[4] Yet whereas the effect of bad weather on operations cannot be seriously disputed, other factors played important roles in hindering Third Army's progress as it struggled to reach the West Wall, including missed opportunities and detrimental situations created by the very design of the November offensive (see Map 10.1).

Historians have long known that Patton's plan itself was to blame for delays in November. Chester Wilmot concluded that his inability to achieve a quick breakthrough in November was less a matter of weather

Map 10.1
Third Army Plan of Advance, November 8, 1944

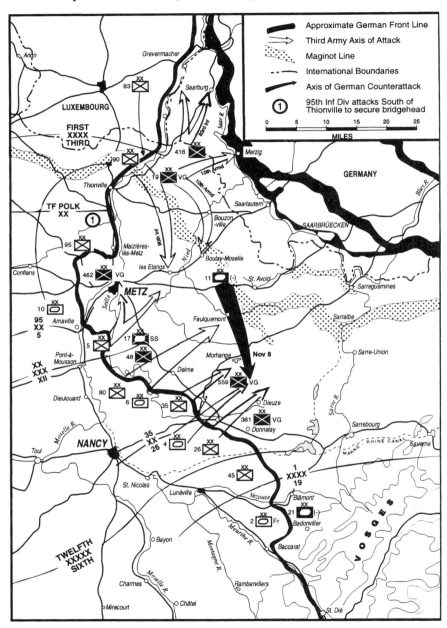

Source: Base map taken from Hugh M. Cole's *The Lorraine Campaign,* U.S. Army in World War II: European Theater of Operations (Washington, D.C., 1984), Map XXII. Altered by Eric Drummie and Bill Traer.

Table 10.1

Weather Conditions in Lorraine, November 8–December 7, 1944

	FAIR	PARTLY CLOUDY	CLOUDY	RAIN	SNOW
NOV 8		X			
NOV 9		X		X	X
NOV 10				X	
NOV 11		X			
NOV 12					X
NOV 13				X	
NOV 14				X	
NOV 15				X	
NOV 16	X				
NOV 17	X				
NOV 18	X				
NOV 19	X				
NOV 20			X	X	
NOV 21			X	X	
NOV 22			X	X	
NOV 23			X	X	
NOV 24			X		
NOV 25			X		
NOV 26	X				
NOV 27	X				
NOV 28			X		
NOV 29			Foggy		X
NOV 30			Foggy		X
DEC 1	X				
DEC 2	X				
DEC 3					X
DEC 4		X			
DEC 5			X	X	
DEC 6			X	X	
DEC 7			X	X	
Total: 30	8	4	12	12	5

Source: Wood, "Writings: Forward to Study on 4th Armored Division," Annex II, "Intelligence," 104.

than an indication of his failure to profit by the lessons of the Normandy campaign. There the Germans had proven their ability to quickly adapt to the broad-based advance of the Allies.[5] From Caen to the Brittany coast German forces checked every thrust of the Allies for two months. Only when Operation "Cobra" smashed their front were the Germans unable to retain their operational balance.

The forty-mile expanse between the German First Army on the Moselle and the forward defenses of the West Wall in November 1944 was a "cushion" that gave Balck and Knobelsdorff the opportunity to employ an elastic defense. The best countertactic against such a defense was "not a coordinated advance along the entire front, but a concerted attack on a narrow sector, followed by a deep penetration."[6] Such an action most likely could not have been checked by Balck's thin reserves.[7] Patton's plan, however, for a general assault all along the line did not follow Wilmot's reasoning. A disregard for the principle of concentration was one serious design flaw of his November offensive.

Another design flaw was that Patton had planned the November campaign with the same ultimate objective of his earlier plans, reaching and securing bridgeheads over the Rhine River. His statement used to open this chapter proves that the distant waterway was still a powerful obsession for him. Directing all effort on a common objective is probably the most important principle of war, but the objective must be obtainable. Successful commanders have been able to project themselves forward in time and space for the purpose of identifying attainable objectives and also for anticipating potential threats to their army. Yet Patton was looking too far afield, partly out of pure ambition and partly because he actually believed that he could reach the Rhine.

Patton's optimism was well founded in August. Eddy observed of Patton after taking command of XII Corps late in the month that he was "about the most optimistic man I have ever seen in my life."[8] But after two months of grueling, primarily infantry combat in Lorraine, marked only by small successes, his confidence was drastically overinflated. That he thought it possible to sustain mobile operations amidst increasing rain, snow, and soggy ground is hard to comprehend. His reasoning, however faulty, is explained in his memoirs. In reflecting on the nature of the November offensive and his hopes for its success, Patton stated that "one of the unfortunate things about this campaign was that it had been planned when the weather was good and the country dry. Therefore, the operations were envisaged as of a blitz nature. When it actually came off, we were in the middle of the greatest flood in eighty years."[9] Yet the weather conditions in Lorraine had revealed their immobilizing effects on armored and infantry movement well before November. Moreover, it was Patton who said a commander should try to make plans to fit the circumstances.

His ultimate decision to attack despite the weather must be applauded, however, simply because in the last instance, it was a difficult one to make. Eddy noted, "I could tell that Gen. Patton had been thinking all day about this decision."[10] Patton read Rommel's *Infantry Attacks* the night of November 7 and recorded, "By chance I turned to a chapter describing a fight in the rain in September, 1914. This was very reassuring because I felt that if the Germans could do it I could."[11] Both Eddy and Grow urged a postponement on November 7 because of the weather, but Patton assured them that the rain would immobilize and trap the Germans.[12]

The chief benefit of this tough decision was the attainment of complete tactical surprise for Eddy's attack on November 8 and Walker's the next day. As von Mellenthin noted, although wireless intercepts had kept the Germans informed of Patton's preparations, "there was a slackening in our ground observation" due to the poor weather.[13] As a result, Balck was unable to defend against Third Army in the way he had originally intended. He wanted to use Ludendorff's World War I scheme of elastic defense to slow Patton's advance in November. His forward line would be lightly manned and prepared to fall back two to three kilometers upon a Main Line of Resistance (MLR) as soon as it was ascertained that Third Army was attacking in strength. The theory was that American ordnance would be wasted on the forward "false positions" while the main German combat elements prepared to hold their ground and counterattack the enemy assault formations.[14] The key element in Balck's defense in November was Wietersheim's 11th Panzer Division, which was broken into *Panzerkampftrupps*, "tank battle teams," consisting of a tank platoon and two panzer grenadier platoons each. As Ganz accurately described them, these panzer battle teams were "fire brigades," Balck's only force capable of intercepting multiple American penetrations.[15] It would be Weitersheim's sorely depleted armored elements that would prevent a complete collapse of First Army's front in the first days of Patton's offensive.

Because of the failure to discern Patton's true intentions, the German divisions facing Third Army, particularly those opposite XII Corps, failed to carry out Balck's "false position" defense and took an unmerciful pounding during the opening artillery barrage on November 8. Utilizing thirty-seven battalions of field artillery (seventeen Corps, twenty divisional), XII Corps fired 21,933 rounds from 540 guns at the 48th Division and the 559th Volksgrenadier Division of Priess's XIII SS Corps and the 361st Volksgrenadier Division of the LXXXIX Corps in the first twenty-four hours. Cole noted that this barrage "smashed the forward enemy positions, destroyed communications, and effectively neutralized most of the German guns."[16] With stunning success, Patton had opened his November campaign with a well-executed set-piece barrage reminiscent of World War I.

The only glitch in XII Corps' operations on November 8 was an apparent misunderstanding between McBride and Irwin over when the 5th Infantry Division would begin its own attack. Cole noted that McBride "launched the 80th Division attack on November 8 with the expectation that the 5th would join in immediately."[17] Irwin had been told by Walker that the 5th Infantry would not attack on the 8th, but McBride was not likewise informed by Eddy. As late as November 4 Eddy was still busy coordinating details between Grow and McBride for the XII Corps offensive, but no mention is made of the 5th Infantry's role in Eddy's diary at this stage.[18] Even Gay recorded a visit to the 5th Infantry on November 8 "where a good view could be had of the proposed site for the crossing . . . at 0600 *the following morning*" [emphasis added].[19] It seems that everyone knew of the timing of Irwin's attack except possibly McBride.

Whatever the reason for McBride's lack of information, this disjointed advance resulted in an exposed left flank for his division, a situation that hampered operations along the intercorps boundary within a few days.[20] The obvious failure to synchronize operations at this stage reflected the *ad hoc* nature of Patton's planning in September. Eddy surely must be held responsible for not hammering out a definite timetable with Walker and passing it on to McBride, but Patton is accountable for not seeing the problems consonant with a disjointed advance in the first place.

Nonetheless, with the exception of Baade's 35th Infantry Division, which moved somewhat behind schedule, XII Corps achieved all its objectives for the first day. Eddy stated that Patton was "very favorably impressed by the gains."[21] He told Eddy to keep pushing as hard as possible. The initial success in the November offensive led Patton to wonder if he had "won another great battle or rather won the opening period,"[22] but it quickly became apparent that the weather would not allow him to bask in the glow of victory for long. Though Eddy had marveled at Patton's good luck and the clear day on November 8, the continually rising waters of the Moselle had washed out every bridge over that river except for one at Pont-à-Mousson in Eddy's sector. Patton described the ground conditions on November 9 as "disheartening."[23] The flood situation had a profound effect on Walker's principal operation on the Corps left wing.

For the first phase of Patton's plan to have any degree of rapid success, Van Fleet's 90th Infantry Division had to accomplish two separate tasks. First, it had to secure a foothold across the Moselle north of Thionville and quickly construct a bridge capable of bearing Morris's 10th Armored Division. Secondly, the 90th needed to rapidly advance southeast some sixteen miles to close one portion of the pincer movement on Metz. Prior to the assault all the officers and men of the 90th Infantry were told of the acute importance of this particular crossing to the overall Corps and Army plan.[24]

Indicative of the crucial nature of Van Fleet's crossing, a total of twenty-eight battalions of field artillery supported his operation, a figure representing the greater total of XX Corps' artillery assets.[25] Extreme care had been taken to assure the secret movement of the artillery from Metz to Thionville. To conceal the movement of Van Fleet's division and its artillery, the 23rd Special Troops maintained the preexisting artillery picture with dummy rubber artillery pieces and simulated flashes using chemical powders. The use of the shoulder patches of the 3rd Cavalry Group, which had been operating in the Thionville area for weeks, helped cover the introduction of 90th Infantry units into that area.[26] Despite this careful preparation and the vital importance placed on the Thionville operation, the high water and terrain in the division's path of advance guaranteed that neither of Van Fleet's tasks would be readily achieved (see Map 10.2).

To a degree the flood conditions actually facilitated the 90th Infantry Division's crossing because the high water inundated large German mine fields on the east bank, a development that gave Van Fleet's infantry tactical surprise.[27] When the crossings began early in the morning of November 9, the river was 300–600 feet wide. By noon, it had swollen to 2,400 feet in width.[28] Van Fleet succeeded in placing eight battalions across the river by the end of November 9 with little interference from Colonel Karl Britzelmayr's 19th Volksgrenadier Division, protecting First Army's front from Koenigsmacker to Metrich, or other German units in the area. Generalleutenant Kurt Pflieger's 416th Division was holding the line from Metrich to the confluence of the Saar and Moselle Rivers. These two divisions, along with Kittel's 462nd Volksgrenadier Division, made up Knobelsdorff's LXXXII Corps.

The construction of a heavy armor bearing bridge, however, was impossible because of the flooding. In fact, the 10th Armored Division would not begin to cross the Moselle until November 14. On the 12th XX Corps engineers began constructing a double-triple Bailey bridge some 180 feet long, but soon discovered that the necessary span needed to be 190 feet, exceeding the longest Bailey in the book by ten feet. There was little choice but to

Map 10.2
90th Infantry Division's Zone of Advance, November 9, 1944

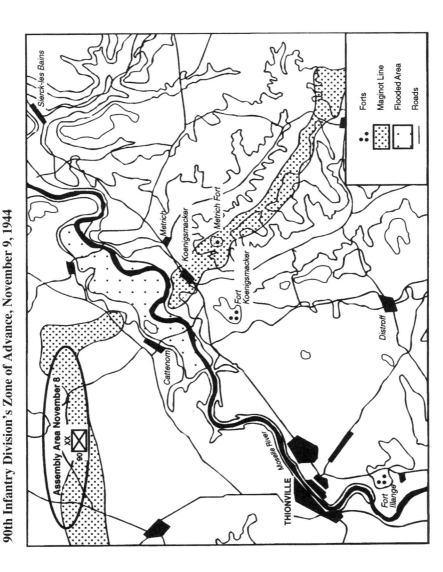

Source: Base map taken from Hugh M. Cole's *The Lorraine Campaign*, U.S. Army in World War II: European Theater of Operations (Washington, D.C., 1984), Map XXII. Altered by Bill Traer.

exceed the limitations and take a calculated risk. Construction continued under enemy mortar fire, which at one point forced work to temporarily cease.[29] Thus the 10th Armored Division sat idle, out of the battle for the first five days of the November offensive, a classic example of the violation of economy of force in the strict sense. Clausewitz's interpretation of economy of force was that "if a segment of one's force is located where it is not sufficiently busy with the enemy, or if the troops are on the march—that is, idle—while the enemy is fighting, then these forces are being managed uneconomically."[30] This definition accurately described Patton's predicament with the 10th Armored Division. Van Fleet commented after the war that "armor is great, but you've got to make it available to roll."[31] Patton's other options with Morris's division at the time were limited. Walker's reservations about sending the division through the Arnaville bridgehead have already been addressed. Passing the division through Pont-à-Mousson was a possibility, but the armor would have had to share the few available hard-surfaced roads with the 4th and 6th Armored Divisions, a situation that guaranteed great confusion.

The flood conditions at Thionville also fowled plans for the employment of the 83rd Infantry Division, which was to cross the Moselle on the heels of the armor and exploit northeast. Moreover, on November 11 Bradley reneged on the use of the division over the river. Weigley stated that the loan was recalled "with exasperating abruptness."[32] According to Gay, Bradley informed Patton that he was "displeased" that Third Army had used the 83rd in a manner different from his written instructions. Gay pointed out, however, that the 83rd had not been committed at all by November 11 and he did not calculate its coming into action until at least the 15th.[33] Bradley later stated that "Patton had given the 83rd so much of a mission that it jeopardized their defensive mission" and added, "You will notice in George's diary that he says that if I'd let him have the 83rd he'd have done wonders, if I hadn't interfered with his use of it. He doesn't bring out the fact that it wasn't his division after all."[34] This was sheer waffling on Bradley's part, and as Robert Allen noted, his decision "completely upset Third Army's operational plan in the midst of battle."[35] On October 1 Gay had sent Walker an almost verbatim directive outlining Bradley's limitations on using the 83rd.[36] Only two regimental combat teams were to be used to clear the Saar-Moselle triangle and seize a bridgehead at Saarburg with the help of some armored elements. The regiments of the 83rd were not to advance beyond Saarburg, and Patton fully understood this.

Bradley's decision to pull the division back may have been simply a lack of faith in Patton's ability to use it before it had to be back in First Army's zone for Hodges' own offensive on November 16 because the division could not have crossed the Moselle until the 15th at the earliest under the current plan. Yet Patton was justifiably upset over the loss of the 83rd in the middle of his offensive. Though Bradley had specifically forbade a separate crossing by the 83rd because that would involve "too much bridging equipment and too much artillery support," this is exactly what he should have allowed Patton to do at the time. A separate crossing of elements of the 83rd would have been made against the weakest division in First Army, Pflieger's 416th Division. Moreover, the Orscholz Switch Line, a series of tank traps, pillboxes, and dragons' teeth that screened the base of the Saar-Moselle triangle could have been outflanked. As it was, Patton would have to attack this well-constructed line frontally later in the month.

Gay, though certainly not an objective witness, noted after the war that "without question" the 83rd assisted by the 10th Armored, and supporting artillery fire from the west bank of the Moselle, could have cleared the triangle and taken Trier. From his perspective, the failure to clear the triangle was the "most serious and far reaching tactical error" made during the war.[37] Patton had more stinging commentary on the event, noting, "I suppose that Hodges and Middleton have been working on Brad for a week and this, added to his natural timidity, caused him to make this decision. I hope history records his moral cowardice."[38] From an operational standpoint, Patton had no illusions about the problems the triangle in German hands presented. "Without it," he declared, "we will not get Saarburg and will have, therefore, to be always bothered by the triangle between the Moselle and Saar Rivers."[39]

The episode was indicative of Bradley's cautious nature and incompatibility with his subordinate's fighting style. Martin Blumenson has written of the professional and personal tension that existed between Bradley and Patton in many of his works. In Normandy, Blumenson stated, they were "less than well synchronized. Their difficulties with each other inhibited forming and implementing a single firm concept, maintaining a strict control over movements and displaying a clear direction toward the proper end."[40] Part of the problem, he felt, was that Bradley had served under Patton in Tunisia and Sicily, and their roles had been reversed in Normandy with negative results. He noted that "it was General Bradley who defined General Patton's missions and roles, and General Patton found it difficult to adjust to his new status, below his subordinate of the previous year."[41] Indeed, although their personal relationship improved somewhat during the remainder of the war, Patton continually criticised Bradley's excessive caution in his diary.[42] This simple fact is an important consideration when assessing Patton's performance.

Despite the obvious negative operational effects of Bradley's about-face with the 83rd Infantry Division, Robert Allen made the revealing observation that Patton did not change his operational plan though the loss of the 83rd "appreciably weakened the impact of the drive" north of Metz.[43] Allen further explained that the November offensive was designed "so that the full weight of both corps could be employed to exploit a breakthrough in whichever sector it occurred."[44] The point is that with the 83rd gone, the possibility of a quick breakthrough in Walker's sector now seemed unlikely, and Patton should have altered his plan accordingly.

With the 10th Armored Division stuck on the wrong side of the river, and the 83rd Infantry Division summarily removed from Walker's control, Van Fleet was left on his own to exploit his well-executed river crossing during the first several days of the Corps offensive. Doing so would not be easy because Patton's flanking of Metz forced Van Fleet's division, once across the river, to fight its way through the northernmost section of the Metz-Thionville Stellung consisting of Metz-type forts. The decision to push the 90th Infantry Division across the Moselle opposite Koenigsmacker was a problem to begin with because the road net east of the river in the division's sector was deficient.[45] Moreover, the heavily forested ridge containing the Maginot Line forts ran parallel to the division's projected route southeast. Two thousand yards to the south of the Maginot ridge ran another ridge line. Both these natural terrain features were fifty to one hundred meters higher than the surrounding terrain, and gave the Germans excellent observation of the crossing site.

No less than nineteen Maginot forts lay in the division's southward route, and within the proposed bridgehead area itself there were three groups of permanent works. At 4,000 yards east of the river sat the Billig Group of forts. Only 1,500 yards east of the river stood the Metrich Group whose fire was tied in with that of the Koenigsmacker Fortified Group located on the southern ridge. One and a half miles south of Thionville itself stood Fort D'Illange, a well-constructed group of three forts with four 100-mm guns. Of all the forts, Fort Koenigsmacker, with a fully manned garrison from the 19th Volksgrenadier Division and four 100-mm guns, was the principal obstacle to overcome.[46] It resembled Fort Driant in that the main works were underground, accessible only by way of steel and concrete sally ports at the ground level. As Cole declared, "The tactical effectiveness of its location forbade that Fort Koenigsmacker be bypassed; it had to be taken, and quickly."[47] Yet even under ideal weather conditions, the area would have presented a formidable defensive position. Fortunately, Van Fleet's division had learned from the errors committed at Fort Driant by the 5th Infantry Division and succeeded in reducing Fort Koenigsmacker by November 11. Weigley pointed out that "Driant had helped teach the Americans not to go down into the tunnels of such works, but to persist in chipping away with satchel charges, thermite grenades, TNT blocks, and dousings of gasoline from above."[48] Van Fleet's operations against the position were well thought out and executed.

With the northern flank of XX Corps held up by high water, forts, and mine fields, Irwin relied on air support to expedite the passage of the 5th Infantry Division past the forts south of Metz (see Map 10.3). The break in the weather on the 9th permitted 689 heavy bombers to strike the southern forts, but the accuracy of this bombing proved negligible as no more than 2 percent of the ordnance dropped hit their targets. Some material damage was done, particularly to Fort Blaise, but the efficiency of the fort was not noticeably impaired.[49] Of more importance than structural damage to the forts was the near complete destruction of German communications in the area. The bombing destroyed communications to such an extent that the battalions of Ostendorff's 17th SS Panzer Grenadier Division defending in front of Irwin were unable to effectively coordinate efforts to repulse the subsequent ground attack.[50]

The intensity of the bombing also had a pronounced effect on troop formations. Third Army later noted that the heavy attack on the forts with two-thousand-lb bombs "helped to disorganize the enemy and for as much as 27 hours later some P/Ws [prisoners of war] in the small towns and open country within the bombed area were definitely dazed."[51] The result of the aerial pounding was that the 17th SS Panzer Grenadier Division stood its ground at very few points during the 5th Infantry's opening attack. Irwin's forces succeeded in crossing the flooded Seille, which had expanded from two hundred to five hundred yards in width, and established a bridgehead some six thousand yards deep.[52]

With both corps firmly engaged, Third Army had achieved much greater success in the initial moves of the November offensive than it had in the opening battles of September. The achievement of tactical surprise played an important part in this, but the detailed preparation done by Patton and his staff had clearly paid dividends. The difficult part of the November operations was to take advantage of the tactical surprise. Walker was not in a good position to effect much penetration at the moment because of the flood, the stranded nature of Morris's division, and Bradley's reneging on

Map 10.3
Air Support Plan, Operation "Madison," November 8–9, 1944

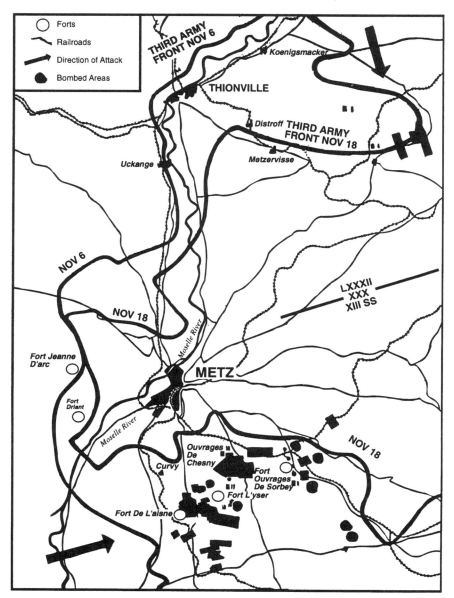

Forts
Railroads
Direction of Attack
Bombed Areas

THIRD ARMY FRONT NOV 6

Koenigsmacker

THIONVILLE

Distroff THIRD ARMY FRONT NOV 18

Uckange

Metzervisse

NOV 6

NOV 18

LXXXII
XXX
XIII SS

Moselle River

Fort Jeanne D'arc

METZ

Fort Driant

Moselle River

Ouvrages De Chesny

NOV 18

Curvy

Fort Ouvrages De Sorbey

Fort L'yser

Fort De L'aisne

Source: Base map taken from "The Effect of Air Power in the Battle of Metz," USAFHRC, microfilm A1175, 159–160. Altered by Bill Traer.

the 83rd. Only Eddy, with his two armored divisions yet to be committed, was in a position to break the front wide open.

By November 9, XII Corps had succeeded in putting several bridges over the Seille River, a necessary requirement prior to the armor entering the battle according to the Corps plan. The armored divisions were to push through the infantry and take the lead, bypassing strong pockets of resistance to make a "hard push" for the Rhine. On the 9th, CCA and CCB, 6th Armored Division passed through McBride's 80th Infantry Division. On the same day, Wood pushed CCB, 4th Armored through the 35th Infantry's positions, and the following day, CCA took the lead in the 26th Infantry Division's sector.

From the outset, the armored combat commands ran into serious trouble due to different factors. To facilitate the movement of Grow's 6th Armored Division, there was only one hard-surfaced road in the entire division area. This was the same road that had to be used by Irwin's 5th Infantry Division, and a certain amount of congestion ensued.[53] Moreover, weather conditions played an important factor. As Cole noted, "the autumn mud nullified a tactical plan based on surprise and speed."[54] Wood fully recognized the difficulties of maneuvering an armored division under such adverse conditions and later stated that he had "no illusions about any rapid advance" at the time.[55] With the fields virtual quagmires, Eddy's powerful armored force was confined to the main hard-surfaced roads where roadblocks, mines, and small groups of determined enemy could slow the armored advance. When Wood quickly informed Eddy on the 9th that terrain conditions had effectively reduced his advance to a one-tank front, Eddy noted, "I have learned to know P. [Wood] very well in the last few months and when he doesn't like something he paints a very black picture indeed."[56] Eddy did not share Wood's pessimism and completely misread the capabilities of armor.

Of the two armored divisions, Grow's 6th Armored achieved greater success, no doubt because of the crippled state of his principal opponent, Casper's 48th Division. Movement was difficult in the early stages of the armored advance, but on November 11, elements of the 6th Armored pushed forward nearly five miles and secured two bridgeheads over the Neid Française River. But by the 13th, Grow had to contend with the 36th Volksgrenadier Division and elements of the 21st Panzer Division, rushed in to bolster the buckling 48th Division. Generalmajor August Wellm's 36th Volksgrenadier Division had been ordered south from the Seventh Army by Rundstedt. A fresh formation, Wellm's division was at full strength and possessed a well-trained artillery regiment equipped with new guns. Most importantly, the majority of the infantry were from the younger classes, and the officers were veterans of the Eastern Front.[57] All things being equal, the 36th was in excellent shape, and according to Weigley, its leader, Wellm, possessed "an exceptional reputation as a tactician."[58]

Feuchtinger's once elite 21st Panzer Division was no better off now than it had been during Manteuffel's counterattack in September. It continued to be nothing more than a scratch infantry formation boosted by small numbers of tanks. When committed to battle against Grow's division, Feuchtinger possessed perhaps nineteen tanks, three assault guns, and four armored infantry battalions consisting of no more than seventy riflemen each.[59] Still, these reserves prevented Grow from reaching his initial objective, the high ground around Faulquemont. On November 16 his armored columns were still almost three miles from the town.

The principal reason for Wood's failure to break out was the commitment by Balck on November 10 of the remnants of Wietersheim's 11th Panzer Division. By November 12 the German armor was in action along a twelve-mile front, a deployment that necessitated a mobile defense.[60] Wood's columns, divided into Task Forces, passed through the 35th Infantry Division's sector and met strenuous opposition less than three miles from their initial launch points from Weitersheim's panzer battle teams. A detachment of German 88s stopped one column cold at Fonteny, a prepared secondary position, while Panzer Grenadiers stubbornly held Viviers and cut off another column.[61] One column of CCA was not even able to start its advance because of the "crowded roadway."[62]

Ganz described another encounter between the German and American armor that generally characterized the nature of Eddy's armored advance. "The American column," he stated, "was road bound, moving up the valley of the flooded Petite Seille. Though the Panthers were technically deadlined, and averaged only six rounds of ammo each, [Lieutenant Walter] Rahn found them a reverse-slope position . . . from where they could engage the American column at 1,500 meters from hull defilade, only the turrets being exposed. Several American tanks and vehicles were knocked out; others drove ahead, while the rest of the column backed up, turned around, and detoured on a secondary road."[63]

Gabel suggested that because Eddy's armor was dispersed, Wietersheim's panzers could "restrict XII Corps' rate of advance with a relatively thin delaying screen and local counterattacks."[64] The panzer battle teams did this to great effect. In fact, by November 12 CCA had been brought to a complete standstill. The marginal success of the armored divisions on the first day caused Patton to comment, "Things are very satisfactory."[65] But on November 11, Eddy stated that both he and Patton were "disappointed in the inability of the armor to make a breakthrough and exploit the rear areas of the enemy, thus cutting off and either killing or capturing the enemy who were not able to withdraw to another delaying position."[66] Interestingly enough, Eddy also recorded that because Patton was an "old tanker," he understood the effect the mud was having on the tanks.

When Eddy finally pulled the armor out of the line after a full week of slugging, the 4th Armored alone had suffered 1,063 casualties, including 220 killed.[67] The division had lost dozens of tanks, and Wood later commented that "this was just another example of the failure of infantry-trained higher commanders to appreciate the possibilities and limitations of armored action."[68] Wood clearly had Eddy in mind when writing this statement. By this time, the relationship between the two had soured considerably. The heavy losses suffered by his division in the recent fighting put a sharp edge on Wood's criticism of Eddy's competence. Eddy had done little to inspire confidence during his poor showing in the bitter infantry struggle in the Gremercy Forest east of Nancy shortly after Patton was forced onto the defensive in late September. Here Eddy proved once again that he was an ill-fitted cog in the Patton fighting machine.

On September 30 Eddy feared the collapse of Baade's 35th Infantry Division, which had been fighting elements of the 553rd, 559th, 19th Volksgrenadier and 15th Panzer Grenadier Divisions commanded by Priess's XIII SS Corps. Eddy ordered a retrograde movement of this unit, as well as the 4th Armored Division, in obvious violation of Patton's staunch conviction that his troops should never yield ground.[69] There are times when retreat is absolutely unavoidable, but the 35th Infantry had not reached that crucial point on September 30. Eddy still had Grow's 6th Armored Division as a reserve, yet he felt the situation untenable and ordered the withdrawal.

In his diary Eddy stated, "I asked the opinion of everyone there (all three regimental commanders, General Baade, General Grow and General Gaffey) on the advisability of withdrawing . . . and got the impression that it was the recommendation of everyone to do so."[70] One would suspect, however, that if this was the case, the officers advocating withdrawal would have stated so in no uncertain terms. Gaffey was adamant in his daily log that "I advised very strongly against this."[71] Eddy himself recorded how Baade was "shocked [to] no end at my decision to withdraw and said he was sure they could hold the ground."[72] No doubt Eddy was a bit shaken when German artillery hit his command post during the day, killing several members of his former 9th Infantry Division staff in North Africa. Apparently, he wished to reverse his withdrawal order after it was discovered that the situation was not as bad as it first looked, but he "didn't think it could be done due to the lack of communications."[73] He then had General Gaffey call Patton, who personally intervened at this point.

Disgusted with virtually everyone involved in the situation, Patton made one of those bold and forceful decisions usually characteristic of his command style and that had been all too absent in September. According to Eddy, he "gave everyone hell over the situation" when he arrived.[74] He sent in the 6th Armored Division to counterattack immediately, which meant as soon as humanly possible, and insisted that he would not give up another foot of ground to the Germans because it would be a great moral victory for them.[75] Eddy had been highly reluctant to commit Grow's armor the previous day because he felt that a failure to restore the line would leave the armor trapped on the far side of the Seille River. Patton reminded him that that was a "damn good reason why they wouldn't fail," adding the historical analogy that Cortez had burned his ships. Patton ordered Baade to lead his division from the front while Grow was to retake the woods "or not come back."[76]

Eddy's status as Corps commander suffered heavily from this incident in the Gremercy Forest. He admitted, "I made a mistake . . . but will certainly see that a re-occurrence never takes place,"[77] but the damage was already done. According to Gabel he lost the confidence of his divisional commanders at this point, although it is doubtful if he ever had Wood's. Patton seriously considered relieving Eddy, declaring, "He worries too much. I will do all the worrying necessary. The corps commanders must fight. I would get rid of him but I do not know of any other any better except possibly [Major General Ernest N.] Harmon, now commanding the 2nd Armored Division."[78] In reality, Patton displayed a great deal of loyalty to his officers despite his fierce reputation as a headcutter and was far behind other American commanders, such as Courtney Hodges, in dismissing subordinates.[79]

Despite Eddy's obvious failings as a fighting corps commander, he was not entirely responsible for the lack of success in the opening days of the November offensive. His decision to commit his two armored divisions so quickly brought with it much criticism both at the time and since, but it must be remembered that Patton fully endorsed this course of action. In reality, there was little unanimity of thought on the proper role of the armored divisions prior to the November offensive. Cole stated that Patton "believed, and stated this belief at every opportunity, that tanks could easily breach the West Wall. . . . But many of the veteran junior officers in the armored divisions were less sanguine and privately held the opinion that the armor would be cut to pieces in the maze of antitank defenses ahead."[80] According to Eddy, Wood fully endorsed the XII Corps plan for "an attack on the part of both the 6th Armored and the 4th Armored, closely followed by the infantry divisions."[81] Wood also proposed that the entire 4th Armored attack through the Dieuze defile, along the Moyenvic-Mittersheim road, but Eddy rejected it because cavalry reports had indicated that considerable enemy forces had gathered there to hold the bottleneck.[82]

In suggesting this scheme of maneuver, Wood was expressing his philosophy of armored action. He apparently did not like the fact that his division was broken up into widely separated combat commands. He believed in concentrating his armor somewhat more and had voiced the same displeasure in September when Eddy would not allow a drive by the entire division north of Nancy. To be fair, Eddy had contemplated pushing the entire 4th Armored north of Chateau-Salins as the spearhead of XII Corps for the November offensive, but the addition of the 6th Armored Division for the corps plan necessitated a "regrouping of Eddy's armored strength."[83]

In considering Eddy's judgment, von Mellenthin felt that "the armored divisions were committed too early, and that Eddy would have done better to wait until his infantry had eaten away more of our main defense zone."[84] The plan completed in early November agreed in principal with this assessment. The armor, stated Cole, was to be committed "as soon as the German forward lines were broken and a favorable position for further exploitation was secured."[85] In referring to the advance of the 26th Infantry Division in the opening stages, Cole believed that the forward German line had been broken, claiming that the infantry had "driven far enough to clear the way for intervention by the armor."[86] Yet this was true only in the sense that room for the deployment of armor had been achieved. An actual breach in Balck's defense, what Patton was really looking for, had not materialized when the armor was committed. Consequently, Gabel's criticism that Eddy's actions reduced Third Army's most powerful concentration of armor to an "infantry support role"[87] was on the money.

The American armored division was not designed to bludgeon an advance forward against fixed defenses, but it was repeatedly used in this capacity. Cole noted that CCB, 4th Armored Division, had made an advance of some four miles into enemy territory and had "broken a way *for the infantry*" [emphasis added]. This was clearly the wrong tactic. Evidence from the first days of the November offensive proved that armor could be held up by small improvised defensive positions. Weigley pointed out that in August a hastily assembled kampfgruppe had managed to stop Patton's 5th Armored Division cold. Favorable defensive terrain and the first hint of rain, which curtailed armored column cover, frustrated Patton's armor. As Weigley observed, "The delay was all the more infuriating because it was imposed by the kind of scratch force that it seemed should have been easy to brush aside."[88]

Eddy's decision to commit his armor so early was based in part on his belief, expressed on October 22 and mirroring that of Patton's, that the German defense would be no more than a "thin, hard shell."[89] Had this actually been the case, the armored divisions might very well have ruptured the German line and achieved unopposed, rapid movement despite the mud and rain. However, the German defense was not thin in depth although thin in manpower. The lull, stated Robert Allen, permitted the Germans to "construct hundreds of fire-covered tank traps, road blocks and mine-fields" making the entire area a "vast network of natural and organized defenses in depth."[90] Only a concentrated strike stood a good chance of overwhelming Wietersheim's tank battle teams.

Colonel Bruce C. Clarke, who so ably led Wood's CCB, had some interesting thoughts on the concentration of armored forces after the war. "The shock effect of the mass use of armor," stated Clarke, "is not a straight-line function based upon the number of tanks used. It varies with some higher power."[91] Though this may sound somewhat abstract, Clarke's argument had a pragmatic side. He continued, "This does not mean that it [an armored division] necessarily moves on a narrow front or on only one road. It may advance on a broad front, but so long as the tactical formations of the division and combat commands are in column, the commanders are ready for any contingency and prompt action can be taken without waiting for higher staff reaction and direction." Most crucially, he believed that "breaking through and out of an enemy defensive zone in a column of combat commands gives as much or even more effective power in the break-through, and at the same time saves . . . uncommitted tactical commands to handle contingencies and to push on promptly in exploitation."[92]

Clarke's statement strongly implied that the "one-tank front" tactic was sound. Most probably, this view was given credence in Lorraine when he managed to penetrate the German line in mid-September to advance straight upon Chateau-Salins. The weather in September, however, was just beginning to affect armored operations, and it was clear in November (if not earlier) that the "one-tank front" could only facilitate short envelopments of a local nature. Only if the American armor were lucky enough to find a truly soft spot in Knobelsdorff's defense, created either by a successful infantry assault or a gap formed by a German inability to maintain links between units, could any deep penetration be achieved.

Ultimately, Eddy could not have waited indefinitely for the infantry to force a gap or relied on opportunism, as Patton had done in Normandy, before committing his armored divisions. Balck was throwing everything he had into the fight within days of XII Corps' advance. It appears that Wood was correct when he stated that Eddy "attempted to retrieve the setback" when it became "apparent that the infantry divisions were bogged down"[93] in the opening stages of the November offensive. This, of course, was not how the plan anticipated using the armored divisions.

For the armored divisions to act as the spearhead of the corps offensive, even in such unenviable circumstances, the XIX TAC needed to provide continuous column cover, but it either snowed or rained from the 9th to the 15th. During the periods of clearing, Weyland's fighter-bombers swooped down to blast German vehicles and guns with fragmentation bombs and napalm, but such instances were too few to maintain the momentum of the armored advance. Moreover, though Clarke's comments on armored concentration had their merits, one cannot overlook the advantages of massing artillery, infantry, and air support on a narrow front to decisively crack Balck's line.

In assessing Patton's overall scheme of maneuver for the November offensive, one historian concluded that "the American disinclination to concentrate power was rarely more apparent."[94] Dominick Graham and Shelford Bidwell agreed, making the broader generalization that "American Army generals, whatever their text books might advise, indulged in the Western Front practice of attacking on as wide a front as possible, for as long as possible, in search of tactical rewards."[95] Indeed, Patton's unwillingness to subject a portion of the German line to an overwhelming concentration of firepower and men allowed Balck to utilize his slender reserves to the utmost. Wilmot's observation concerning American attacks in Normandy was accurate for Lorraine as well; attacking all along the line succeeded only in pushing the Germans back a few miles. On November 16, for example, the 361st Volksgrenadier Division conducted a general withdrawal in front of Paul's 26th Infantry Division and succeeded in regaining contact with the 11th Panzer Division.[96] All along the front the Germans were able to plug holes and withdraw in fairly good order.

The conscious choice on Patton's part to forego concentration, coupled with the fact that he was attacking without support on his flanks from First and Seventh Armies, further negated much of Third Army's power beyond that already canceled out by the weather. Patton made an astute observation about the nature of Third Army's offensive on November 6 when he commented, "I will bring the whole pack [of Germans] in on me" if Hodges delayed too long in launching his own offensive with First Army.[97] He brushed this possible development off by adding "well all the more glory," but he was essentially correct in his observation. Because of the idle posture of Hodges' First Army until November 16, the Germans were able to move the 36th Volksgrenadier Division from opposite Hodges into Third Army's zone by the 13th. This division successfully intervened to solidify a gap in the German line created by the complete collapse of the 48th Division shortly after the offensive started.

Similarly, the Sixth Army Group did not initiate its advance until November 13. This permitted Balck to move Feuchtinger's 21st Panzer Division north to further assist the 48th Division. The German high command even succeeded in throwing in elements of the 25th Panzer Grenadier Division against Van Fleet on November 12.[98] Gay observed on November 22 that the Germans were managing to replace their casualties to the point where their force opposing Third Army was "practically as strong as it was when the Metz Campaign started."[99] The ability of these German reserves to play the role of spoiler for Third Army's advance was possible for three reasons: their relative freedom to act, the weather, and Patton's insistence on attacking widely dispersed with much of his combat power tied up at Metz.

Though concentration of effort on a narrow sector was the only way to guarantee a quick and decisive rupture of the German defenses, sufficient to allow the armor to roll with some impunity, battering ram tactics did achieve results. The situation arising from the combined attacks of McBride's 80th Infantry Division and Grow's 6th Armored Division against Casper's 48th Division was a rare opportunity for exploitation during the November offensive and serves to illustrate one of the "might have beens" of the campaign. The 48th Division proved itself to be the weak link in First Army's defensive front. The situation was so precarious for Casper's unit that elements of the 361st Volksgrenadier Division were rushed north from opposite Paul's infantry and Wood's armor on the 10th. Indeed, by November 13 the division was "at its last gasp," and Balck lumped it with the remnants of von Muehlen's 559th Volksgrenadier Division.[100]

The fighting in McBride's sector at this point was essentially a pursuit, but just when a power drive might have split Priess's XIII SS Corps front wide open, Eddy altered the scheme of maneuver for XII Corps on November 12. This change involved an advance on the wings of the corps, which meant that Baade's 35th Infantry Division would be "pinched out." Most importantly, Grow suddenly had to widen his frontage to the south to cover the space, and after November 11, CCB, 6th Armored had dual responsibilities: holding the bridgehead across the Neid Française and maintaining contact between XII Corps and the south flank of XX Corps. As Cole pointed out, "Its proximity to a boundary between two corps whose main axes of advance were tangential resulted in confused orders and considerable delay."[101]

The flaw in the use of Grow's division was obvious. Its momentum was stopped by subsidiary assignments. Cavalry could have filled the gap; Grow should have been sent forward with one order, penetrate. He and McBride were further handicapped by the fact that Eddy had to purposely slow the advance until the 5th Infantry Division could be brought across the Neid River.[102] Eddy, however, had already determined to slow the advance on his own, notifying McBride on the 13th to prepare to consolidate his present position.[103] Eddy would have stopped short of the corps objective, Faulquemont, had not Patton ordered it taken the next day, telling Eddy that it was "easier to defeat the Germans there than later on the Saar or on the West Wall."[104] Apparently, Patton had now abandoned his old formula of bypassing strong points. In a revealing statement on November 14, he appeared to have given up on a lightning thrust to the West Wall, commenting that because of the rain and its subsequent hindrances, including trench foot, the campaign had become a question of "mutual crucifixion."[105]

Generalleutnant der Waffen SS Max Simon, who took over command of the XIII SS Corps from Priess on November 15, characterized Third Army operations at this stage as "very cautious and systematic." The operations were "prepared thoroughly," and the commanders "took advantage of every opportunity offered by the terrain." Most importantly, he noted that the Americans advanced only when they had "secured control of the first ground taken."[106] This sounds remarkably like the type of warfare practiced by Patton's great rival, Field Marshal Montgomery. There can be little doubt that completing the encirclement of Metz was Patton's foremost concern in mid-November. Eddy noted that Eisenhower had called Patton to "emphasize the fall of Metz."[107] Morris's 10th Armored Division was divided in two when it finally crossed the Moselle on November 15. CCB struck due east for a Saar crossing at Merzig, a mission beyond the power of a single combat command, while CCA was used to protect the left flank of Van Fleet's 90th Infantry Division as it struck for Bouzonville and the encirclement of Metz.

By November 19, Van Fleet had met up with Irwin east of Metz, and the escape route for German units stuck in and around the city was closed. Investing the city proper was left to General Twaddle, who formed a task force on November 15 out of elements of his 95th Infantry Division, which had been operating on the east bank in support of Van Fleet's division since

November 8, and elements of Irwin's division.[108] Though various forts would continue to hold out till early December, Third Army had finally succeeded in enveloping Metz eleven days after the start of the November offensive. Fort St. Quentin capitulated on December 6, followed the next day by Fort Plappeville. Fort Driant succumbed on the 8th, and Jeanne d'Arc, the last fort to fall, surrendered five days later.[109] However, the bag of prisoners that Patton had hoped for in his pincer movement did not materialize; he managed to trap only six thousand.[110]

Though Gay observed on the 13th that "At this time . . . it appears that the enemy is withdrawing or partially withdrawing from Metz,"[111] Balck did not make a definite move in this direction until some days later. He had no intention of carrying out the spirit of Hitler's November 7 declaration designating Metz a fortress to be defended to the last man. Leaving Kittel's 462 Volksgrenadier Division (which now contained several thousand mostly overaged men) with no heavy weapons and limited food, the rest of First Army broke contact with the Metz garrison and fell back to the Neid River on the night of November 17.[112] Patton cracked the Metz defensive system, but Balck withdrew his entire line in good order through the XX Corps pincer movement to prepare for Third Army's next onslaught.

Concerning the role of Metz in the overall defense of Lorraine, von Mellenthin observed that "in view of the weakness of the garrison, Metz put up a credible resistance and played its part in tying up considerable American forces."[113] Indeed, it had taken the 5th, 90th, and 95th Infantry Divisions along with half the 10th Armored Division to finally overwhelm the city's substantial defenses. Yet in and of itself, the Metz operation in November was highly successful. Regardless of the fact that it was not even necessary to capture the city, one nevertheless sees a vast improvement in Third Army's handling of the fortifications. As Cole put it, this operation was "skillfully planned," marked by "thorough execution" and was an excellent example of a prepared battle for the reduction of a fortified position."[114] Less stellar, however, was Patton's overall coordination of his two principal maneuver bodies, XX and XII Corps, a problem that would persist during the final stages of the Lorraine Campaign.

NOTES

1. Martin Blumenson, *The Patton Papers* (Boston: Houghton Mifflin, 1974), II: 570.

2. Ibid., II: 576.

3. Christopher R. Gabel, *The Lorraine Campaign: An Overview, September–December 1944* (Fort Leavenworth, Kans.: Combat Studies Institute, 1985), 24.

4. Robert S. Allen, *Lucky Forward: The History of Patton's Third U.S. Army* (New York: Vanguard Press, 1947), 167.

5. Chester Wilmot, *The Struggle for Europe* (London: Collins, 1957), 565.

6. Ibid., 565–566.

7. Ibid.

8. Manton S. Eddy Diary, August, 29, 1944, U.S. Army Infantry School, National Infantry Museum (NIM), Fort Benning, Ga.

9. George S. Patton, *War as I Knew It* (Boston: Houghton Mifflin, 1947), 136.

10. Eddy Diary, November 7.

11. Patton, *War as I Knew It*, 128.

12. Eddy Diary, November 7.

13. Major General F. W. von Mellenthin, *Panzer Battles: A Study of the Employment of Armour in the Second World War* (Norman: Oklahoma University Press, 1971), 325. Von Mellenthin described German intelligence at the time as "pretty good" despite the complete absence of air reconnaissance because the Americans were "careless about telephone conversations and signals security."

14. Hugh M. Cole, *The Lorraine Campaign*, U.S. Army in World War II: European Theater of Operations (Washington, D.C.: Center for Military History, 1984), 307. The soft spots in the MLR were to be defended by massed guns of stationary fortress antitank companies. Beyond the MLR, field artillery was concentrated on tactical checkpoints.

15. A. Harding Ganz, "11th Panzers in the Defense," *Armor* (March–April 1994): 35.

16. Cole, *Lorraine Campaign*, 318–319.

17. Ibid., 425.

18. Eddy Diary, November 4.

19. Hobart R. Gay/Hugh J. Gaffey Diary, November 8, 1944, Special Collections, United States Military Academy Library, West Point (WP).

20. Cole, *Lorraine Campaign*, 425.

21. Eddy Diary, November 8.

22. Blumenson, *Patton Papers*, II: 572.

23. Patton, *War as I Knew It*, 128. Patton stated that trucks and airplanes were marooned by the water and that things looked "bad."

24. John Colby, *War from the Ground Up: The 90th Division in World War II* (Austin, Tex.: Nortex Press, 1991), 285.

25. XX Corps AAR, "The Reduction of Fortress Metz 1 September–6 December, 1944," Box 64, Patton Papers (PP), Library of Congress (LC), 15.

26. Colby, *War from the Ground Up*, 284–285; "Reduction of Fortress Metz," 15. The breakdown in artillery assets for the Thionville crossing were as follows: The XX Corps Artillery allocated its 18 2/3 battalions, which included the eight French 100-mm guns of the fortress Guentrange, the three battalions of

the 10th Armored Division, two battalions from the 83rd Infantry Division, and the four battalions of the 90th Infantry itself.

27. Colby, *War from the Ground Up*, 286; Gabel, *The Lorraine Campaign*, 26.

28. Charles E. Wright, "Moselle River Crossing at Cattenom," *Armored Cavalry Journal* (May–June 1948): 52.

29. William C. Hall, "Bridging at Thionville," *Military Engineer* (April 1948): 169–171.

30. Carl von Clausewitz, *On War*, edited and translated by Michael Howard and Peter Paret (Princeton, N.J.: Princeton University Press, 1976), 213.

31. Conversation between General James A. Van Fleet and Colonel Bruce H. Williams, Senior Officers Debriefing Program, Van Fleet Papers, United States Army Military History Institute (USAMHI), Carlisle Barracks, Pa., 69.

32. Russell F. Weigley, *Eisenhower's Lieutenants: The Campaign of France and Germany 1944–1945* (Bloomington: Indiana University Press, 1981), 398.

33. Gay/Gaffey Diary, November 11.

34. Bradley's Commentary/WWII As Recorded By Chester Hanson, BP, USAMHI.

35. Allen, *Lucky Forward*, 184.

36. Gay/Gaffey Diary, November 11. See Appendix E, Third Army Operational Directives, November 1.

37. Hobart R. Gay to A. R. Hartman, November 23, 1948, Historical Division Combat Interviews (HDCI), National Archives (NA), Washington, D.C.

38. Blumenson, *Patton Papers*, II: 573.

39. Ibid.

40. Martin Blumenson, "Bradley-Patton: World War II's 'Odd Couple,' " *Army* (December 1985): 56.

41. Ibid., 59.

42. Ibid., 64.

43. Allen, *Lucky Forward*, 184.

44. Ibid., 167.

45. Cole, *Lorraine Campaign*, 381. Cole's words were "hardly adequate."

46. Colby, *War from the Ground Up*, 283–284.

47. Cole, *Lorraine Campaign*, 380.

48. Weigley, *Eisenhower's Lieutenants*, 393.

49. "The Effectiveness of Third Phase Tactical Air Operations in the European Theater, May 5, 1944–May 8, 1945," United States Air Force Historical Records Center (USAFHRC), microfilm A1175, 161, 164.

50. Ibid., 165. Two guns, one in each casement of Fort Blaise, were put out of operation, and two direct hits on one of the casements had penetrated the roof.

51. Ibid., 164.

52. Cole, *Lorraine Campaign*, 426.

53. Ibid., 357.

54. Ibid., 355.
55. John S. Wood, "Things Remembered and Things Considered," Box 8, Wood Papers, Bird Library, Syracuse University (SU), 66.
56. Eddy Diary, November 9.
57. Cole, *Lorraine Campaign*, 367.
58. Weigley, *Eisenhower's Lieutenants*, 392.
59. Cole, *Lorraine Campaign*, 365. The 4th Armored was further hindered by its commitment so close to the boundary between the Third and Seventh Armies. Because the Third Army boundary was subject to continual alteration, Wood's division had to "constantly alter its axis of advance in order to stay within the proper zone, and even, on occasion, to double back on its tracks."
60. Ibid., 328.
61. Ganz, "11th Panzers in the Defense," 35.
62. Cole, *Lorraine Campaign*, 326.
63. Ganz, "11th Panzers in the Defense," 35. The column in question was Bill Hunter's 37th Tank Battalion of Creighton Abrams' CCA. This delaying action forced Hunter to bivouac for the night. American losses at Fonteny included fifteen tanks, ten half-tracks, and three assault guns.
64. Gabel, *The Lorraine Campaign: An Overview*, 26.
65. George S. Patton Diary, November 9, 1944, Special Collections, United States Military Academy Library, West Point (WP).
66. Eddy Diary, November 11.
67. A. Harding Ganz, "Patton's Relief of General Wood," *The Journal of Military History* LIII, 3 (July 1989): 266.
68. Wood, "Things Remembered and Things Considered," 68.
69. Patton, *War as I Knew It*, 314.
70. Eddy Diary, September 30.
71. Gay/Gaffey Diary, September 30.
72. Eddy Diary, September 30.
73. Ibid.
74. Ibid.
75. Blumenson, *Patton Papers*, II: 559.
76. Patton, *War as I Knew It*, 112; Blumenson, *Patton Papers*, II: 558–559.
77. Eddy Diary, September 30.
78. Blumenson, *Patton Papers*, II: 559.
79. Patton, *War as I Knew It*, 98. Of the thirteen corps and divisional commanders relieved from command in Twelfth Army Group during the war, General Hodges led the way with no less than ten dismissals. He relieved Major General Charles R. Corlett for lack of aggressiveness against the West Wall and Major General John Millikin for problems at the Remagen Bridge. General William H. Simpson relieved no one. Robert H. Berlin, "United States Army World War II Corps Commanders: A Composite Biography," *The Journal of Military History*, LIII (April 1989): 163–166.

80. Cole, *Lorraine Campaign*, 318.

81. Eddy Diary, October 18.

82. Cole, *Lorraine Campaign*, 325.

83. Ibid., 326.

84. Mellenthin, *Panzer Battles*, 325–326.

85. Cole, *Lorraine Campaign*, 317.

86. Ibid., 324.

87. Gabel, *The Lorraine Campaign: An Overview*, 25.

88. Weigley, *Eisenhower's Lieutenants*, 243.

89. Eddy Diary, October 22.

90. Allen, *Lucky Forward*, 168.

91. Colonel Bruce C. Clarke, "Principles of the Employment of Armor," Box 1, Wood Papers, SU.

92. Ibid.

93. Wood, "Things Remembered and Things Considered," 66.

94. Weigley, *Eisenhower's Lieutenants*, 390.

95. Dominick Graham and Shelford Bidwell, *Coalitions, Politicians, and Generals: Some Aspects of Command in Two World Wars* (London: Brassey's, 1993), 287.

96. Cole, *Lorraine Campaign*, 333.

97. Blumenson, *Patton Papers*, II: 569.

98. Cole, *Lorraine Campaign*, 390.

99. Gay/Gaffey Diary, November 22.

100. Cole, *Lorraine Campaign*, 367.

101. Ibid., 366.

102. Ibid., 368.

103. Eddy Diary, November 13.

104. Patton Diary, November 14.

105. Blumenson, *Patton Papers*, II: 574.

106. ETHINT 33, "XIII SS Inf Corps in the Lorraine Campaign," an Interview with Genlt (W-SS) Max Simon, August 17, 1945, Donald S. Detwiler, with Charles B. Burdick and Jurgen Rowher, eds., *World War II German Military Studies* (New York: Garland Publishing, 1979), II.

107. Eddy Diary, November 14.

108. On November 8 General Twaddle sent a battalion across the Moselle at Uckange three miles south of Thionville to act as a diversion for Van Fleet's crossing the next day. Eventually, Twaddle increased this force to two battalions and some armored elements and sent them north to clear various forts in Thionville. Therefter, Task Force Bacon was established on November 15 with the purpose of driving into Metz.

109. Cole, *Lorraine Campaign*, 449.

110. Stephen E. Ambrose, *Citizen Soldiers: The U.S. Army from the Normandy Beaches to the Bulge to the Surrender of Germany* (New York: Simon and Schuster, 1997), 165.

111. Gay/Gaffey Diary, November 13.
112. Mellenthin, *Panzer Battles*, 329–330.
113. Ibid., 330.
114. Cole, *Lorraine Campaign*, 449.

Chapter 11

Advance to the West Wall

I wish things would move faster in this Army.
                              —Patton, November 21, 1944[1]

I believe that the enemy has nearly reached his breaking point. As a matter of fact, we are stretched pretty thin ourselves.
                              —Patton, December 5, 1944[2]

The final encirclement of the Metz fortress system seemed to foreshadow the imminent collapse of the entire German defense of Lorraine. Indeed, it had only been because of the natural strength of the Metz position that the Germans were able to hold Third Army up at all in September and October. Eliminating Metz should have torn a huge hole in Balck's defense, and to a certain extent it did, but Patton's offensive also merely pushed the Germans back into rearward positions hastily constructed all through October.[3] The Germans could not stabilize a line of resistance in front of XX Corps, but desperate rearguard actions combined with the slowness of Walker's advance after the encirclement made the hole less of a problem than it should have been for the them.[4]

Metz had bought Balck precious time and he used it well, but the reason for the failure by Third Army to capture more of the German divisions caught in the Metz pocket was the slowness of the advance. Kittel's 462nd Volksgrenadier Division was the only division written off by the Germans after the battle even though at one time the 19th Volksgrenadier and 17th SS Panzer Grenadier Divisions had been threatened with complete encirclement around Metz. General Pflieger, commander of the 416th Division, observed after the war that Patton's operations north of Metz should have been completed in half the time.[5] This is a biased assessment, but most of the

German commanders involved in the November battle for Metz generally concurred in Pflieger's opinion that Third Army might have moved faster. Moreover, Cole himself admitted that Patton's operations could not be characterized as going for the jugular, observing that "it is true that the events of September and early October had made the Americans wary of high losses and dramatic failures, such as the first attempt to take Fort Driant, and prompted a widespread use of cautious and slow-moving tactics in which crushing superiority in men, guns, and tanks was concentrated wherever the enemy showed signs of standing his ground."[6]

Patton had every reason to fear high casualties. Despite not coming into contact with the German forces in the Metz area proper until almost the final hours of the encirclement operation, Van Fleet's division sustained 2,300 casualties in the first seven days.[7] In fact, there can be little doubt that there would have been a lengthening of the operation, with a corresponding increase in American casualties, if Balck had determined to carry out Hitler's orders to the letter. Moreover, Weigley was right to assert that Patton also retained his "long-standing doubts about the aggressiveness of American infantry."[8] Sustained casualties, poor weather, deteriorating logistics, German resistance, and an increasing tendency within Third Army to regroup before each new push combined to choke Patton's advance in the following weeks.

Of the numerous factors mentioned here, Patton really only had control over whether or not his subordinates indulged in excessive periods of rest and reorganization. To generate and sustain momentum, Patton needed to be firm with his corps and divisional commanders. On December 7 he would make the general comment that "regrouping is the curse of war and a great boon to the enemy,"[9] and he had once sarcastically noted that regrouping seemed to be the chief form of amusement in the British Army. The same ailment now seemed to plague his forces.

The noticeable thing is that Patton never moved to decisively rectify the problem. He increased his presence at the front during November and December as Table 11.1 indicates but commented on November 19, "I find that if one goes up too often, one becomes a nuisance."[10] In his own estimation he got "out where it is unhealthy oftener than any general, to include divisional commanders,"[11] yet it was a function of his command philosophy to choose his moments for direct intervention into operational matters and the performance of his subordinates very carefully. He considered one of the toughest tasks he, or any other general, had was "not to interfere with the next echelon of command when the show is going all right."[12] Of course, he played a role at the front, as when he personally told General Paul to push his men as hard as possible at the beginning of the November offensive, and on the 19th when he informed Irwin that the 5th Infantry was not as good as it had been and for Irwin to improve it.[13] But to suggest, as one study of the Metz campaign does, that "Patton's personality permeated the battle. He was everywhere! He forced, pushed and, at times, directed forward operations"[14] overstates his role in orchestrating the battle at the front. November 18 was the ideal moment for Patton to take the initiative and give powerful impetus and direction to Walker and the divisional commanders of XX Corps, but he did not do so. His reasoning was that there was no need to be at the front, because everyone was "doing a swell job."[15]

The fate of Metz was sealed long before November 18, and Patton should have directed the encircling units to head east much sooner. The slowness of the advance after the encirclement of Metz was not so much the fault of

Table 11.1
Patton's Visits to Corps and Divisions during November–December 1944

November 8	Patton—26th, 35th, and 80th Inf Divs
November 9	Patton— XX Corps, 5th Inf Div
November 10	
November 11	Patton—XII Corps, 6th Armd Div
November 12	
November 13	Patton—XII Corps, 26th Inf Div
November 14	Patton—XX Corps, 90th and 95th Inf Divs
November 15	Patton—XII Corps, 35th and 26th Inf Divs
November 16	
November 17	Patton—6th Armd, 80th Inf Divs
November 18	
November 19	Patton—5th Inf Div
November 20	Patton—XII Corps
November 25	Patton—XX Corps, 5th, 90th, 95th, and 10th Armd Divs
November 29	Patton—XII Corps
December 2	Patton—XX Corps, 90th, 95th, and 10th Armd Divs
December 4	Patton—XV Corps
December 12	Patton—4th Armd, 26th and 87th Inf Divs

Source: Gay/Gaffey Diary; Blumenson's The Patton Papers, II; Patton's memoirs *War as I Knew It*; Eddy's daily diary; and typescript copies of Patton's daily diary, which contain information not included in Blumenson's work.

divisional commanders as it was of the consequences of the design of the November offensive. With the escape routes east of Metz closed by November 19, Walker quickly made plans to reorient his corps for a drive due east against Merzig. His eagerness to head east caused Patton to comment that he was displaying considerable drive, but the 95th Infantry Division, scheduled to spearhead the corps advance against the West Wall, was "jammed in and around" Metz along with the 5th Infantry Division.[16] Boundary lines had to be altered to extract the division, a process estimated to take some four days. Walker thus rescheduled the renewed advance for November 25th.

Patton has been condemned by Appleman for allowing Twaddle and Walker to regroup for what amounted to six days, November 19–25, remarking that this was a "complete failure of command planning" and a "profound failure of the commander to give direction and to *supervise* the tactics and operations of his army units" [*emphasis added*].[17] The army plan certainly lost a measure of focus after the Metz operation. In the overall scheme of things there existed little coordination between Walker and Eddy with the subsequent result that each of their respective advances took on the character of semi-independent operations. An efficient way of extracting the divisions in and around Metz could have been worked out before hand.

While Walker was somewhat handicapped by his lead division being stuck in Metz, Eddy halted XII Corps operations on the 16th on his own initiative, but did so quietly because "if I just told Georgie that I was going to stop he would raise the roof." Eddy, always obsessed with closing loose ends, remarked, "I consider this reorganization and regrouping absolutely imperative."[18] After the regrouping period, XII Corps struck out on November 18, just when XX Corps was gearing down for its own maintenance period, with the intention of seizing a bridgehead across the Saar at Saarbruecken. McBride's entire 80th Infantry Division remained at Faulquemont to screen the area while Paul and Baade attacked generally east and northeast on a narrower corps front.

Reflecting the scheme of maneuver used at the outset of November, Eddy held the 4th and 6th Armored Divisions in reserve. He enjoyed good initial success on the 18th, as he had on November 8, causing Patton to later reflect that "things looked so good that I could almost picture myself going through the Siegfried Line any day" but with the added qualification that he had been "slightly overoptimistic."[19] Eddy, repeating his own unwarranted optimism, bet General Paul a quart of scotch that the 26th Infantry Division would be on the Rhine in seven days after jumping off.[20] Even Gay recorded that the general army picture indicated that the "enemy is beaten in the area of the Third

Army west of the Saar River" and that the action had now "become a pursuit to that point."[21] Gay's comment was far from accurate. It was true that the Germans were withdrawing northeast to gain the better defensive terrain along the Saar River, but it was a fighting withdrawal and they soon began to once again hold tenaciously against XII Corps.

Eddy felt confident enough to commit his armor on the 19th even though the infantry divisions only had one day to work on the German positions. On the 20th Grow informed him that a blitz was out of the question, but that the armor could continue to advance by executing short envelopments and could punch ahead if aided by large quantities of artillery.[22] Clearly, however, such limited objective methods would not produce a quick breakthrough to the Rhine. The situation the armor was placed in was less than advantageous, and Eddy was soon confronted by Wood on the matter.

On the 18th Eddy recorded that Wood "had blown off a little steam when I told him how I wanted his columns set." The next day, Eddy informed Patton that Wood "is going to have to take his commands from the Corps or I am going to have to be allowed to get someone who will take and execute the orders I give him." Eddy had "seen this coming for quite some time" and as the casualties in the 4th Armored rose due to the poor weather and mud, stressed the point that "it has gotten so that at times he has been to the point of belligerency over the use of the armor. Many, many times I have had to curb my own temper."[23] The disagreement between the two over tactics continued.

Eddy ordered Wood northeast on the Corps' right flank on the 22nd to attack Saare-Union, and A. Harding Ganz pointed out that "To Wood the order made no sense."[24] He felt the route chosen by Eddy incapable of sustaining an armored division and quickly decided to cross the boundary line between the Third and Seventh Armies and use the better terrain east of the Saar in Wade Haislip's XV Corps zone. He approached Wade Haislip of XV Corps, now a part of Patch's Seventh Army, and received permission for the move and then "presented the plan to Eddy as a *fait accompli*."[25] Wood's later justification for the move was that "such lines [army boundaries] meant little to me and I went where the going was good."[26] His action was pure improvisation, and Patton fully endorsed the scheme because he had himself tried to persuade Bradley that he could "rapidly and cheaply" outflank the Saar River line if Haislip's XV Corps was reattached to Third Army.[27] Patton noted that Eisenhower liked the plan but Bradley thought it could be accomplished by moving the Army Group line north into XII Corps' zone. Patton objected, "on the grounds that the zone of advance of the Third Army is natural and self-contained, and that to put an Inter-Army boundary within it is a tactical mistake of the highest order."[28] On November 25 Bradley officially refused the request. Patton remarked that Bradley's "thesis is that all four American Armies should consist of 12 divisions. This is absurd. An Army should be the size necessary to accomplish its task in the theater of operations where it is committed."[29] Once again, Patton and Wood were on the same page, and Eddy had trouble keeping up. Cole described Wood's plan to fight in the rear of the German formations holding the Saar before returning to XII Corps' zone "tentative and opportunistic,"[30] a characterization sufficient to explain Patton's entire plan of advance at this stage of the campaign.

Sound though Wood's reasoning was for venturing into the XV Corps sector, on the 23rd his combat commands ran head on into elements of Generalleutenant Fritz Bayerlein's Panzer Lehr Division released by the high command to patch the Seventh Army breakthrough in the Saverne area. Once an elite division, Panzer Lehr had suffered grievously in Normandy and in the retreat and was now weak in tanks, possessing only one battalion of thirty-four Mark IVs and thirty-eight Panthers and no tank destroyers. Other assets included two battalions of artillery, two regiments of armored infantry, a reconnaissance battalion, an understrength engineer battalion, and one 88-mm antiaircraft battery.[31] Though outnumbered in men and tanks, Bayerlein's division would give a good account of itself against Wood's 4th Armored and elements of XV Corps, although one Panzer Lehr officer has recorded that the American 90-mm tank destroyers "inflicted heavy losses" on the division's armor.[32] By the 26th, Panzer Lehr had expended much of its offensive capability and assumed defensive lines to screen a German withdrawal before being relieved by the 25th Panzer Grenadier Division the next day.

On November 23 Patton met with his two corps commanders to discuss the Army's situation and develop further operations. Eddy described Patton at this meeting as depressed over the progress to date. Two days earlier Patton lamented, "I wish things would move faster in this Army," but this sentiment was partly the product of professional jealousy, for elements of Devers' Sixth Army Group had closed up to the Rhine at Strasbourg on the same day. After fifteen days of hard fighting, Third Army had advanced no more than twenty miles, and this chiefly in Eddy's sector.

The fact that the Germans had flooded the country in front of the 26th Infantry Division was partly responsible for the sluggish advance. According to General Simon, XIII SS Corps commander, this was the "main reason why the American tanks had such difficulty and did not get through"[33] in Eddy's sector. However, Patton also understood that his personal belief that his soldiers could attack continuously for sixty hours had been surpassed many times during the campaign. He noted on the same day that "the impetus of our attack is naturally slackening due to the fatigue of the men."[34] The only way to rest the units that had been doing the heavy fighting since November 8 was to put the divisions into column and narrow the front of each corps. This would have given the additional advantage of focusing his combat power more, but he noted on the 21st, "I doubt whether we can do it."[35] The next day, however, he had decided to have the 26th and 35th Infantry Divisions "stand fast" and "refit to what degree is possible."[36]

His scheme of maneuver finalized at the November 23rd meeting was a broad advance still aimed at securing bridgeheads across the Rhine. With the left flank of the army secured by the Moselle River,[37] he intended to jab at the Saar River from Saarburg to well south of Saarbruecken hoping to secure at least one bridgehead for each corps.[38] Though Saarburg was some twenty miles north of the main corps axis of advance, Patton felt that a movement in this direction would pull German forces away from the main thrust of Walker's new offensive on the 25th. Furthermore, he stated that a river crossing "should be made on a wide front with the hope that somewhere, somehow a foothold will be gained."[39]

To effect this plan, the 10th Armored Division and one combat team of the 90th Infantry Division were to try for Saarburg and Merzig, an operation already in progress at the time of the November 23 meeting between Patton and his corps commanders. The rest of the 90th and the entire 95th Infantry Division were to attack east towards Saarlautern. The 80th Infantry Division and 6th Armored Division, along with one combat team of the 35th Infantry Division, were to attack towards Saarguemines while Wood's division attempted its own "end run" across the Saar. The fact that the 5th Infantry Division, "less one combat team in Metz," was to follow "whichever [XX Corps] assault makes a hole" clearly proved that Patton, even at this late stage, continued to shun concentration in favour of opportunism, an operational method that the Germans had long since demonstrated to be bankrupt in Lorraine. Additional confirmation of this tendency was the fact that Patton made no plans to decisively reinforce Grow and McBride even though he was convinced that their operations had "the best chance" of success.[40]

In his diary at the time, Patton could not "refrain from again regretting the fact that Bradley did not let me use the 83rd in the attack on Sarrbourg [Saarburg]."[41] Yet he still insisted on carrying out his original plan for XX Corps' left flank even though the circumstances under which the plan had first been designed no longer existed. Incredibly he commented, "I doubt if the 10th Armored's northern thrust is really efficacious, due to the slowness imposed on it by weather conditions."[42] Thus he committed an entire armored division and a good portion of perhaps his best infantry division to an operation that he had no faith in. Patton suspected that his "jabs" against the Saar would have to be accomplished in jumps rather than a continuous attack. At the moment, his only jab was being made by Eddy's XII Corps, but his renewed push of the 18th had once again spent itself some twelve days later except for Wood's continued fight to outflank Saare-Union.

On the 30th XII Corps still stood some five miles from Saareguemines on a twenty-five mile front with its left wing touching XX Corps around St. Avold.[43] Von Mellenthin believed that "Patton would have done better if the 4th and the 6th Armored Divisions had been grouped together in a single corps,"[44] but the American army had never shown any inclination toward this type of corps structure. Even if it had, there was a practical problem with von Mellenthin's criticism. Cole rightly pointed out that near the frontier the roads were poorly constructed and would have quickly broken down under the use of two armored divisions. This is precisely what happened during the battles between 4th Armored and Panzer Lehr.

Eddy's offensive may have bogged down further during this period if Patton had not had a change of attitude about McBride's 80th Infantry Division passively screening Faulquemont. Although army orders had clearly specified that the division would contain the town, Patton had a spontaneous reaction to a division sitting doing nothing and ordered it forward. Once McBride got moving again, his division made a solid advance of nearly eighteen miles. Eddy's original reason for holding up the 80th at Faulquemont was simply to give the division some much needed rest after 102 consecutive days in contact with the enemy. By the end of the month the division had sustained 513 killed, 2215 wounded, and 373 missing since November 8. In fact, all of Eddy's divisions had suffered heavily. Baade's 35th Infantry Division casualty list ran to 349 killed, 1,549 wounded, and 115 missing. Grow's division lost 162 killed, 725 wounded, and 47 missing. The new 26th Infantry Division sustained the most casualties of any unit in XII Corps, including 661 killed, 2,154 wounded, and 613 missing. Incidence of trench foot, which was high in all the divisions, reached 2,898 men in the 26th Infantry during November.[45]

These figures strongly suggest that the principal reason for XII Corps' slow advance was the blunting of its cutting edge. Patton calculated Third Army's replacement shortage at nine thousand men on November 29, a figure to increase to eleven thousand four days later (see Appendix C).[46] The replacement crisis forced Patton to twice draft 5 percent of Army headquarters personnel to retrain as riflemen. As he explained it, because 92 percent of Third Army's casualties occurred in the rifle companies, a division that lost four thousand men "has practically no riflemen left." This calculation meant that with eleven thousand men short in a nine-division army, "we are closely approaching a 40% shortage in each rifle company."[47] Cole suggested that at this point Patton had "gradually abandoned the hope of a quick break-through to the Rhine" and seemed to have been "concerned simply with driving steadily forward, going as far as his strength and supplies would permit."[48] The sharp decline in the fighting power of his army may have been too obvious for even Patton to dismiss.

While XII Corps battled its way toward the Saar and preparations were underway for XX Corps' main effort, cavalry elements and CCA, 10th Armored Division attempted to clear the Saar-Moselle triangle, originally the objective of the 83rd Infantry Division. Confronting CCA, and later elements of the 90th Infantry Division at the base of the triangle, was the fortified east-west extension of the West Wall, known as the Orscholz Switch Line (see Map 11.1). Designed to provide a barrier against any northward advance into the Saar-Moselle triangle, this defensive position consisted of field works, antitank barriers, reinforced concrete pillboxes, and bunkers. On November 17, elements of Pflieger's 416th Division started withdrawing northward to garrison the Orscholz position.[49] With the triangle in enemy hands, German forces sat squarely on XX Corps' northern flank.

Any operations against German forces in the triangle designed not to be decisive was a waste of dwindling Third Army assets, but Morris's armored attack on November 21 was essentially a reconnaissance in force because intelligence on the line was nil. Weigley noted that although Walker's G-2 section was aware of the existence of the line, "both the XX Corps and the Third Army had issued orders as if altogether ignorant of it."[50] The network of artificial defenses, including dragon's teeth, augmented by German defenders fighting on their own soil for the first time, forced the armor to quickly give way to Van Fleet's infantry. For three grueling days the infantry made advances but at considerable cost. One battalion was reduced to a mere one hundred men, and although several pillboxes and bunkers were destroyed, no clear breach of the line was made.[51]

Patton was not yet prepared to give up with the 10th Armored. On the 25th he noted that the division "is very self-confident and while it is not moving fast, it is progressing, so I decided to let them keep on toward Saarburg for a little longer."[52] By November 27, however, he finally realized that Walker did not have the necessary strength assembled along the

Map 11.1
The Orscholz Switch Line

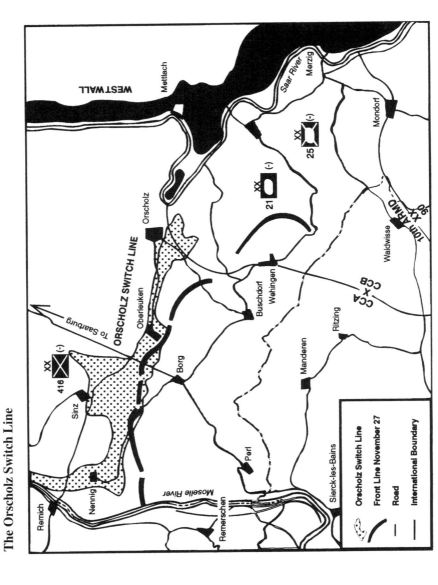

Source: Base map taken from Hugh M. Cole's *The Lorraine Campaign*, U.S. Army in World War II: European Theater of Operations (Washington, D.C., 1984), Map XXII. Altered by Bill Traer.

Orscholz Line to crack it and canceled further attempts to clear the triangle. Once this was decided, Walker reoriented CCA for the push eastward.

The battle against the Orscholz Line highlighted Patton's loose grip on the campaign. CCB, 10th Armored Division had crossed the frontier to within three thousand yards of the Saar and Merzig on November 19 and sat there for several days as CCA and valuable infantry assets were expended in fighting ninety degrees off the main corps axis of advance. Von Mellenthin believed that Patton "made a bad mistake in dispersing this division [10th Armored] in isolated attacks along the corps front, and the order to concentrate for an advance on Merzig was given too late to achieve any important breakthrough."[53] That Patton allowed such a large portion of the combat power of XX Corps to hack away on a divergent axis reinforces the idea that he was relying on improvisation. He hoped that the armor could quickly penetrate the line and swiftly cross the Saar, thus bringing him that much closer to the Rhine. Here is a good example where his obsession with the Rhine had a negative tactical result on his overall operations because it prevented a quick concentration of power in the direction Patton chiefly wanted to go. Incidentally, where Patton wanted to go happened to be the strongest sector of the West Wall.

Patton believed an attack against the West Wall defenses between Merzig and Saarlautern would produce a rapid result "because a straight line is the shortest distance between points and also it is so strong that it is probably not too well defended."[54] His theory that an inherently strong position might allow the enemy to employ weak forces there had its merits, but the overwhelming evidence from the Orscholz Line and Metz battles indicated that lightly manned fixed positions were formidable obstacles nonetheless. In reality, the sector was not lightly defended. Walker's own intelligence indicated that Balck and Knobelsdorff had assembled some ten thousand men from elements of the 559th and 36th Volksgrenadier and 347th Divisions to oppose Twaddle's crossing in the sector of the West Wall, which they too considered to be the strongest.

Before the West Wall could be attacked, Van Fleet and Twaddle had to first get there. Their progress to the famed fortifications may have taken even longer than it did had not Patton personally examined their scheme of maneuver on the 25th, the day the XX Corps advance was to begin. "I thought the plan I inspected this morning," stated Patton, "was over-timid and said so. They are talking about seizing successive objectives and closing up on them. As it is, there is nothing to oppose them from marching straight forward."[55] Patton was right. On the 26th, Twaddle advanced some five miles and repeated this performance the next day against the newly committed 347th Division. By the 28th his division had crossed the frontier.[56] Van Fleet had also closed to within two to three miles of the Saar at this point. With these forces in place the battle to penetrate the West Wall was about to begin.

In early September, Patton had urged Bradley and Eisenhower to let him charge through the West Wall, which at the time was completely unmanned and suffered from several years of complete neglect. Patton was adamant that any delay in taking advantage of the opportunity to breach the line uncontested would have dire consequences later on. What could have been taken cheaply in September was now to cost Third Army heavy casualties and cause Patton further frustration. At the end of November only Walker's XX Corps was in a position to make a breach of the West Wall. The inability of the Germans to make a more determined stand against XX Corps after retreating from Metz was a function of the terrain, which diminished in defensive terms towards the Saar River. The Germans made little use of the Maginot Line fortifications as they continued to fall back. Forced to deploy on the more open ground east of Metz, the retreating divisions were quite vulnerable.

It was a considered judgment on the part of both Balck and Rundstedt that the best place to make another stand against XX Corps was along the Saar Heights Position (*Saar-Hoehen Stellung*), a natural defensive feature laying in front of the West Wall just west of the Saar. Both men betted heavily on the strength of the position to hold up Third Army.[57] This terrain feature rose gradually to the Saar to form a series of heights whose reverse sides generally broke away abruptly to the river. In the 95th Infantry Division's sector around Saarlautern the heights were quite rugged and terminated well short of the Saar forming a natural bridgehead of low ground. Most of Saarlautern sat in this area and was not a part of the West Wall. The suburbs of the city on the eastern side, however, were firmly integrated into the line's defenses.

In tactical terms the Saar Heights represented the last major German defensive line in front of the Saar River and was sufficient to both "cover the movement of field forces into the West Wall fortifications or to screen deployment and maneuver for counterattacks launched to deflect any frontal attack against the main works of the West Wall."[58] The heights boasted no permanent concrete works but did have temporary field works. Here, German resistance again stiffened against XX Corps. When the 95th Infantry Division first attacked the heights on November 29, it received ten counterattacks throughout the day by a special assault group from Panzer Lehr. So determined were Balck and Knobelsdorff to protect the western approaches to Saarlautern, that Van Fleet's division, attacking in tandem with Twaddle's, met little resistance further north and succeeded in pushing patrols to the Saar on the 29th.[59]

Despite the good defensive quality of the Saar Heights position, Balck was afraid that the numerous small attacks being made against his line (as opposed to what he earlier characterized as a few powerful attacks at different points) would be more than his scant mobile reserves could cope with. Feuchtinger, Bayerlein, and Weitersheim simply did not possess enough armor to deflect multiple penetrations. As a result, Balck, though quickly reprimanded by Rundstedt, ordered a general withdrawal of the LXXXII Corps, First Army's right wing opposing XX Corps, to the Saar in preparation for garrisoning the West Wall.[60] On December 1 he extended the order to the XIII SS Corps, which brought its right flank to the west side of the river. Everything Balck had was now being thrown into a last-ditch attempt to hold the West Wall.

The condition of Balck's forces opposing XX Corps at this point was not good. Of the four nominal divisions in Hoernlein's LXXXII Corps, the 416th Division was safely entrenched in the Orscholz Line, but Britzelmayr's 19th Volksgrenadier Division had only 630 riflemen left. Most of its heavy equipment had been lost west of the Saar and its replacements, a motley assortment of all types, were rated as poor. A few riflemen of this battered division, along with the remnants of Muehlen's 559th Volksgrenadier Division and Casper's decimated 48th Division were grouped together to form Kampfgruppe Muehlen and numbered but 360 men all ranks. Feuchtinger's 21st Panzer Division was woefully understrength, containing some 200 armored infantry in the whole division by December 4. The 347th Division was for all intents and purposes destroyed and had to be reinforced by a regiment from the 36th Volksgrenadier Division. It was only the reinforced concrete of the West Wall, serving to augment their diminished numbers and fighting quality, that prevented these decimated units from being completely destroyed, even by a much weakened Third Army.

Patton's solution to the problem of the fixed fortifications of the West Wall was the same as at Metz, the use of massive aerial bombardment in support of a traditional combined arms attack. On November 29 Bradley informed him that since both the First and Ninth Army advances had stalled, Third Army would get their allotted air support if a breakthrough of the West Wall could be achieved.[61] It was perhaps because of this welcomed support that Patton reaffirmed his conviction that the West Wall was not impregnable. However, as Blumenson suggested, "this was nothing more than the old Patton flash, the Patton spirit; he was really not so sure."[62] Indeed, there was little cause for optimism, but Walker was soon preparing for the first assaults against the line.

Walker had assured Gay on the 29th that he could launch a full assault across the Saar at any moment and that if no air support was available, he would attack regardless no later than December 3.[63] To assist XX Corps, Weyland drew up Operation "Hi-Sug," a carpet bombing of the eastern portion of Saarlautern by eight groups of medium bombers (five hundred aircraft) from the IX Bombardment Division. XX Corps was also to receive priority on fighter-bombers and the guns of the III Corps artillery, sent forward from Metz to assist the 95th Infantry Division in its crossing.[64] If and when Twaddle's division secured a breach, the 90th Infantry and 10th Armored Divisions were to follow through the gap.

Weyland secured the use of the bombers on December 1, but only four groups succeeded in finding their targets because of a guidance failure, and the ground observers reported that the bombing had not been very effective.[65] This was a moot point, however, because despite Walker's assurances to the contrary, Twaddle's troops were not close enough to the river to take rapid advantage of the bombing effect. Even when Weyland managed to organize an additional strike the next day, the 95th still was not in position to take full advantage of the carpet bombing. The city's electrical system was crippled in this second attack, and the infantry did succeed in securing the portion of Saarlautern on the west side of the Saar as well as two bridges, but the fight to expand the bridgehead quickly degenerated into a two week house-to-house battle.[66] The main German defenses had been built so close to the east bank of the Saar that proper tactical deployment of Twaddle's forces in front of the fortified area for an assault was virtually impossible.[67]

While the 95th Infantry Division anchored the corps' right flank with a crossing at Saarlautern, the 90th Infantry Division struggled to secure a crossing farther north. Forced to battle both the Germans and a flooded Saar that expanded from two hundred to three hundred feet in its sector, and continued to rise, Van Fleet's efforts to cross the Saar resembled the earlier crossing of the Moselle at Koenigsmacker. Complete surprise was achieved on December 6 under a XX Corps artillery barrage from over six hundred guns (field artillery, tank destroyers, and regimental cannon) that fired eight thousand rounds in forty-five minutes. A bridgehead had been established at Dilligen and Pachten, but by the next day most of the newly arrived 719th Division, originally committed in the Saarlautern sector on the 4th, and tanks from the 11th Panzer Division, were committed against the bridgehead.

The fighting conditions for both the 90th and 95th Infantry Divisions were atrocious. One account of the crossing made by Van Fleet's infantry stated that heavy rains "turned the eastern bank of the river into a sea of mud for nearly a mile inland. The entire area was literally studded with enemy pillboxes and advances were measured not in feet or yards but in the number of pillboxes taken."[68] Once across the river, Cole noted that the infantry faced a situation where "nearly every pillbox or bunker captured by the Americans entailed some reduction in the actual rifle strength on the firing line. At no time were sufficient explosives available to demolish any large number of these enemy works. . . . Bitter experience soon taught the Americans that each captured pillbox or bunker must be occupied to prevent German infiltration and the reoccupation of a presumably 'dead' work."[69] The long duration of the close combat in the Saarlautern bridgehead, and in the Dilligen area as well, resulted in numerous combat casualties, and was particularly distinguished by a high rate of sick and combat-fatigue cases.[70]

Van Fleet's division quickly found itself in a precarious situation. Already weakened by heavy fighting, the infantry battalions were subjected to continual counterattacks and had to rely on resupply by way of vehicular ferrys, assault boats, and air drops. It was absolutely impossible to build a vehicular bridge due to insecure anchorages on the muddy banks, the swift current, and the volume and deadly accuracy of German artillery. The 90th never did succeed in establishing a vehicular bridge across the Saar in the remaining days of the campaign.[71] No bridge meant that, like at the Moselle in early November, Morris's 10th Armored Division had to sit and watch the battle unfold.

Another division that had to sit and wait was Irwin's 5th Infantry. On December 1 Walker put into motion a plan to put the division into the XX Corps line along a narrow front south of the 95th Infantry Division as soon as the bulk of it could be relieved from the Metz forts. On December 5 the bulk of the division began moving east, and on the 7th its final relief at Metz by the new 87th Infantry Division was underway.[72] Irwin was positioned behind the 95th Infantry Division on December 9 and prepared to relieve Twaddle's weakened forces. By the 17th, Irwin had assumed command of the Saarlautern bridgehead, but the 5th Infantry Division never had the opportunity to fully take part in the fighting at the West Wall before it was ordered to head north into the Ardennes. Containing the active forts of Metz was a necessary evil, but the fighting strength of Irwin's division was sorely missed at the West Wall as casualties mounted.

Indicative of the strength of the West Wall opposite XX Corps was the reaction of Balck to another crisis on December 11. Patch's Seventh Army was threatening the West Wall south of XII Corps, an area where the line was not strongly fortified. Aware of the line's strength in the Saarlautern sector, Balck shifted Feuchtinger's 21st Panzer Division remnants and the 404th Volks Artillery Corps to reinforce the threatened area despite objections from the new commander of First Army, General der Infanterie Hans von Obstfelder, who replaced Knobelsdorff on the 4th. All but the rear elements of these units had left the Saarlautern area by December 15.[73] The loss of these forces did not noticeably impair the defense of the West Wall in XX Corps' sector.

The prospect of cracking the West Wall was growing dimmer for Patton in the face of the tremendous enemy resistance and his own diminishing fighting power. Walker's lead division, the 95th, was described by the Corps G-3 Periodic Report for December 2 as "tired," with four of the infantry battalions reduced to 55 percent normal strength.[74] Van Fleet's division was not much better off. Clearly, Third Army could not force a penetration of the West Wall fortifications, a defensive system certainly as strong if not stronger than the fortifications of Metz, by generating fighting power and momentum on the stamina and courage of its dwindling pool of infantrymen. Twice, on December 6 and again on the 15th, Patton took the exceptional step of drafting 5 percent from the various corps and army headquarters staffs to retrain as riflemen at Metz. Yet although these draftees, numbering some 6,500 men, fleshed out the ranks of the divisions, their lack of full training was a serious problem in the line and led to many casualties.[75]

In addition to the acute manpower deficiencies at the West Wall was a growing problem once again of ammunition shortages. At the end of November Patton bitterly noted that "how the hell we can fight a war without men and ammunition I don't know."[76] The lack of sufficient 240-mm artillery ammunition was keenly felt as Third Army attempted to blast its way into the fortified cities along the Saar. Yet even if abundant quantities had been available, Cole noted that the great superiority of the American artillery was "partially erased when the ground fogs and lowering clouds of the late months cut down observation, thus somewhat restoring an equilibrium between the 1944 gun or howitzer and the 1940 bunker."[77] The only alternative to artillery was air power, and Patton was to get enormous support in the last stages of the campaign.

On December 5 Eisenhower gathered the Allied air commanders together to devise a strategy for employing the strategic air forces to achieve an early decision on the Western Front. Brigadier General Weyland attended this conference and was instrumental in persuading Eisenhower that the heavy bomber force could best be used by assisting Third Army in a tactical role along the Saar.[78] The next day, Generals Carl Spaatz, Jimmy Doolittle, and Hoyt S. Vandenburg visited Third Army to offer Patton direct bomber support for his attack on the West Wall.[79] By way of interest, Patton was also offered the services of Lieutenant General Lewis Brereton's First Airborne Army, but he was not sold on the value of airborne troops. "The trouble with the Airborne Army," he stated, "is that it is too ponderous in its methods."[80] He felt that smaller contingents available on short notice would be of much greater tactical value. Ultimately, he did not plan to use any airborne troops at the West Wall.

The plan devised by the bomber generals would later be described by Patton as "the most ambitious air blitz ever conceived."[81] Indeed, it would be bigger than "Cobra" or "Goodwood." Designated Operation "Tink" by Weyland, this air blitz was to consist of a massive bombardment of Zweibruecken in assistance of XII Corps.[82] The mediums from the IX Bombardment Division were to be augmented by the striking power of the heavies of both the U.S. Eighth Air Force and RAF Bomber Command. The date for the massive offensive was set for December 19 to be followed four days later by Seventh Army's own air Operation, "Dagger."[83] Third Army had to be completely deployed along the West Wall by this date, a projection that caused Patton to note that the operations on Eddy's front had thus become a "horse-race against time."[84] But it was a race Patton could not win. Moreover, the choice of Zweibruecken as the area of concentration was questionable.

Zweibruecken was not a part of the West Wall and actually stood some miles in the rear of the line. There was no large city integrated into the line in XII Corps' zone other than Saarguemines. Weyland's philosophy, endorsed by Patton, was no doubt that XII Corps could crack the weaker section of the West Wall in its sector. If Zweibruecken, which lie in the Corps' path, were suppressed by massive bombardment, some degree of momentum might be generated. In his memoirs, Patton stated that the focus of the bombing was to be Kaiserlautern, but this was probably an error on his part because Kaiserlautern was more than twenty miles inside Germany and was not a part of the main West Wall fortifications. It was simply too far away to have helped the ground forces.[85] If Zweibruecken could be pounded into submisson, however, there was the possibility of rolling up the West Wall from the south and attacking it from the rear. But the entire operation hinged on whether of not Eddy could get to the West Wall in strength.

On November 30, when Eddy halted his forces once again, XII Corps stood some six miles from the West Wall at its closest point. At its farthest point, on the Corps' right flank where the 4th Armored was fighting, the distance ran to over fifteen miles (see Map 11.2). Incredibly, nineteen days later, Eddy still had barely managed to close to the German border, and in only one sector did he actually penetrate the frontier, striking proof of the level of German resistance on their own soil, the inherently strong nature of the terrain, and the diminishing fighting power of XII Corps (see Map 11.3). On December 2 the 26th Infantry Division was still fighting for Saare-Union, and it was not even until the 7th that the 35th Infantry Division was prepared to tackle Saareguemines, an important rail and industrial center that had been a constant target for American and British bombing. This continual aerial pounding forced the German defenders to build extensive concrete shelters, which, when added to the numerous large factory buildings, essentially made the city a demifortress.[86]

According to Eddy, Patton, on leaving the XII Corps CP on December 3, stated that the attacks had to continue "even if we had to go on until there was just one rifleman left in each company," at which point the infantry were to dig in. Only at this point, added Eddy, would he "permit us to stop our advance."[87] Patton overlooked the fact that if he exhausted XII Corps' already weak infantry strength just getting to the West Wall, the bombing would make little difference. Eddy noted that he justified his demand for keeping up the pressure by quoting Grant, "when he said that there are times in every battle when both sides think they are licked, but the side that continued the attack won the battle."[88] In truth, both sides were nearing the end of their strength.

The German units opposing XII Corps by this time (36th Volksgrenadier, 17th SS Panzer Grenadier, and 11th Panzer Divisions) had long since reached a state of exhaustion themselves. All three divisions in Simon's XIII SS Corps were described as being in "poor condition" and "greatly outweighed in numbers and material." Simon would also shortly lose the Panzer Lehr Division and the valuable 401st Volks Artillery Corps to the imminent Ardennes offensive. The high command, now obsessed with this strategic operation, could only send 5,700 replacements to First Army. Moreover, the army was only capable of firing some 7,000 rounds per day.[89] In stark contrast to First Army's artillery expenditure, XII Corps had gone from firing 9,000 rounds per day from December 1–3 to 22,575 rounds on the 4th, the day that Eddy launched a three-division attack (35th and 80th Infantry, 6th Armored Divisions) to correct the Corps line as it approached the West Wall. Baade and Grow closed on Saareguemines on the 6th and were finally in a position to tackle the city's defenses the next day.

By December 7, however, Eddy's infantry divisions had clearly lost their offensive capacity in the short term. The 26th and 80th Infantry Divisions

Map 11.2
Third Army's Battle Line, November 30, 1944

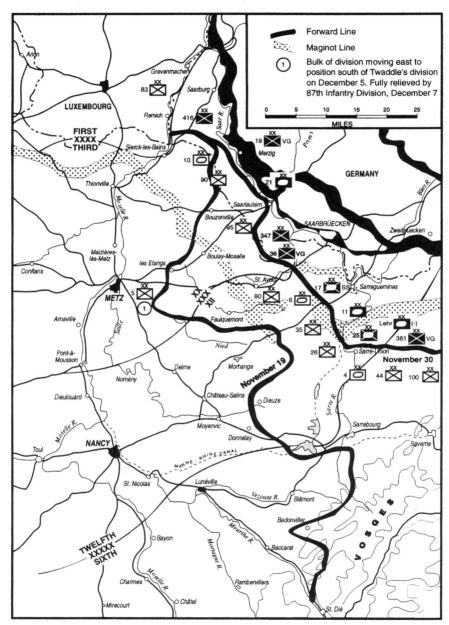

Source: Base map taken from Hugh M. Cole's *The Lorraine Campaign*, U.S. Army in World
War II: European Theater of Operations (Washington, D.C., 1984), Map XXII. Altered
by Eric Drummie and Bill Traer.

Map 11.3
Third Army's Battle Line, December 19, 1944

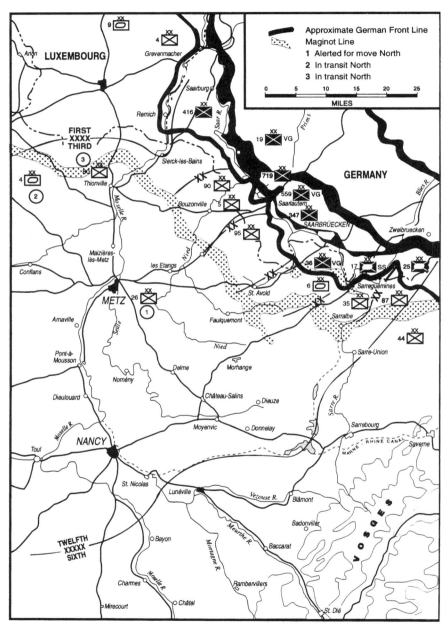

Source: Base map taken from Hugh M. Cole's *The Lorraine Campaign*, U.S. Army in World
War II: European Theater of Operations (Washington, D.C., 1984), Map XXII. Altered
by Eric Drummie and Bill Traer.

were 51 and 60 percent short of riflemen respectively and when he brought up the crisis with Patton, he was told that only five hundred replacements were on the way.[90] Eddy hoped to get the new 87th Infantry Division as soon as possible because "a new division at full strength is just what I need to keep the advance rolling."[91] The day before, Grow's 6th Armored Division finally left the line in rough shape. On the 8th, the exhausted 4th Armored Division was relieved by the newly arrived 12th Armored Division temporarily loaned from Haislip's XV Corps. In effect, however, Eddy's fighting strength was absolutely reduced because Haislip declined to commit the 12th Armored to full-scale operations until it had gained some experience.[92]

By the time the 4th Armored was pulled out, it had been without its energetic and brilliant commander, General Wood, for five days. On the advice of Eddy, Patton finally relieved Wood from command of the division on the 3rd and sent him home on a sixty-day leave. As Patton said of Wood, "Unquestionably, in a rapid moving advance, he is the greatest division commander I have ever seen, but when things get sticky he is inclined to worry too much, which keeps him from sleeping and runs him down, and it makes it difficult to control his operations."[93] The high casualties suffered by the division in atypical armored fighting had been a major cause of Wood's growing belligerency with Eddy and hurt the division's effectiveness. Some companies had a 100 percent turnover in officers, but the loss of valuable tank crews was the most serious problem because the replacements available were "converted riflemen or headquarters personnel who knew nothing about tanks."[94] Command of the 4th Armored subsequently fell on Major General Hugh J. Gaffey, the Third Army Chief-of-Staff.

The 4th Armored Division, despite its high casualties sustained slugging it out with Panzer Lehr, had nonetheless succeeded in rolling up the German defense line along the Saar for nearly twenty miles across XII Corps' zone of advance, but Eddy could not take advantage of this fact. Saareguemines was finally secured on the 11th, and XII Corps had ten vehicular bridges across the Saar, but the 26th Infantry Division had just managed to clear the Maginot Line the day before to stand a frustrating ten miles from the West Wall. This division was soon replaced by the new 87th Infantry Division, but it too had trouble advancing, as did the 35th Infantry Division. Numerous small woodlots and forests stood in their path, and as Cole noted, "Here again the German grenadier proved himself an able woods fighter." The 35th Infantry Division, severely reduced in rifle strength due to the fact that it had been in the line for 162 consecutive days, lacked the endurance to "drive home successful attacks on any but narrow frontages."[95] Indeed, the advance of XII Corps to the West Wall had taken its toll of both the men in the line and even the corps commander. Patton had Eddy "come in and spend the nights of the 13th and 14th, as he is tired and nervous and should relax."[96] By the 16th, Patton seriously considered putting Eddy on a few days leave and giving XII Corps to Gaffey.[97]

It is difficult to see how Patton could have succeeded in penetrating the West Wall in force deployed as he was. His intention to exert pressure all along the line made sense, and Balck recognized the threat this tactic posed, but the principle was negated when the defensive qualities of the West Wall were taken into account. The Germans, though necessarily spread thin by attempting to offer at least a degree of resistance along the entire front, were compensated in their efforts by the natural strength of the West Wall. Conversely, Third Army, by spreading itself thin actually lessened its own ability to combat those fortifications and drive home hard won successes.

Though the Germans disparaged the West Wall as outdated, any combination of fixed fortifications, field works, antitank traps, and dragon's teeth, constructed in depth with a keen sense of the existing terrain, was going to present a formidable challenge to an army tired from continuous fighting and short of infantry. Unlike Metz, Patton could not outflank the West Wall. The only way to break through, to use the advice of Wade Haislip, was to put one's combat power in the place you wanted to go and "punch it through."[98] This tactic would have been considerably more successful for XX Corps if not attempted against a strongly fortified city like Saarlautern.

Patton's decision to once again make a large city the principal axis of attack for XX Corps was a highly questionable one, especially after his experience with Metz. Aerial bombardment of cities was a double-edged sword tactically. Communications and troop formations may be destroyed, but the resulting debris inhibited mobility and offered the defender numerous defensible positions. Stalingrad and Caen clearly proved this. Patton's concern with road nets and rail centers was justified, but anticipating quick success against a city in which every building became a defender's dream was fantasy. He later noted that although the casualties were low in this type of fighting, which they were not, it was a "tedious" operation, as one might suspect.

When one looks at the maps displaying Patton's line at points in time during the campaign, a pattern is quickly apparent. In effect, German forces in Lorraine were able to dictate his rate of advance because of three principal anchor positions: Metz, the Orscholz Line, and the section of the West Wall extending from Saarlautern through Merzig to the Orscholz Line. The possession of Metz allowed German forces to pivot, slow the rate of advance of XII Corps, and withdraw in relatively good order once the Moselle line was breached south of Nancy. The successful holding of the Orscholz Line prevented XX Corps from driving into the Saar-Moselle triangle thereby flanking the strongest section of the West Wall and funneled its advance straight into the Saarlautern-Merzig area. Possession of this sector allowed German forces to continue the tactical pivot and again dictate the rate of advance of XII Corps.

The German defense at the West Wall was further augmented by another important factor. With XII Corps besieging Saarguemines and XX Corps attacking Saarlautern, the angle between the axis of advance for the two corps had widened the distance between their main forces, a development not completely controllable by Patton. Separating the two corps was a heavily forested and rugged area dominated by a mining town and shafts. The French General Staff prior to World War II had considered the area unfeasible for offensive operations, and Patton agreed.[99]

As Third Army continued to hammer away at the West Wall in Walker's sector, and struggled simply to close to the fortifications in Eddy's sector, Patton lamented that although his advance was going forward by short leaps, it was "not very brilliant."[100] He fully realized that if he failed to get through the West Wall with the final set-piece air-ground attack scheduled for the 19th, he would have to once again go on the defensive and await reinforcements. Any hopes he may have had in cracking the West Wall in December 1944 vanished when General Levon C. Allen, Bradley's Chief of Staff, informed Patton on December 16 that he would have to give the 10th Armored to First Army to repulse the initial German penetrations of the Ardennes offensive. During the 17th and 18th the true scope of the offensive manifested itself, and on the 19th at a conference in Verdun Eisenhower told Patton to head for Luxembourg and take command of the battle for the southern side of the German salient.

Thus the three-month campaign by Third Army on the German border came to an end. As armored and infantry divisions hurriedly pulled out of Third Army's line along the Saar to race north into the Ardennes, Patton left behind the muddy, flooded battlefield of Lorraine. Though the enemy had been cleared from the area between the Moselle and the Saar, the campaign had been one of personal and professional frustration from beginning to end. The Rhine was still seventy miles away.

NOTES

1. Martin Blumenson, *The Patton Papers* (Boston: Houghton Mifflin, 1974), II: 576.

2. Ibid., 587.

3. Hugh M. Cole, *The Lorraine Campaign*, U.S. Army in World War II: European Theater of Operations (Washington, D.C.: Center for Military History, 1984), 450.

4. Russell F. Weigley, *Eisenhower's Lieutenants: The Campaign of France and Germany 1944–1945* (Bloomington: Indiana University Press, 1981), 397–398.

5. Cole, *Lorraine Campaign*, 415, footnote 68.

6. Ibid., 449, footnote 57.

7. Ibid., 416.

8. Weigley, *Eisenhower's Lieutenants*, 397.

9. Blumenson, *Patton Papers*, II: 588.

10. Ibid., 576.

11. Ibid.

12. Ibid., 575.

13. George S. Patton Diary, November 25, 1944, Special Collections, United States Military Academy Library, West Point (WP).

14. R. Stephenson et al., "The Battle of Metz," Battlebook 13–A, (Fort Leavenworth, Kans.: Combat Studies Institute, 1984), 36.

15. Blumenson, *Patton Papers*, II: 575.

16. Cole, *Lorraine Campaign*, 499.

17. Major Roy E. Appleman, "Comments on Grow's Study 'Narrow Front vs Broad Front,' " October 15, 1952, Box: "General Grow, Special Studies on World War II," United States Army Military History Institute (USAMHI), Carlisle Barracks, Pa.

18. Manton S. Eddy Diary, November 16, 1944, U.S. Army Infantry School, National Infantry Museum (NIM), Fort Benning, Ga.

19. George S. Patton, *War as I Knew It* (Boston: Houghton Mifflin, 1947), 135.

20. Eddy Diary, November 16.

21. Hobart R. Gay/Hugh J. Gaffey Diary (Gay/Gaffey Diary), November 18, 1944, Special Collections, WP.

22. Cole, *Lorraine Campaign*, 459, footnote 18.

23. Eddy Diary, November 18–19.

24. A. Harding Ganz, "Patton's Relief of General Wood," *The Journal of Military History* LIII, 3 (July 1989): 268.

25. Ibid.

26. Hanson Baldwin, *Tiger Jack* (Fort Collins, Colo., 1979), 94.

27. Patton Diary, November 23.

28. Blumenson, *Patton Papers*, II: 582.

29. Ibid.

30. Cole, *Lorraine Campaign*, 463.

31. ETHINT 67, "Critique of Normandy Breakthrough Pz Lehr Div from St. Lo to the Rhur," an Interview with Genlt Fritz Bayerlein, August 15, 1945, Don-

ald S. Detwiler, with Charles B. Burdick and Jurgen Rowher, eds., *World War II German Military Studies* (New York: Garland Publishing, 1979), III.

32. Helmut Ritgen, *The Western Front 1944: Memoirs of a Panzer Lehr Officer* (Winnipeg: Federowicz, 1995), 237.

33. ETHINT 33, "XIII SS Infantry Corps in the Lorraine Campaign," an Interview with Genlt der Waffen-SS Max Simon, August 17, 1945, Detwiler et al., *World War II German Military Studies*, II.

34. Blumenson, *Patton Papers*, II: 576.

35. Ibid.

36. Patton Diary, November 22.

37. Cole, *Lorraine Campaign*, 488.

38. Gay/Gaffey Diary, November 23.

39. Patton Diary, November 22.

40. Ibid.

41. Ibid.

42. Ibid.

43. Cole, *Lorraine Campaign*, 521.

44. Major General F. W. von Mellenthin, *Panzer Battles: A Study of the Employment of Armour in the Second World War* (Norman: Oklahoma University Press, 1971), 334.

45. Cole, *Lorraine Campaign*, 462, 479–480, 485.

46. Blumenson, *Patton Papers*, II: 583.

47. Ibid., 586.

48. Cole, *Lorraine Campaign*, 520.

49. Ibid., 487.

50. Weigley, *Eisenhower's Lieutenants*, 399.

51. Joe I. Abrams, *A History of the 90th Division in World War II* (Baton Rouge, 1946), 40. Abrams stated that during the initial attack of November 23 the 358th Infantry Regiment made good progress but soon came under a "violent" artillery barrage. Considering the general layout of the line, he remarked that "Pillboxes with well-defended communications trenches located in carefully selected positions provided the enemy with a perfect defense."

52. Patton Diary, November 25.

53. Mellenthin, *Panzer Battles*, 335.

54. Blumenson, *Patton Papers*, II: 585.

55. Patton Diary, November 25.

56. Gay/Gaffey Diary, November 26–28.

57. Cole, *The Lorraine Campaign*, 501, footnote 15.

58. Ibid., 501.

59. Ibid., 508.

60. Ibid., 511.

61. Patton, *War as I Knew It*, 139.

62. Blumenson, *Patton Papers*, II: 586.

63. Gay/Gaffey Diary, November 29; Patton, *War as I Knew It*, 139.

64. Cole, *Lorraine Campaign*, 513.

65. Ibid., 512. The four bomber groups hit Saarlautern and two other cities while the XIX TAC interdicted targets three to four miles east of the river.

66. Gay/Gaffey Diary, December 3; Cole, *Lorraine Campaign*, 573.

67. Cole, *Lorraine Campaign*, 573.

68. John Colby, *War from the Ground Up: The 90th Division in World War II* (Austin, Tex.: Nortex Press, 1991), 326.

69. Cole, *Lorraine Campaign*, 573.

70. Ibid.

71. Colby, *War from the Ground Up*, 346.

72. Gay/Gaffey Diary, December 5–7.

73. Cole, *Lorraine Campaign*, 587. The 526th Replacement Division was to replace these units, but only small elements arrived by December 15.

74. Ibid., 515. Against the regiments of the 95th Infantry Division, German resistance was particularly fanatical. Simon, the commander of the XIII SS Corps, stated that the 87th Regiment of the 36th Volksgrenadier Division and the remnants of the 347th Division fought "tooth and nail" against Twaddle's division. See footnote 41.

75. Blumenson, *Patton Papers*, II: 588; Cole, *Lorraine Campaign*, 595.

76. Blumenson, *Patton Papers*, II: 584.

77. Cole, *Lorraine Campaign*, 551.

78. Spires, *Air Power for Patton's Army*, 255. First and Ninth Army representatives at the meeting wanted to employ the strategic bomber force against the Roer dams.

79. Richard G. Davis, *Carl A. Spaatz and the Air War in Europe* (Washington, D.C.: Center for Air Force History, 1992), 517.

80. Patton, *War as I Knew It*, 139.

81. Ibid., 141.

82. Spires, *Air Power for Patton's Army*, 256.

83. Ibid., 263. The bombers were scheduled to hit thirty-four targets over three consecutive days. Eighth Air Force bombers were to bomb twenty-six supply depots while Weyland's own aircraft were to hit all communications centers behind the point of assault immediately following the bombers to confuse the enemy.

84. Patton, *War as I Knew It*, 142.

85. Ibid., 141.

86. Cole, *Lorraine Campaign*, 528–529.

87. Eddy Diary, December 3.

88. Ibid.

89. Cole, *Lorraine Campaign*, 526, 534.

90. Eddy Diary, December 7.

91. Ibid., December 6.

92. Cole, *Lorraine Campaign*, 533, footnote 23. The 12th Armored Division operated in XII Corps' zone but remained under XV Corps command.

93. Blumenson, *Patton Papers*, II: 587.

94. Cole, *Lorraine Campaign*, 532, footnote 20.

95. Ibid., 546.

96. Blumenson, *Patton Papers*, II: 591.

97. Patton Diary, December 16.

98. Wade H. Haislip, "Corps Command in World War II," *Military Review* (May 1990): 32.

99. Cole, *Lorraine Campaign*, 570.

100. Patton, *War as I Knew It*, 145.

Chapter 12

Assessment

It is true that this enemy counteroffensive worked to deflect General Patton's divisions short of the Rhine and brought the Lorraine Campaign to an abrupt conclusion. But the German forces had been so badly shattered in Lorraine that the Third Army was able to disengage on this front with relative ease as it turned to intervene in the battle of the Ardennes.

—Official History[1]

I have known commanders who considered that once their plan was made and orders issued, they need take no further part in the proceedings, except to influence the battle by means of their reserves. Never was there a greater mistake. . . . To succeed, a C.-in-C. must ensure from the beginning a very firm grip on his military machine; only in this way will his force maintain balance and cohesion and thus develop its full fighting potential.

—Field Marshal Montgomery[2]

The Lorraine Campaign tested Patton's generalship like no previous or subsequent campaign. It was, as Blumenson noted, "dogged, grim, and dirty, lacking glamour,"[3] quite a change from the improvisational nature of his audacious end run around the German Seventh Army in Normandy. Throughout August Patton enjoyed perfect weather and terrain conditions under which to practice his preferred method of waging war. The rolling open countryside of his operational area allowed his army to move with remarkable speed. What followed in Lorraine was a study in contrast. Fighting conditions held slight resemblance to those encountered in August.

Patton did achieve varying degrees of mobility, but movement was quickly confined to short spurts by German counteraction. To reduce the area encompassed by the Moselle and Saar Rivers required an advance of only forty-sixty miles, yet in the end Patton needed over three months to complete the task. He never did reach his stated objectives of Frankfurt and the Rhine. In the long grinding process of reaching the West Wall, Third Army sustained fifty thousand casualties, approximately one-third of its entire war total. Thus the series of battles fought by Third Army in Lorraine throughout the Fall and Winter of 1944 serves as an excellent case study for examining his generalship on a restricted armored battlefield.

Patton's campaign in Lorraine was chiefly framed by his perception of the nature of the war on his front. In August, those on the ground could be forgiven their belief that the hard fighting lay behind them in the shattered hedgerows and smoldering ruins of Normandy. The rest of the war was, or so it seemed, a matter of pursuit. This sentiment infected everyone, including Patton, who was probably more susceptible to it than anyone else because he already possessed great personal confidence and optimism about the end result of his actions.

His failure to heed Koch's ominous appraisal of enemy capabilities at the beginning of September is understandable in light of his philosophy of attacking regardless of time, location, or conditions. Eisenhower acknowledged that he was never affected by doubts or caution, and that ultimately he was a "one-sided individual," an aggressive combat commander.[4] As admirable a quality as aggressiveness is for a combat commander, this characteristic, when reinforced by the great success of August, produced tunnel vision and unwarranted optimism in Patton. His failure of perception in early September manifested itself on two connected levels: he did not fully appreciate the drastic change in terrain, and he completely misread the ability of the German army to stand and fight.

Contrary to Patton's belief, the German forces assembled in front of the West Wall to hold Third Army were far from beaten. In fact, they displayed tremendous powers of resiliency. The German army had not fought well following the utter collapse of their front in late July, and the Allies had chased them across France throughout August. But Lorraine became that crucial area where German retreat finally linked up with German reinforcement. At the doorstep of the Reich the Wehrmacht stopped running and turned to fight. To be sure, the army that dug in to fight in front of the West Wall was by degrees inferior to the army that conquered Poland, France, and advanced to the gates of Moscow, but it was no longer handicapped by defending on the relatively open plains of Normandy. If Clausewitz's observation that "it is easier to hold ground than to take it"[5] is true, and virtually no one would disagree, then it follows that it is easier to defend on significant tactical heights than rolling open countryside. To be sure, the open spaces of Normandy had yielded some advantage, especially to German armor when it could engage Allied armor at long ranges, but the terrain at the border was more rugged and *de facto* more defensible. First Army, aided by numerous rivers and generally favorable terrain, managed to overcome its initial reliance on a thin linear defense to organize defense in depth by the end of the campaign. Practical opportunities for "digging in" presented themselves much more readily than they had in Normandy. Defensible terrain, in combination with Allied logistical weakness, saved the German army in the fall of 1944.

Moreover, Patton ended up fighting the strongest concentration of German forces in the West. He enjoyed a numerical superiority in virtually every category, but Lorraine had the effect of balancing the playing field somewhat, and as Richard Overy observed, "The line between material resources and victory on the battlefield is anything but a straight one."[6] In Lorraine Patton fought elements of three different German armies—the First, Nineteenth, and Fifth Panzer Armies—comprising eight different corps and eighteen divisions. This assemblage still had some teeth. The six normal infantry divisions were far from first class, but the five volksgrenadier and four panzer grenadier divisions gave solid performances. The four new panzer brigades, built around the superior Panther tank, could have been potent had their training matched their equipment. Still, three of the best panzer divisions in the west—Weitersheim's 11th Panzer, Bayerlein's Panzer Lehr, and Feuchtinger's 21st Panzer Divisions—provided good, if drastically overstrained, mobile defense.

German forces in Lorraine were also fairly well led. Grow felt that Third Army was opposed by a "veteran foe led by skillful and resourceful leaders who thoroughly understood the principles of defense even though they did at times apply them illogically or ineffectively."[7] Many of the German commanders in Lorraine had fought in Russia where a premium was placed on defensive tactics, but it is difficult to adequately judge the value of their eastern experience to the defense of Lorraine for the simple reason that they did not fully appreciate the annihilating power of Allied air power, a misperception that frequently had disastrous results.

Third Army still counted on the highly effective system of direct ground support and interdiction of the XIX TAC despite the poor weather. German air power played virtually no role in the campaign. The absolute American dominance of the skies over Lorraine, and indeed in the West, simply cannot be paid mere lip service. That the Germans could mount an effective defense under such adverse conditions is indicative of their resiliency. But this fact should surprise no one because they did the same thing throughout the Normandy Campaign for two months.

The chief weakness of the German forces opposing Patton, beyond a devastated supply system and manpower shortages, was Hitler's constant "operational" interference. It crushed initiative and suppressed sound tactical thinking. In particular, Hitler's handling of scarce resources in counterattacks was disastrous. Immediate counterattacks to check enemy penetrations and regain lost ground were an integral part of German defensive doctrine, but the premature commitment of the 106th and 112th Panzer Brigades and most of the armored element of Manteuffel's Fifth Panzer Army at Hitler's insistence in September was futile.[8] Instances of successful low-level counterattacks are numerous. When involving well-executed infantry assaults supported by armor against key points and vulnerable areas such as forests or the defense of a hastily established bridgehead under cover of fog, the results were often quite good. Moreover, seen as a means to an end, German counterattack doctrine worked well in Lorraine because it served Hitler's strategy of buying time for the Ardennes offensive. Had the time been taken to carefully coordinate Manteuffel's counterattack against Patton as he pushed Wood's 4th Armored Division to the limit to reach the West Wall, it might have had devastating results.

Despite the handicaps under which they fought, German field commanders nonetheless managed to achieve a relatively successful integration of terrain factors and tactical defensive doctrine. This enabled them to achieve a degree of elasticity in their defense despite the fact that, due to wartime exigencies, "greater reliance was placed on linear 'passive' defenses."[9] Grow concluded that "the German defense of Lorraine as a whole was flexible which is not inconsistent with the fact that it included rigid features."[10] Thus German forces were able to absorb a tremendous amount of punishment and roll with Third Army's punches. They were continually helped in this regard by Patton's almost exclusive tactic of attacking on a broad front.

Patton's "thin crust" hypothesis was essentially correct in September; Knobelsdorff's line had no depth. But he took the wrong lesson from this fact, believing that Third Army could slice through a dispersed defense with sustained pressure all along the front and that he, not the Germans, could dictate the nature of the fighting. Yet with Third Army continually repulsed at the river in the opening stages, it is questionable who had the initiative. He pressed the Moselle too thinly, and as Nat Frankel observed, "even Patton's idolaters admit his tactical miscalculations at this juncture."[11] Patton had criticized Bradley in mid-July for his failure to recognize the need for concentration as First Army struggled to break out of the hedge-row country in Normandy. He confidently asserted at the time, "I could break through in three days if I commanded. They try to push all along the front and have no power anywhere. All that is necessary now is to take chances by leading with armored divisions and covering their advance with air bursts. Such an attack would have to be made on a narrow sector."[12]

Bradley later built on Patton's concentration theme in designing "Cobra," but Weigley made the interesting point that the principle of concentration of effort was never extensively utilized by American commanders, including Patton, during the fighting in Northwest Europe. Following the successful example of "Cobra," noted Weigley, American commanders "reverted to assaults on a broad front, not only strategically but operationally, within a single army."[13] The first and only time in the campaign Patton attempted concentrated action on a large scale was after Wood's penetration to Chateau-Salins.

The solution to the problem of an enemy capable of reforming his line relatively quickly based on fixed anchor positions was a clean breach that did not allow the line to reform. Patton had been lucky to pierce Knobelsdorff's line with a single combat command as part of an effort along a broad front, and in doing so, he achieved a *break-in* and a *breakthrough* of the German defense in one rapid slicing motion. His plan to exploit the Chateau-Salins success represented his best idea in September and ultimately of the entire campaign and characterized the speed at which he could change gears when an opportunity presented itself.

The principal characteristic of the proposed maneuver was a greater concentration of effort on a narrower front utilizing armored forces aided by motorized infantry. When the time came to concentrate behind Wood, the vanguard of Third Army was poised to begin another breakin operation against the West Wall, and Patton quickly proposed an attack on a small section of the West Wall nine miles wide, but there were some problems with the scheme of maneuver. With the Germans presenting a solid front and knowing from which direction Third Army had to advance, Patton had to seek surprise in time and scale. This was why it was so important to transfer the 7th Armored to Eddy quickly. Eddy needed the reinforcement. Patton hesitated in doing so because he was trying to execute two decisive operations simultaneously, one with XX Corps at Metz and one with XII Corps. The result was the incorrect employment of the 7th Armored Division and the failure to reinforce the true opportunity afforded by Wood's penetration.

Patton failed to definitely state his intentions regarding the employment of Silvester's 7th Armored Division. Walker and the Third Army staff had designed a plan to push Silvester's armor through the Arnaville bridgehead to cut off Metz from the rear. The planned employment of the armor remained in effect even after Bradley was satisfied that enough of Third Army had crossed the river by the 14th to allow it to continue offensive operations. Kemp called the plan "Real Pattonesque" but noted a number of difficulties. Only one need be mentioned here. The principal flaw was that XII Corps was not in a position to guard Silvester's right flank at the time. More importantly, XX Corps was not in a position to guard Eddy's left flank if and when he started for the West Wall. On September 16, all three combat commands of Silvester's division were engaged in the bridgehead area, and this operation continued well past the September 17 date for Patton's offensive with XII Corps.[14] This was a perfect example of the less-than-stellar coordination achieved between his corps in Lorraine.

Another problem in the scheme of maneuver at this point was the intention to deal with Knobelsdorff's defense in depth with armor leading. At Avranches Patton had successfully led the breakout with armor, but there was no subsequent need to deal with a continuous man-made defensive line in depth beyond that point. The West Wall, on the other hand, was a prepared defensive position. His first concern was getting there as quickly as possible so that he might go through it "like shit through a goose" as he had promised, but at no time did Patton consider a pitched battle against the West Wall a possibility. Proof lies in his instructions to Eddy, who once through the line was to drive XII Corps "straight to the Rhine in the vicinity of Worms" and "grab a bridgehead before it [the bridge] is blown up."[15] The West Wall was an afterthought.

In mid-September it was true that the West Wall was still unprepared, but the axis of Patton's advance would take him straight into the strongest portion of the line. The lessons derivable from Silvester's experience butting his head against the permanent fortifications around Metz suggested that Wood might not crack the West Wall so easily. Grow observed that in order for Patton to have penetrated the West Wall with Wood and Baade and exploited the success, there had to be both initial power and follow-up strength "proportional to the width and depth of the penetration."[16] Eddy did not have the strength to penetrate and sustain a fight through the West Wall without reinforcement. The addition of the 7th Armored to XII Corps was thus crucial. It, together with the 4th and 6th Armored Divisions (Patton still had Leclerc's 2nd French Armored Division as well) represented a potent striking force.

Only maximizing the element of surprise could guarantee capturing a bridgehead over the Rhine. To achieve surprise, XII Corps' advance had to be relatively fluid from the start and uninterrupted by German resistance. Patton stood a good chance of succeeding in this on September 17. If the Germans could not achieve a rapid, coordinated effort against the vanguard of Third Army on their own terms, as Manteuffel's offensive proved, there was little prospect of containing the 4th Armored Division and the follow-on elements once involved in a running battle for the West Wall. Knobelsdorff would have had a difficult time coping with Patton had he been able to turn the campaign from a static one to a fluid one.

Patton was on the verge of accomplishing this very feat, but at the critical moment he deferred to Eddy's timetable rather than insisting on his own. Gaffey was sent in to get things going but came back convinced that Eddy was right. A serious problem with Patton's operations on the Moselle was his failure to keep a tight grip on developments. He tried desperately hard not to micromanage the campaign, and the result was too great a reliance on his mobile battle philosophy of minimal interference. Many of the difficulties arising throughout the campaign can be traced directly to this tendency. The moment was opportune for Patton to exert the ruthless driving power that has made him famous, but he declined. XII Corps was well positioned for a strike deep into Knobelsdorff's defense, and an excellent opportunity was missed by the master of opportunism. However, there are appropriate questions to ask in regard to the ability of Third Army to sustain such an advance from a supply perspective.

Third Army still suffered from gasoline and artillery shortages as Wood prepared to move against the West Wall, but by September 14 the army had received its first delivery of gasoline supplied by rail. The army After Action Report recorded this development as a "great help."[17] Nevertheless, at the same time, the rationing system was reworked, allotting five thousand gallons per day for the infantry divisions and twenty-five thousand gallons per day for the armored divisions. Even with the rationing, Third Army had less than a half-day supply of gasoline at any one time and would not even approach two days' supply until late October.[18] With only a quarter of the fuel that had been expended per day in August now available, it is likely that the gasoline rationing would have impeded Wood's division from "racing" to the West Wall unless all available army fuel stocks were thrown behind his drive. This was unlikely as Patton was still pressing hard at Metz.

Artillery ammunition remained a serious problem as well, with Patton noting on the 18th that "we are very short."[19] Though his enthusiasm for the plan continued unabated until Mantueffel's counterattack revealed its true scale, Wood had already become concerned with the effect the logistical situation would have on the proposed advance. He stated that "this job of getting supplies across the river [Moselle] and on the roads is getting to be a major problem." Consequently, he believed that "this will not be a very fast operation—no blitz."[20] Coming from Patton's best armored commander, this was not an encouraging forecast.

Third Army's logistical shortfalls covered a wide range of important items. On September 24 Patton's assistant Adjutant General, Lieutenant Colonel E. W. Hartman, sent Bradley a short letter strongly suggesting that the shortage of 60-mm mortars and .30 caliber rifles was "seriously affecting the combat efficiency of the Third Army units."[21] He indicated that the army was short 475 rifles, 290 mortars, and nearly 830 .30 caliber machine guns. McBride had notified Patton in writing on September 20 that his infantry were short these items (see Table 12.1). Nothing had been done to correct the problem, he stated, even though the items were listed as a "critical shortage in the Daily G-4 report."[22]

Such shortages were generally reflective of all the infantry divisions of Third Army. To sustain the kind of rapier Patton envisaged the 4th Armored and the follow-on elements to be, he might have had to strip some of the stay-behind divisions, namely the 5th and 90th Infantry Divisions, of all sorts of minor ordnance. Though able to stretch his supplies farther than his fellow army commanders, the logistical situation threatened to be a real problem for Patton's proposed advance on September 14.

More than continued shortages of vital supplies plotted to hinder Patton's plans. By September 17, the day Montgomery launched his great airborne offensive into Holland, the weather became a factor in Patton's

Table 12.1
80th Infantry Division Ordnance Shortages, September 1944

Item	Short
Gun, machine, cal. .30, light	31
Gun, machine, cal. .30, heavy	11
Launcher, grenade, M7	79
Launcher, rocket, AT	42
Mortar, 60mm, with mount	28
Rifle, cal. .30, M1903A4, Sniper	14
Rifle, Browning, automatic, cal. .30	100
Tank, medium	12

Source: "80th Infantry Division List of Critical Shortages as of September 1944," 80th Infantry Division AAR, September 1944, MMRB.

Lorraine campaign in a significant way. He appears to have recognized this, stating on the 17th that "the ground is so slippery that it has adversely affected our tanks."[23] The previous day he recorded that it was so wet that the tanks had to be winched up hill. But he saw the weather in relative terms. "I always feel," he added, that "it is just as hard on the enemy, harder, as he is less well equipped,"[24] a sentiment previously voiced in Tunisia. The obvious observation about the weather was that it would only deteriorate as winter approached. Compared to the terrible flood conditions of November, September still held the best opportunity to make a swift-moving strike against the West Wall work.

Ultimately, the question of the feasibility of Patton's plan is problematical because the logistical element always threatened to strangle his options in September. Yet attacking as planned would have meant, at the very least, the retention of the initiative for Third Army. Had a great success been achieved, perhaps including an exploitable breach of the West Wall, who can say what support Eisenhower and Bradley may have thrown behind Third Army and its superaggressive commander. Bradley already had his hopes pinned on his former boss as he became more disillusioned with Eisenhower's deference to Montgomery. The chief obstacle to Third Army's advance, however, was Metz, and Patton consistently failed to handle the city properly on the operational level.

In his memoirs, Patton admitted to making only one mistake during the war, his raid on Hammelburg to rescue American prisoners. According to Harkins, however, he also admitted that "his insistence upon directly assaulting instead of bypassing Metz" was an error.[25] Indeed, Metz was the key to the entire campaign, and the long siege there was of his own making, but it may have had a great psychological effect on Patton who simply refused to allow the American army to be rebuked by an old fortress.

The best tactic against Metz was to screen it. Lieutenant General Guy Simonds, commander of the II Canadian Corps, had wanted to screen Boulogne, Dunkirk, and other coastal fortresses to free up forces for a drive on Antwerp. Proof that the Metz fortifications were containable was evident by the fact that the largest and most powerful forts—Driant, Jeanne d'Arc, and others—remained operational and were successfully screened by Irwin's 5th Infantry Division long after the envelopment was complete. A rapid envelopment in September, when the ground still permitted good mobility, would have completely disrupted the German defense of the entire area. Grow believed that such action could have given Patton an opportunity to concentrate a strike against the West Wall. "If one infantry division and one armored division," he stated, "had been directed straight at the West Wall from Thionville, with no regard to the Metz operation, and a second armored division had been initially in reserve to exploit a break in the Wall, we should have had an example of attack on a narrow front with a good chance of major success."[26]

Patton's decision to completely reduce Metz made any quick movement eastward impossible and seriously hindered the flow of Third Army operations. He gave the difficult operation to Walker and told him to get on with it. "It is hard to resist the conclusion," noted Hogg, "that in this affair Patton was out of his depth and knew it."[27] More likely, he had no idea what he was up against, but this should not have precluded a tight reign on operations as they continued to falter through September. He allowed the battle at Metz to drift and was noticeably absent from the operations, not visiting XX Corps headquarters or any division in the corps until September 16, a full ten days after operations had started and a period characterized by small advances (see Table 12.2). He ventured forth to discuss developments with Walker only once during the month. When XX Corps got bogged down at Metz, he was not quite sure what to do. As he had done in Tunisia when the going got tough, he set his mind to grinding it out. As Appleman stated, "Patton's operation in the vicinity of Metz . . . was poor and showed a lack of imaginative generalship."[28]

Though Patton incorrectly maintained his focus on Metz, the initial failures there, especially at Fort Driant, opened his eyes to the necessity for a comprehensive plan for reducing the fortifications and subsequently developed a good learning curve for the art of the set-piece battle against fixed defenses. By mid-October, much time and effort had been expended on the various plans for systematically reducing Metz. When viewed in isolation, Patton's final operations against Metz showed a good deal of skill. He was more than capable of conducting a tedious set-piece attack against a fortified position. Yet additional problems arose after the Metz operation had been completed.

After Metz had been enveloped, Patton had difficulty in coordinating the thrusts of his two corps. Gabel labeled the campaign after Metz on the corps level as a "disjointed affair, with little cooperation between corps, and little continuity from one operation to the next."[29] The difficulty stemmed directly from Patton's insistence that Metz be physically occupied rather than simply screened. The necessity of having the 5th Infantry Division turn inward toward the city's center, instead of moving east in conjunction with Eddy's left wing, meant that the corps advances were staggered from the start. This situation could have been fixed but Patton never saw the need,

Table 12.2
Patton and Staff Visits to Divisions and Corps during September 1944

September 5	Patton	XX Corps
September 6	Gay	XII Corps
September 7	Gaffey	XX Corps, 5th Inf Div
September 8	Patton	XII Corps
September 9	Gaffey	XV Corps
	Harkins	XX Corps
September 11	Gaffey	12th AG
September 12	Patton	12th AG
	Gaffey	12th AG, XX Corps
September 13	Patton	XII Corps, XV Corps
September 14	Gaffey	XX Corps
September 15	Patton	12th AG
September 16	Patton	XX Corps, 7th Armd Div, 5th Inf Div
	Gay	XII Corps, XV Corps
September 17	Gaffey	XII Corps
September 18	Patton	XII Corps, XV Corps
	Gaffey	XX Corps
September 19	Patton	XII Corps, 4th Armd Div
	Gay	XX Corps
September 20	Patton	12th AG
	Gaffey	XII Corps, XV Corps
September 21	Patton	SHAEF
	Gaffey	XII Corps
September 22	Patton	90th Inf Div
	Gaffey	XX Corps
September 23	Patton	12th AG
	Gaffey	XX Corps
	Harkins	XII Corps
September 24	Patton	XII Corps
	Gaffey	XII Corps
September 25	Patton	12th AG

Source: Hobart Gay's daily diary; Hugh J. Gaffey's daily log entries; Blumenson's *The Patton Papers*, II; Patton's memoir *War as I Knew It*; and typescript copies of Patton's daily diary that contain information not included in Blumenson's work.

and the problem was further exacerbated by allowing Walker and Eddy to repeatedly stop their offensives at different times.

Carlo D'Este characterized the ill-defined yet vital ingredient for a successful commander as "the ability to sense instinctively the right course of action on the field of battle" and believed that Patton possessed this essential trait to a "marked degree."[30] According to Hogg, however, Patton instinctively chose the correct course of action only when he had his enemy off balance and constantly moving. But "if [the] enemy . . . prepared defensive positions, Patton's touch was less sure and he was prone to reinforce his own weakness and persist in courses of action even when they had been demonstrated to be wrong or ineffective."[31]

Eisenhower remarked many years after the war that Patton intensely disliked "the heavy fighting necessary to break through. . . . When we got into dirty . . . fighting [on] the Moselle and later when he was trying to fight his way to the relief of Bastogne, he was apt to become pessimistic and discouraged."[32] He felt Patton's successes in open situations attributable to his "emotional tenseness and impulsiveness."[33] One can see how these characteristics would not mesh well with the intricate movement required in a tight battle like that at the Moselle. There is no question that Patton could be highly creative, particularly when he had the enemy on the run. The fact nevertheless remains that he did not respond to the difficulties in Lorraine with the bold and daring imagination reminiscent of the amphibious hops in Sicily or the breakout at Avranches.

Napoleon once said that a commander had to be guided by his own experience or genius. Patton's armored genius is beyond doubt, but his limited experience in static fighting prior to Lorraine was a disadvantage. He had to learn the art of the set-piece battle from scratch. Blumenson stated that the American army commanders in Europe "showed a decided tendency to stay within the odds, the safe way of operating, and refrained from opting for the imaginative and the unexpected."[34] He intended this criticism for everyone *but* Patton, yet in a very real sense the censure reflected Patton's performance in Lorraine and brings the discussion to one final point—and that concerns Patton's role in the campaign, the larger strategic picture, and his relationship with Bradley and Eisenhower.

Patton's operations in Normandy were intended to achieve decisive results at the sharp end of Allied thrusts. Eisenhower had retained him in command after the incident in Sicily because he envisioned Patton spearheading the drive out of the Normandy bridgehead. Patton's task in Lorraine, however, was meant to be completely diversionary. Eisenhower never entertained any serious consideration of using Third Army again as his lead horse until the very end of the campaign when Patton received the support of the strategic air forces. In his secondary role, Patton became a magnet for German reserves. As the official history noted, "The battle for Lorraine had forced the German high command to divert substantial forces from the defense of the Rhur. This dispersion of enemy resources, especially armor, had been particularly telling in the early phases of the battle for the Aachen gateway."[35]

Patton was still on probation when he entered Lorraine. According to Wood the whole Patton-Bradley-Eisenhower command relationship affected Patton's performance in Northwest Europe. Wood was adamant in his postwar writings that Patton was reluctant to "assert himself too strongly" after the slapping episodes of 1943.[36] Eisenhower still deemed it essential that he be kept under control. Bradley was Patton's great restraint. Though their relationship was cordial, Patton had little faith in Bradley's intuitive understanding of operational warfare and resented his repeated interference. Bradley disrupted Patton's operations in early November when he withdrew use of the 83rd Infantry Division, but Patton failed to adapt to the circumstances and continued on as if nothing had changed. This reflected his belief in Tunisia that one should be careful of ever changing a plan.

The result was caution on Patton's part. At a press conference on September 7 he stated, "I am one of the most cautious people because I have been shot twice. I haven't any ambition to be shot more, and I don't take chances at all."[37] As early as August 9 Patton wrote, "If I were on my own, I would take bigger chances than I am now permitted to take."[38] Blumenson has reinforced this idea, claiming that "bound to execute the plans formulated by his superiors, Patton suffered from his helplessness. . . . He rid himself of frustration and resentment in his diary and in his letters to his wife by castigating his bosses for their inability to think big and brilliantly."[39]

Although he regained some of his swagger after the success of the Normandy campaign, Patton certainly never brought his full improvisational style to bear in Lorraine. But excuses cannot be made for his failure to make sound tactical decisions. His difficulties were produced by a failure to sometimes face the obvious but also due to the incompatibility of his established battle philosophy with battle conditions in Lorraine, particularly his concepts of minimal interference and the utilization of speed. However, had he not abandoned his most cherished concept, that of avoiding the enemy's main strength, his operations might have been far more successful.

NOTES

1. Hugh M. Cole, *The Lorraine Campaign*, U.S. Army in World War II: European Theater of Operations (Washington, D.C.: Center for Military History, 1984), 607.

2. B. L. Montgomery, *The Memoirs of Field Marshal the Viscount Montgomery of Alamein* (London: Collins, 1958), 81.

3. Martin Blumenson, *Patton: The Man behind the Legend, 1885–1945* (New York: William Morrow, 1985), 241.

4. Alfred D. Chandler, ed., *The Papers of Dwight D. Eisenhower: The War Years* (Baltimore: Johns Hopkins University Press, 1970), II: 1357.

5. Carl von Clausewitz, *On War*, edited and translated by Michael Howard and Peter Paret (Princeton, N.J.: Princeton University Press, 1976), 357. Blaskowitz stated, "[W]e wished we had had fortifications in the interior of France, particularly along the Seine and Somme Rivers. Our withdrawal . . . would have been much more satisfactory." ETHINT 32, "The Defense of Metz," an Interview with Genoberst Johannes Blaskowitz, July 20, 1945, Donald S. Detwiler, with Charles B. Burdick and Jurgen Rowher, eds., *World War II German Military Studies* (New York: Garland Publishing, 1979), II.

6. Richard Overy, *Why the Allies Won* (London: Johnathan Cape, 1995), 316.

7. Robert W. Grow, "Flexibility in Defense," Hist 314.7, Box: "General Grow, Special Studies on World War II," United States Army Military History Institute (USAMHI), Carlisle Barracks, Pa.

8. For all his military ineptness there seems to be some validity in the argument that Hitler saved the German army from disintegration twice—once in December 1941 by demanding that it stand its ground in front of Moscow, and again in September 1944 in front of the West Wall. See John Strawson, *Hitler as Military Commander* (London: Batsford, 1971), 235.

9. Keith E. Bonn, *When the Odds Were Even: The Vosges Mountains Campaign, October 1944–January 1945* (Novato, Calif.: Presidio, 1994), 39.

10. Grow, "Flexibility in Defense."

11. Nat Frankel and Larry Smith, *Patton's Best: An Informal History of the 4th Armored Division* (New York: Hawthorn, 1978), 65.

12. Martin Blumenson, *The Patton Papers* (Boston: Houghton Mifflin, 1974), II: 482.

13. Russell F. Weigley, *Eisenhower's Lieutenants: The Campaign of France and Germany, 1944–1945* (Bloomington: Indiana University Press, 1981), 729.

14. Cole, *Lorraine Campaign*, 161–177.

15. Blumenson, *Patton Papers*, II: 549.

16. Robert W. Grow, "Broad Front vs Narrow Front," Hist 314.7, Box: "General Grow, Special Studies on World War II," USAMHI.

17. Third Army After Action Report (AAR), Special Collections, United States Military Academy Library, West Point (WP), I: 73.

18. Ronald G. Ruppenthal, *Logistical Support of the Armies*, U.S. Army in World War II: European Theater of Operations (Washington, D.C.: Department of the Army, 1959), II: 194.

19. George S. Patton Diary, September 18, 1944, Special Collections, WP.

20. Cole, *Lorraine Campaign*, 223.

21. E. W. Hartman to Commanding General, Twelfth Army Group, September 24, 1944, Modern Military Reference Branch (MMRB), Suitland, Maryland.

22. Major General H. L. McBride to Commanding General, Third Army, September 20, 1944, MMRB. McBride noted that "to date no replacements have been received for items lost one month ago." Though all the divisions were having supply problems, Eddy singled out McBride's division in late October for its supply discipline. "This division uses more gas than any other," noted Eddy, "and they seem to loose [*sic*] a great many weapons." Manton S. Eddy Diary, October 23, 1944, U.S. Army Infantry School, National Infantry Museum (NIM), Fort Benning, Ga.

23. Blumenson, *Patton Papers*, II: 550.

24. Ibid.

25. Paul D. Harkins, *When the Third Cracked Europe: The Story of Patton's Incredible Army* (Harrisburg, Pa.: Army Times Publishing, 1969), 57.

26. Grow, "Broad Front vs Narrow Front."

27. Ian V. Hogg, *The Biography of General George S. Patton* (New York: Hamlyn, 1982), 123.

28. Roy E. Appleman, "Comments on Grow's Study 'Broad Front vs Narrow Front,' " Hist 314.7, Box: "General Grow, Special Studies on World War II," USAMHI. Table 12.2 reveals that Patton made no less than five trips to see Bradley at Twelfth Army Group Headquarters and one trip to SHAEF, partly to develop further operational plans and partly to hold on to the resources the shift in strategic priority had left him with. He might have gone forward more often if not for the numerous trips to Bradley's headquarters, but this is only speculation.

29. Christopher R. Gabel, *The Lorraine Campaign: An Overview, September–December 1944* (Fort Leavenworth, Kans.: Combat Studies Institute, 1985), 36.

30. Carlo D'Este, *Bitter Victory: The Battle for Sicily, 1943* (New York: HarperCollins, 1988), 61.

31. Hogg, *Biography of George S. Patton*, 153.

32. Eisenhower to Frank McCarthy, January 6, 1966, copy in personal possession of Alan Aimone, Chief of Special Collections, West Point Library. Eisenhower wrote this personal and confidential assessment of Patton for McCarthy, the director of the film *Patton*. In discussing army boundaries with Bradley and Hodges on August 5, Patton recorded his preference to avoid close fighting. "I succeeded in getting the boundary . . . I desire," he wrote, "as it keeps me on the outside—on the running edge." Blumenson, *Patton Papers*, II: 501.

33. Dwight D. Eisenhower, *Crusade in Europe* (Garden City, N.Y.: Doubleday, 1948), 181.

34. Martin Blumenson, "America's World War II Leaders in Europe: Some Thoughts," *Parameters: US Army War College Quarterly* XIX, 4 (December 1989): 3.

35. Cole, *Lorraine Campaign*, 607.

36. John S. Wood, "Thing Remembered and Things Considered," Box 8, Wood Papers, SU, 73. Wood added that there was no worse way to conduct armored operations than those in Brittany. "George Patton knew better, but for some reason was unable to perform as I thought he would," stated Wood, and could only "attribute it again to his being outweighed and submerged by the preponderence and rigidity of the infantry-minded people over him."

37. Blumenson, *Patton Papers*, II: 542.

38. Ibid., 505.

39. Martin Blumenson, *The Battle of the Generals* (New York: William Morrow, 1993), 271–272.

Third Army Order of Battle[1]

III Corps
Major General John Millikin
(October 31–)
87th Infantry Division
(Nov 25–Dec 4, III Corps, XII Corps, Dec 11–)
Major General Frank L. Cullin, Jr.

345th Infantry Regiment

346th Infantry Regiment

347th Infantry Regiment

334th Field Artillery Battalion (105mm) [How Trk-D]

335th Field Artillery Battalion (155mm) [How Trac-D]

336th Field Artillery Battalion (105mm) [How Trk-D]

912th Field Artillery Battalion (105mm) [How Trk-D]

87th Reconnaissance Troop, Mechanized

610th Tank Destroyer Battalion (Dec 14–) [M36]

312th Engineer Combat Battalion

87th Counter Intelligence Corps Detachment

787th Ordnance Light Maintenance Company

XII Corps
Major General Manton S. Eddy
26th Infantry Division
(Oct 12–)
Major General Willard S. Paul

101st Infantry Regiment

104th Infantry Regiment

328th Infantry Regiment

101st Field Artillery Battalion (105mm) [How Trk-D]

102nd Field Artillery Battalion (105mm) [How Trac-D]

180th Field Artillery Battalion (155mm) [How Trk-D]

263rd Field Artillery Battalion (105mm) [How Trk-D]

26th Reconnaissance Troop, Mechanized

761st Tank Battalion (Oct 29–Dec 12)

602nd Tank Destroyer Battalion (Oct 23–Dec 12) [M18][2]

610th Tank Destroyer Battalion (Nov 12–Dec 12) [M36]

691st Tank Destroyer Battalion (Oct 15– Dec 7) [M36]

704th Tank Destroyer Battalion (Oct 14–Oct 16) [M18]

390th AAA Auto-Wpns Battalion

101st Engineer Combat Battalion

26th Counter Intelligence Corps Detachment

726th Ordnance Light Maintenance Company

35th Infantry Division
Major General Paul W. Baade

134th Infantry Regiment

137th Infantry Regiment

320th Infantry Regiment

127th Field Artillery Battalion (155mm) [How Trac-D]

161st Field Artillery Battalion (105mm) [How Trk-D]

216th Field Artillery Battalion (105mm) [How Trk-D]

219th Field Artillery Battalion (105mm) [How Trk-D]

35th Reconnaissance Troop, Mechanized

737th Tank Battalion (Sept 11–Nov 22, Nov 27–   )

654th Tank Destroyer Battalion [M10–M36]

691st Tank Destroyer Battalion (Sept 5–Sept 9) [M36]

448th AAA Auto-Wpns Battalion

60th Engineer Combat Battalion

35th Counter Intelligence Corps Detachment

80th Infantry Division
Major General Horace L. McBride

317th Infantry Regiment

318th Infantry Regiment

319th Infantry Regiment

313th Field Artillery Battalion (105mm) [How Trk-D]

314th Field Artillery Battalion (105mm) [How Trk-D]
315th Field Artillery Battalion (155mm) [How Trac-D]
905th Field Artillery Battalion (105mm) [How Trk-D]
80th Reconnaissance Troop, Mechanized
702nd Tank Battalion
610th Tank Destroyer Battalion (Nov 23–Dec 6) [M36]
691st Tank Destroyer Battalion (Sept 16–Sept 18) [M36]
808th Tank Destroyer Battalion (Sept 25–   ) [M36]
633rd AAA Auto-Wpns Battalion
305th Engineer Combat Battalion
780th Ordnance Light Maintenance Company
80th Counter Intelligence Corps Detachment

4th Armored Division
Major General John S. Wood (–Dec 3)
Major General Hugh J. Gaffey (Dec 3–   )

8th Tank Battalion
35th Tank Battalion
37th Tank Battalion
10th Armored Infantry Battalion
51st Armored Infantry Battalion
53rd Armored Infantry Battalion
22nd Armored Field Artillery Battalion (105mm)
66th Armored Field Artillery Battalion (105mm)
94th Armored Field Artillery Battalion (105mm)
25th Cavalry Reconnaissance Squadron, Mechanized
504th Counter Intelligence Corps Detachment
489th AAA Auto-Wpns Battalion
24th Armored Engineer Battalion

6th Armored Division
(Sept 20–Dec 11, Dec 11–   , III Corps)
Major General Robert W. Grow

15th Tank Battalion
68th Tank Battalion
69th Tank Battalion
737th Tank Battalion (Nov 22–Dec 3)
9th Armored Infantry Battalion
44th Armored Infantry Battalion

50th Armored Infantry Battalion
128th Armored Field Artillery Battalion (105mm)
212th Armored Field Artillery Battalion (105mm)
231st Armored Field Artillery Battalion (105mm)
86th Cavalry Reconnaissance Squadron, Mechanized
506th Counter Intelligence Corps Detachment
777th AAA Auto-Wpns Battalion
128th Armored Ordnance Maintenance Battalion
25th Armored Engineer Battalion

12th Armored Division
(Dec 8–)
Major General R. R. Allen

23rd Tank Battalion
43rd Tank Battalion
714th Tank Battalion
17th Armored Infantry Battalion
56th Armored Infantry Battalion
66th Armored Infantry Battalion
493rd Field Artillery Battalion
494th Field Artillery Battalion
495th Field Artillery Battalion
92nd Cavalry Reconnaissance Squadron, Mechanized
512th Counter Intelligence Corps Detachment
572nd AAA Auto-Wpns Battalion
134th Armored Ordnance Maintenance Battalion
119th Armored Engineer Battalion

XX Corps
Major General Walton H. Walker
5th Infantry Division
Major General S. Leroy Irwin

2nd Infantry Regiment
10th Infantry Regiment
11th Infantry Regiment
19th Field Artillery Battalion (105mm) [How Trk-D]
21st Field Artillery Battalion (155mm) [How Trac-D]
46th Field Artillery Battalion (105mm) [How Trk-D]
50th Field Artillery Battalion (105mm) [How Trk-D]

5th Reconnaissance Troop, Mechanized
735th Tank Battalion (–Oct 20, Nov 1–)
774th Tank Destroyer Battalion
(Sept 14–Sept 24, Nov 5–Nov 22) [M36]
818th Tank Destroyer Battalion [M10–M36]
449th AAA Auto-Wpns Battalion (–Nov 23, Nov 29–)
7th Engineer Combat Battalion
5th Counter Intelligence Corps Detachment
705th Ordnance Light Maintenance Company

83rd Infantry Division
(Sept 21–Oct 12,   –Nov 11)
Major General R. C. Macon

329th Infantry Regiment
330th Infantry Regiment
331st Infantry Regiment
322nd Field Artillery Battalion (105mm) [How Trk-D]
323rd Field Artillery Battalion (105mm) [How Trk-D]
324th Field Artillery Battalion (155mm) [How Trac-D]
908th Field Artillery Battalion (105mm) [How Trk-D]
83rd Reconnaissance Troop, Mechanized
774th Tank Battalion
802nd Tank Destroyer Battalion [Towed AT]
453rd AAA Auto-Wpns Battalion
308th Engineer Combat Battalion
83rd Counter Intelligence Corps Detachment
783rd Ordnance Light Maintenance Company

90th Infantry Division
Major General Raymond S. McLain
Major General James A. Van Fleet

357th Infantry Regiment
358th Infantry Regiment
359th Infantry Regiment
343rd Field Artillery Battalion (105mm) [How Trk-D]
344th Field Artillery Battalion (105mm) [How Trk-D]
345th Field Artillery Battalion (155mm) [How Trac-D]
915th Field Artillery Battalion (105mm) [How Trk-D]
90th Reconnaissance Troop, Mechanized

712th Tank Battalion (–Sept 20)

607th Tank Destroyer Battalion (–Nov 2, Nov 20–Nov 27) [M36]

773rd Tank Destroyer Battalion (Nov 2–   ) [M10–M36]

537th AAA Auto-Wpns Battalion

315th Engineer Combat Battalion

90th Counter Intelligence Corps Detachment

790th Ordnance Light Maintenance Company

95th Infantry Division
(Oct 18–   )
Major General Harry L. Twaddle

377th Infantry Regiment

378th Infantry Regiment

379th Infantry Regiment

358th Field Artillery Battalion (105mm) [How Trk-D]

359th Field Artillery Battalion (105mm) [How Trk-D]

360th Field Artillery Battalion (155mm) [How Trac-D]

920th Field Artillery Battalion (105mm) [How Trk-D]

95th Reconnaissance Troop, Mechanized

735th Tank Battalion (Oct 20–Nov 29)

778th Tank Battalion (Nov 11–   )

607th Tank Destroyer Battalion (Nov 1–   ) [M36]

614th Tank Destroyer Battalion (Nov 22–Nov 23) [Towed AT]

705th Tank Destroyer Battalion (Oct 15–Nov 2) [M18]

773rd Tank Destroyer Battalion (Oct 25–Nov 7) [M10–M36]

774th Tank Destroyer Battalion (Oct 20–Oct 26) [M36]

818th Tank Destroyer Battalion (Oct 20–Oct 26) [M10–M36]

547th AAA Auto-Wpns Battalion

320th Engineer Combat Battalion

95th Counter Intelligence Corps Detachment

795th Ordnance Light Maintenance Company

7th Armored Division
(–Sept 25)
Major General Lindsay McD. Silvester

17th Tank Battalion

31st Tank Battalion

40th Tank Battalion

814th Tank Destroyer Battalion [M10–M36]

23rd Armored Infantry Battalion

38th Armored Infantry Battalion

48th Armored Infantry Battalion

434th Armored Field Artillery Battalion (105mm)

440th Armored Field Artillery Battalion (105mm)

489th Armored Field Artillery Battalion (105mm)

87th Cavalry Reconnaissance Squadron, Mechanized

507th Counter Intelligence Corps Detachment

203rd AAA Auto-Wpns Battalion

129th Armored Ordnance Maintenance Battalion

33rd Armored Engineer Battalion

10th Armored Division
(Nov 2–)
Major General William H. H. Morris, Jr.

3rd Tank Battalion

11th Tank Battalion

21st Tank Battalion

20th Armored Infantry Battalion

54th Armored Infantry Battalion

61st Armored Infantry Battalion

419th Armored Field Artillery Battalion (105mm)

420th Armored Field Artillery Battalion (105mm)

423rd Armored Field Artillery Battalion (105mm)

90th Cavalry Reconnaissance Squadron, Mechanized

510th Counter Intelligence Corps Detachment

609th Tank Destroyer Battalion (Oct 16–) [M18]

638th Tank Destroyer Battalion (–Oct 15) [M18]

796th AAA Auto-Wpns Battalion

132nd Armored Ordnance Maintenance Battalion

55th Armored Engineer Battalion

XV Corps
Major General Wade H. Haislip
(September 9–September 29)
79th Infantry Division
(September 9–September 29)
Major General Ira T. Wyche

313th Infantry Regiment

314th Infantry Regiment

315th Infantry Regiment

310th Field Artillery Battalion (105mm) [How Trk-D]

311th Field Artillery Battalion (105mm) [How Trk-D]

312th Field Artillery Battalion (155mm) [How Trac-D]

904th Field Artillery Battalion (105mm) [How Trk-D]

79th Reconnaissance Troop, Mechanized

191st Tank Battalion (Dec 1–   )

773rd Tank Destroyer Battalion (Sept 9–Oct 12) [M10–M36]

813th Tank Destroyer Battalion (–Sept 9, Oct 12–   ) [M10–M36]

463rd AAA Auto-Wpns Battalion

304th Engineer Combat Battalion

79th Counter Intelligence Corps Detachment

779th Ordnance Light Maintenance Company

2nd French Armored Division[3]
(September 9–September 29)
Major General Jacques Leclerc

12 Cuirs Armored Regiment

12 R.C.A. Armored Regiment

501 R.C.C. Armored Regiment

I Infantry Battalion

II Infantry Battalion

III Infantry Battalion

3 Regimental Artillery (Colonial)

40 Regimental Artillery (Nord Afric)

64 Regimental Artillery (OB)

1 Light Antiaircraft Artillery Regiment

1st Regiment B Fusilers Marins

1 Tank Destroyer Regiment

Divisional Reconnaissance Armored Regiment

(Armored Cars)

1 Regiment Spahis Marocains

13 Engineer Battalion

NOTES

1. Compiled from Shelby L. Stanton, *World War II Order of Battle* (New York: Galahad, 1991).

2. The designations for the tank destroyers include the early model M10 "Wolverine," the newer M18 "Hellcat" with a 76-mm gun like the M10, and the truly formidable M36, which possessed a 90-mm gun. The designation M10–M36, represents sequential outfittings meaning that the battalion initially went into battle as an M10 unit and was converted to M36 equipment.

3. Taken from Eddy Florentin, *Battle of the Falaise Gap* (London: Elek Books, 1965), end papers. In total, the 2nd French Armored Division contained 514 officers, 12,830 other ranks, 300 tanks (Shermans and Stuarts), 460 guns, and 3,120 vehicles.

German Order of Battle[1]

Supreme Commander
OB West

Field Marshal Gerd von Rundstedt

Army Group B[2]

Field Marshal Walter Model

Army Group G

Generaloberst Johannes Blaskowitz (–Sept 21)
General der Panzertruppen Hermann Balck (Sept 21–   )

First Army

General der Panzertruppen Otto von Knobelsdorff (–Dec 4)
General der Infanterie Hans von Obstfelder (Dec 4–   )

401st Volks Artillery Corps
(–Dec 5)

5 Artillery Battalions

404th Volks Artillery Corps

LXXXII Corps[3]

General der Artillerie Johann Sinnhuber
General der Infanterie Walter Hoernlein

25th Panzer Grenadier Division[4]

35th Panzer Grenadier Regiment

19th Volksgrenadier Division

Colonel Karl Britzelmayr
59th Regiment
73rd Regiment
74th Regiment

416th Division

Generalleutenant Kurt Pflieger
713th Regiment
714th Regiment

XIII SS Corps

Generalleutenant der Waffen-SS Herman Priess (–Nov 15)
Generalleutenant der Waffen-SS Max Simon (Nov 15–)

21st Panzer Division
(Nov 13–)

Generalleutenant Edgar Feuchtinger
22nd Panzer Regiment
125th Panzer Grenadier Regiment
192nd Panzer Grenadier Regiment

48th Division[5]

Generalleutenant Carl Casper
128th Regiment

36th Volksgrenadier Division
(Nov 13–)

Generalmajor August Wellm
87th Regiment
118th Regiment
165th Regiment

347th Division[6]
(November 17–   )

17th SS Panzer Grenadier Division

Generalleutenant der Waffen-SS Werner Ostendorff
37th SS Panzer Grenadier Regiment
38th SS Panzer Grenadier Regiment

559th Volksgrenadier Division

Generalmajor Kurt Freiherr von Muehlen
1125th Regiment
1126th Regiment
1127th Regiment

Division Number 462[7]

Generalleutenant Walther Krause
Generalleutenant Heinrich Kittel (Nov 11–   )
Fahnenjunkerschule (Officer Candidate School) Regiment [1,800 men]
Unterfuehrerschule (NCO School) Regiment [1,500]
1010th Security Regiment [600]
2 Replacement Battalions
1 Machine Gun Company
1 Engineer Battalion
1–2 Flak Battalions
1 Artillery Battalion
4 Companies Waffen-SS Nachrichtenschule troops
(Signal School)
Few Luftwaffe troops
IV FLAK CORPS (2 Battalions)
22nd and 25th Fortress Regiments Staffs

XLVII Panzer Corps[8]

General der Panzertruppen Heinrich Freiherr von Luettwitz

3rd Panzer Grenadier Division[9]

General Hans Hecker
8th Panzer Grenadier Regiment
29th Panzer Grenadier Regiment

553rd Volksgrenadier Division[10]

1119th Regiment

1120th Regiment

1121th Regiment

First Parachute Army

(Elements)

15th Panzer Grenadier Division

Generalleutenant Eberhard Rodt

104th Panzer Grenadier Regiment

115th Panzer Grenadier Regiment

111th Panzer Brigade

112th Panzer Brigade

LXXXIX Corps[11]

General der Infanterie Gustav Hoehne

361st Volksgrenadier Division
(Oct 23–)

Colonel Alfred Philippi

951st Regiment

952nd Regiment

953rd Regiment

First Army Reserve
(September)

106th Panzer Brigade

Nineteenth Army

General der Infanterie Friedrich Weise

IV Luftwaffe Field Corps

16th Division

Generalleutenant Ernst Haeckel
221st Regiment
223rd Regiment
225th Regiment

LXXXV Corps

LXIV Corps

Fifth Panzer Army[12]

General der Panzertruppen Hasso von Manteuffel

LVIII Panzer Corps

General Walter Krueger

113th Panzer Brigade

719th Division

Generalleutenant Felix Schwalbe
723rd Regiment

11th Panzer Division[13]

Generalleutenant Wend von Wietersheim
15th Panzer Regiment
110th Panzer Grenadier Regiment
111th Panzer Grenadier Regiment

Panzer Lehr Division
(November 21–December 5)

Generalleutenant Fritz Bayerlein

Mischellany

9th Flak Division[14]

3rd Parachute Replacement Regiment
92nd Luftwaffe Field Regiment
268th Artillery Regiment
761st Artillery Regiment

NOTES

1. Constructing a German order of battle for Lorraine is difficult in that many of the divisions identified were committed piecemeal throughout the campaign. The appelations of "division" or "corps" often times misrepresent exactly what such units contained as far as troops and equipment. This order of battle has been constructed from information contained in Cole's official history and is not meant to be exhaustive. The chief object is to provide the reader with as clear a picture as possible of the different divisions employed against Third Army. In most cases, only the division is identified, with regimental and other attached units provided when available.

2. Model's command included First Army until September 8 when it, along with General der Infanterie Friedrich Weise's Nineteenth Army, were placed under command of Blaskowitz's Army Group G.

3. On September 7 the staff of this corps would move north. The troops in the area thus fell under command of the XIII SS Corps.

4. Eventually under command of General der Infanterie Erich Peterson's XC Corps.

5. Remnants of this division were combined with remnants of the 559 Volksgrenadier Division to form Kampfgruppe "Muehlen" shortly after the November offensive started.

6. Remnants.

7. Upgraded to 462 Volksgrenadier Division and given an extra infantry regiment in November to include the 1215th, 1216th, and 1217th Regiments.

8. Left Lorraine for Ardennes offensive in October.

9. Ranks nearly full, but like all panzer grenadier divisions at this time it lacked the organic tank battalion.

10. The 553rd Volksgrenadier Division was given command of the First Parachute Army troops in the area.

11. Replaced Luettwitz's XLVII Panzer Corps in October.

12. Manteuffel took command of Fifth Panzer Army on September 11. He and the headquarters staff of the Army left the Lorraine area in October to prepare for the Ardennes offensive.

13. 11th Panzer Division, First Army reserve on November 8.

14. Apparently guns only.

Appendix C

Casualties and Replacements[1]

A: Third Army

Casualties

Battle	Non-Battle	Total	Replacements
September 1–September 4		3,635	3,117
		Difference	−518
Phase I: September 5–September 25			
13,357	5,290	18,647	17,088
		Difference	−1,559
Phase II: September 26–November 7			
9,052	11,524	20,576	22,440
		Difference	+1,864
Phase III: November 8–December 2			
22,879	14,785	37,664	27,601
		Difference	−10,063

B: German Army

Actual			Estimated			
P/Ws	Buried	Total	P/Ws	K	W	Total
Phase I: September 5–September 25						
13,462	354	13,816	20,310	11,525	23,790	55,625
Phase II: September 26–November 7						
5,341	1,007	6,348	6,400	8,800	28,000	43,200
Phase III: November 8–December 2						
26,490	1,928	28,418	26,500	13,300	36,500	76,300

[1] Compiled from the Third Army G-1 Section Daily Casualty Reports No. 32, September 1 to No. 124, December 2, 1944, Box 48, PP, LC.

Appendix D

Material Losses[1]

A: Third Army

	Tanks		Artillery	Vehicles, All Types
Light		*Medium*	*75mm & Over*	
Phase I: September 5–September 25				
41		113	16	368
Phase II: September 26–November 7				
17		34	6	120
Phase III: November 8–December 2				
38		101	7	400

B: German Army

Tanks	Artillery	All Types	Vehicles, Total
Phase I: September 5–September 25			
410	392	1,006	1,808
Phase II: September 26–November 7			
176	55	432	663
Phase III: November 8–December 2			
104	382	288	774

[1]Compiled from the Third Army G-1 Section Daily Casualty Reports No. 32, September 1 to No. 124, December 2, 1944, Box 48, PP, LC.

Third Army Operational Directives

5 September 1944

1. Third US Army will—

a. Advance to the east with two Corps abreast; one Corps initially covering right flank and later advancing to the east.

b. Seize bridgehead east of the MOSELLE RIVER.

c. Continue advance to the east to seize a bridgehead east of the RHINE RIVER from KOBLENZ to KARLSRUHE.

2. XX Corps (5th Inf Div, 90th Inf Div, 7th Armd Div and supporting troops) will, without delay—

a. Seize METZ, advance east of the MOSELLE RIVER within zone, continue advance rapidly to the northeast to seize MAINZ and secure a bridgehead east of the RHINE RIVERwithin zone.

b. Be prepared to continue advance to seize FRANKFURT, on Army order.

c. Maintain contact with First US Army on the left.

3. XII Corps (35th Inf Div, 80th Inf Div, 4th Armd Div and supporting troops) will, without delay—

a. Seize Nancy and secure a bridgehead east of the MOSELLE RIVER within zone.

b. Protect south flank of Army until relieved by elements of XV Corps.

c. Be prepared to continue advance rapidly to the northeast, on Army order, to seize MANNHEIM and secure a bridgehead east of the RHINE RIVER within zone.

4. XV Corps (79th Inf Div, 83rd Inf Div, 2nd Fr Armd Div and supporting troops) will, without delay—

a. Move Corps troops and 2nd Fr Armd Div (upon release by First US Army) to an area southeast of TROYES.

b. Protect the south flank of the Army from MONTARGIS to the east, relieving elements of XII Corps.

c. Move 79th Inf Div (upon release by First US Army) to a concentration area southeast of TROYES.

d. Direct the 83rd Inf Div (upon release by VIII Corps) to move to an area selected by XV Corps.

e. Seize line of MOSELLE RIVER within zone.

f. Be prepared to—

(1) Continue advance to the northeast to seize KARLSRUHE and secure a bridgehead east of the RHINE RIVER within zone, or

(2) Move through bridgeheads secured by XII Corps or XX Corps.

5. Army Reserve—

6th Armd Div (upon being released by VIII Corps) will be moved to an area east of TROYES as Army Reserve.

16 September 1944

1. *Boundaries.*

a. Corps boundaries given in Operational Directive, this headquarters, dated 5 September 1944, as changed by Amendment No. 1, this headquarters, dated 11 September 1944, are further changed as shown on attached operations overlay.

b. Boundary between First and Third US Armies remains unchanged.

c. Boundary between Third and Seventh Armies will be announced later.

2. *Missions.*

a. XX Corps—

(1) Continue advance to seize FRANKFURT.

(2) Maintain contact with First US Army on the left.

b. XII Corps—Continue advance rapidly to the northeast, to seize DARM-STADT and secure a bridgehead east of the RHINE RIVER within zone.

c. XV Corps—

(1) Advance to the northeast on Army order, echeloned to the right rear of XII Corps.

(2) Protect right flank of the Army and maintain contact with Seventh US Army.

(3) Be prepared to:

(a) Seize MANNHEIM and secure a bridgehead east of the RHINE RIVER within zone, or

(b) Move through bridgeheads secured by XII Corps or XX Corps.

28 September 1944

1. *Information.*

(Details of the movements of armies and army groups flanking Third Army).

2. *Third US Army will:*

(1) Improve present positions by local counter-attacks to seize and secure the line of departure delineated in Letter of Instruction No. 4, Headquarters Third US Army, 25 September 1944.

(2) Continue aggressive reconnaissance.

(3) Be prepared to resume the advance to the northeast to secure crossings of the RHINE and seize the FRANKFURT-DARMSTADT area.

Boundary Changes.

3. *Corps Missions.*

a. XII Corps will:

(1) (a) Seize and secure high ground in vicinity of CHATEAU SALINS and along general line VIGNY–MONCHEUX–LANEUVEVILLE-EN-SAULNOIS.

(b) Improve position from CHATEAU SALINS to boundary between Sixth and Twelfth Army Groups to contact elements of Seventh Army in vicinity of AVRI-COURT.

(c) Maintain aggressive reconnaissance.

(2) Protect right flank of Army and maintain contact with Seventh US Army.

(3) Be prepared to resume advance to secure RHINE crossings and seize DARMSTADT.

b. XX Corps will:

(1) (a) Reduce enemy forts to consolidate line shown on overlay.

(b) Seize and hold bridgehead east of SEILLE RIVER along general line MARLY–FLEURY–VIGNY.

(c) Maintain aggressive reconnaissance.

(2) Be prepared to:

(a) Continue advance to secure RHINE crossings and seize WEISBADEN and FRANKFURT.

(b) Protect left flank of the Army.

c. Priority for support of Corps Missions:

(1) First Priority—XX Corps (Forts).

(2) Second Priority—XII Corps (CHATEAU SALINS).

(3) Third Priority—XII Corps (high ground along general line VIGNY–MONCHEUX–LANEUVEVILLE-EN-SAULNOIS.

X. Under the supervision of the Army Artillery Officer, all possible avenues of tank attack will be plotted and data prepared. These concentrations will be numbered from north to south and the accomplished fire charts will be given proper distribution so that a maximum amount of artillery fire and air support can be brought to bare on any zone.

12 October 1944

Confirming verbal orders issued 11 October 1944, XX Corps will:

1. Contain enemy defenses in the METZ area, withdrawing force from FORT DRIANT.

2. Employ newly-assigned divisions to replace divisions which have been continuously engaged to permit:

a. Resting of troops.

b. Reorganization, refitting and preparation for further offensive action.

c. Training of newly-assigned divisions.

3. Maintain aggressive reconnaissance and continue coverage of all possible avenues of tank approach.

4. Maintain contact with Ninth US Army on left.

18 October 1944
OUTLINE PLAN 'A' FOR THE RESUMPTION OF THE OFFENSIVE

1. *PURPOSE:* To present two plans for the resumption of the offensive which may be used as a basis for detailed planning by Third US Army Staff Sections and by Corps. The Operational Directive which will be issued by this headquarters to effect the resumption of the offensive will conform to one of these two plans.

2. *ASSUMPTIONS:* It is assumed that:
a. Third US Army will consist of three Corps, six infantry divisions and three armored divisions as follows:
(1) III Corps, XII Corps and XX Corps.
(2) 5th, 26th, 35th, 80th, 90th and 95th Infantry Divisions.
(3) 4th, 6th and 10th Armoured Divisions.
b. The boundary between First and Third US Armies will remain as shown on attached overlay.
c. The boundary between Sixth and Twelfth Army Groups will be changed to make MANNHEIM inclusive to Sixth Army Group as shown on the attached overlay.
d. The XVIII Corps (Airborne) consisting of the 82nd and/or 101st Airborne Divisions may assist the advance by seizing a bridgehead east of the RHINE RIVER in the general area MAINZ-MANNHEIM.
e. The XIX Tactical Air Command will furnish adequate air support and medium and heavy bombardment will be available.

3. *TENTATIVE PLAN:*
a. *General Plan*: Third US Army will:
(1) Envelop METZ defensive works from north and south.
(2) Advance northeast within zone to seize MAINZ-FRANKFURT-DARMSTADT area.
(3) Be prepared for further offensive action to the northeast.
b. *Scheme of Maneuver*:
(1) *Phase One—*
(a) Contain METZ on the West.
(b) Cross MOSELLE RIVER north of METZ and seize rail and road facilities in the vicinity of BOULAY.
(c) Advance northeast from vicinity of PONT-A-MOUSSON and seize rail and road facilities in vicinity of FALKENBERG (FAULQUEMONT).
(d) Destroy enemy forces withdrawing from METZ area and isolate METZ defensive works.

(2) *Phase Two*—(After METZ area has been neutralized).

(a) Advance northeast with two Corps abreast. One Corps will remain initially in the area northwest of BRIEY, advancing on Army order echeloned to the left rear.

(b) Continue advance rapidly to—

1. Establish a bridgehead east of the RHINE RIVER between MAINZ and MANNHEIM.

2. Seize the MAINZ-FRANKFURT-DARMSTADT area.

(c) Be prepared for further offensive action to the northeast.

4. *CORPS MISSIONS:*

a. XX Corps (5th Inf Div, 90th Inf Div, 95th Inf Div, 10th Armd Div and supporting troops) will—

(1) Contain METZ defensive works west of the MOSELLE RIVER.

(2) Cross the MOSELLE RIVER in the vicinity of THIONVILLE with a minimum of one infantry and one armored division and seize rail and road facilities in vicinity of BOULAY.

(3) In conjunction with XII Corps, destroy any enemy forces withdrawing from METZ area and be prepared for further advance to the northeast.

(4) Continue advance rapidly to the northeast to:

(a) Establish a bridgehead east of the RHINE RIVER between MAINZ and OPPENHEIM.

(b) Seize MAINZ-FRANKFURT area.

(5) Be prepared for further advance to the northeast.

b. XII Corps (26th Inf Div, 35th Inf Div, 80th Inf Div, 4th Armd Div, 6th Armd Div and supporting troops) will—

(1) Advance northeast from vicinity of PONT-A-MOUSSON with a minimum of one infantry and one armored division and seize rail and road facilities in vicinity of FAULQUEMONT.

(2) In conjunction with XX Corps, destroy any enemy forces withdrawing from METZ area and be prepared for further advance to the northeast.

(3) Continue advance rapidly to the northeast to:

(a) Establish a bridgehead east of the RHINE RIVER between OPPENHEIM and MANNHEIM.

(b) Seize DARMSTADT area.

c. III Corps (and supporting troops) will—

(1) Assemble in an area northwest of BRIEY.

(2) Assume command of troops as may be assigned by Army order.

(3) Advance northeast on Army order, echeloned to left rear.

d. (1) In the advance Corps will be disposed in depth with armor in lead; armor to be reinforced by motorized infantry. These leading elements will pass around obstacles and points of resistance wherever possible in order to continue the advance to the RHINE RIVER. Infantry forces following will advance rapidly, clear enemy resistance and consolidate gains.

(2) Reconnaissance will be pushed to maximum in order to seize intact all possible crossings of major river obstacles (e.g. the SAAR and RHINE rivers).

OUTLINE PLAN 'B' (Assumptions and General Plan same as Plan 'A')
1. *SCHEME OF MANEUVER:*

a. *Phase One—*

(1) Contain Metz on the West.

(2) Seize and secure all possible crossings of the MOSELLE RIVER in the vicinity of THIONVILLE, and advance on BOULAY.

(3) Attack northeast, with two Corps abreast, from the PONT-A-MOUSSON–NANCY area to seize rail and road facilities in the vicinity of FAULQUEMONT-BOULAY.

(4) Destroy enemy forces withdrawing from the METZ area and isolate METZ defensive works.

b. *Phase Two—*(After METZ has been neutralized).

(1) Advance northeast with two Corps abreast, one Corps advancing on Army order, initially echeloned to the left rear.

(2) Continuation of the advance to be the same as Plan 'A.'

2. *CORPS MISSIONS:*

a. XX Corps (1 armored division, 2 infantry divisions and supporting troops) will—

(1) Attack northeast from vicinity of PONT-A-MOUSSON with one armored and two infantry divisions and—

(a) Seize rail and road facilities in vicinity of FAULQUEMONT.

(b) Seize rail and road facilities in vicinity of BOULAY.

(2) In conjunction with III Corps, destroy any enemy forces withdrawing from METZ area and be prepared for further advance to northeast.

(3) Continuation of the advance to be the same as Plan 'A.'

b. XII Corps (2 infantry divisions, 2 armored divisions and supporting troops) will—

(1) Attack northeast from NANCY area destroying the enemy on its front and protect the south flank of Third US Army.

(2) Assist XX Corps in seizing rail and road facilities in vicinity of FAULQUE-MONT.

(3) Continuation of the advance to be the same as Plan 'A.'

c. III Corps (2 infantry divisions, 1 tank group—to be of tank battalions detached from infantry divisions—and 1 tank destroyer group) will—

(1) Contain METZ defensive works west of the MOSELLE RIVER.

(2) With a minimum of one infantry division, one tank group and one tank destroyer group, seize and secure all possible crossings in the THIONVILLE area.

(3) Attack southeast and assist XX Corps in seizing rail and road facilities in vicinity of BOULAY.

(4) Assist XX Corps in destroying any enemy forces withdrawing from METZ area.

(5) Be prepared to advance to the northeast in XX Corps zone echeloned to the left rear.

(6) Protect left flank of Third US Army.

November 1, 1944
MEMORANDUM:
TO: Major General Walker, Commanding General, XX Corps.

Communication from the Headquarters Twelfth Army Group under date of 30 October 1944, reference the use of the 83rd Division, in substance is herewith *paraphrased*:

In order to make it absolutely clear to everyone concerned as to just what use is to be made of this division, I would like to state it here. The 83rd Division is placed under your operational control to the extent that follows:

This division is not to make a separate river crossing, as this would involve too much bridging equipment and too much artillery support. The initial river crossing of this division should be made through the bridgehead already established by your own divisions. After a bridgehead has been established by your divisions, one regimental combat team could be used to cross over in the bridgehead and then turn to the northeast to protect that flank and to advance up the east side of the Moselle River. As it advances, it will wipe out the defenses facing the right regimental combat team of this division now in the front line. As this right regimental combat team is freed by the advance up the other side of the river, it can also be brought down, put through the bridgehead and used on the east side of the Moselle to give the original attack by the regiment of the 83rd more depth and power. These elements of the 83rd Division may be used to clean out the terrain between the Moselle River and the Saar River which runs through Saarburg, and seize crossings of the Saar River in the vicinity of Saarburg for future use by your other division. No elements of the 83rd should be used beyond this point.

Selected Bibliography

Primary Sources, Unpublished

Documents

Division After Action Reports, U.S. National Archives (NA), Modern Military Reference Branch (MMRB), Suitland, Maryland.
Historical Division Combat Interviews (HDCI), NA, Washington, D.C.
Third Army After Action Report (AAR), Special Collections, United States Military Academy Library, West Point (WP).
Third Army G-3 Section: Report of Operations, MMRB.
Third Army Headquarters Memorandum, MMRB.
Third Army Operational Directives, MMRB.
Third Army Terrain Area Analyses, MMRB.

Studies

Air Effects Committee 12th Army Group and General Omar N. Bradley, Military Advisor. United States Strategic Bombing Survey, "Effect of Air Power on Military Operations, Western Europe," U.S. Air Force Historical Research Center (USAFHRC). July 15, 1945, microfilm C 5169.
The Army Air Forces Evaluation Board. "The Effectiveness of Third Phase Tactical Air Operations in the European Theater, May 5 1944–May 8 1945," USAFHRC. August 20, 1945, microfilm A1175.
The Army Air Forces Evaluation Board."The Effect of Air Power in the Battle of Metz," USAFHRC. January 19, 1945, microfilm A1174.
Board, General. European Theater of Operations. "The Tactical Air Force in the European Theater of Operations," File R373/1 Study #54. Prepared by Brigadier General Ralph F. Stearly, Brigadier General Robert M. Lee, and Colonel James C. McGehee. Office of the Chief of Military History (OCMH), Washington, D.C., no date.

Edwards, Major Meyer A., Major Harry V. Heim et al., "Armor in the Attack of Fortified Positions," Research Report prepared at the Armored School, Fort Knox, Kentucky, 1949–1950, OCMH, Washington, D.C.

Grow, Robert W. "Broad Front vs Narrow Front," Study based on *The Lorraine Campaign* by Hugh M. Cole. Office of the Chief of Military History, 1952 Hist 314.7, Box: "General Grow, Special Studies on World War II," United States Army Military History Institute (USAMHI).

———. "Mobility Unused," Study based on *The Lorraine Campaign* by Hugh M. Cole. OCMH, Oct 1, 1952. Hist 314.7, Box: "General Grow, Special Studies on World War," II, USAMHI.

Stephenson, R. et al. *The Battle of Metz* Battlebook 13–A. Fort Leavenworth, Kans.: Combat Studies Institute, 1985.

Personal Papers

Abrams Papers, USAMHI
Bradley Papers, USAMHI
Bradley Papers, WP
Dager Papers, USAMHI
Eddy Diary, U.S. Army Infantry School, National Infantry Museum (NIM), Fort Benning, Ga.
Gay Papers, USAMHI
Gay/Gaffey Diary, Special Collections, WP
Harkins Papers, USAMHI
Koch Papers, USAMHI
Patton Papers, Library of Congress (LC), Washington, D.C.
Sylvan Papers, USAMHI
Van Fleet Papers, USAMHI
Wood Papers, Special Collections, Bird Library, Syracuse University (SU)

PRIMARY SOURCES, PUBLISHED

Blumenson, Martin, ed. *The Patton Papers*. 2 vols. Boston: Houghton Mifflin, 1972, 1974.

Chandler, Alfred D., ed. *The Papers of Dwight D. Eisenhower: The War Years*. Baltimore: Johns Hopkins University Press, 1970.

Detwiler, Donald S., with Charles B. Burdick and Jurgen Rohwer, eds. *World War II, German Military Studies*. 24 vols. New York: Garland Publishing, 1979.

MEMOIRS

Allen, Robert S. *Lucky Forward: The History of Patton's Third U.S. Army*. New York: Vanguard Press, 1947.

Bradley, Omar N. *A Soldier's Story*. New York: Henry Holt and Company, 1951.

Bradley, Omar N., and Clay Blair. *A General's Life.* New York: Simon and Schuster, 1983.

Butcher, Harry C. *My Three Years With Eisenhower.* New York: Simon and Schuster, 1946.

Codman, Charles R. *Drive.* Boston: Little, Brown, 1957.

Luck, Hans von. *Panzer Commander: The Memoirs of Colonel Hans von Luck.* New York: Praeger, 1989.

North, John, ed. *The Alexander Memoirs 1940–1945.* London: Cassell, 1962.

Patton, George S. *War as I Knew It.* Boston: Houghton Mifflin, 1947.

Ritgen, Helmut. *The Western Front 1944: Memoirs of a Panzer Lehr Officer.* Winnipeg: J. J. Federowicz, 1995.

Truscott, Lucian K. *Command Missions: A Personal Story.* New York: Arno Press, 1979, original publication in 1954.

SECONDARY SOURCES

Books

Abrams, Joe I. *A History of the 90th Division in World War II June 6 1944 to May 8 1945.* Baton Rouge: Army and Navy Publishing Company, 1946.

Ambrose, Stephen E. *The Supreme Commander: The War Years of General Dwight D. Eisenhower.* Garden City, N.Y.: Doubleday, 1970.

———. *Citizen Soldiers: The U.S. Army from the Normandy Beaches to the Bulge to the Surrender of Germany.* N.Y.: Simon and Schuster, 1997.

Bennett, Ralph. *Ultra in the West: The Normandy Campaign of 1944–1945.* New York: Scribner's, 1979.

Blumenson, Martin. *Breakout and Pursuit.* U.S. Army in World War II: European Theater of Operations. Washington, D.C.: Department of the Army, 1961.

———. *Patton: The Man behind the Legend, 1885–1945.* New York: William Morrow, 1985.

———. *The Battle of the Generals: The Untold Story of the Falaise Pocket— The Campaign That Should Have Won World War II.* New York: William Morrow, 1993.

Bonn, Keith E. *When the Odds Were Even: The Vosges Mountains Campaign, October 1944–January 1945.* Novato, Calif.: Presidio, 1994.

Brownlow, Donald G. *Panzer Baron: The Military Exploits of General Hasso von Manteuffel.* North Quincy, Mass.: The Christopher Publishing House, 1975.

Clausewitz, Carl von. *On War*, edited and translated by Michael Howard and Peter Paret. Princeton, N.J.: Princeton University Press, 1984, original publication in 1976.

Colby, John. *War from the Ground Up: The 90th Division in World War II.* Austin, Tex.: Nortex Press, 1991.

Cole, Hugh M. *The Lorraine Campaign*. U.S. Army in World War II: European Theater of Operations. Washington, D.C.: Center for Military History, 1984, original publication in 1950.

Creveld, Martin van. *Supplying War: Logistics from Wallenstein to Patton*. Cambridge: Cambridge University Press, 1977.

———. *Fighting Power: German and U.S. Army Performance, 1939–1945*. Westport, Conn.: Greenwood Press, 1982.

D'Este, Carlo. *Bitter Victory: The Battle for Sicily, 1943*. New York: HarperCollins, 1988.

———. *Patton: A Genius for War*. New York: HarperCollins, 1995.

Doubler, Michael D. *Closing with the Enemy: How GIs Fought the War in Europe, 1944–1945*. Lawrence, Kans.: University Press of Kansas, 1994.

English, John A. *A Perspective on Infantry*. New York: Praeger, 1981.

Essame, H. *Patton: A Study in Command*. New York: Charles Scribner's Sons, 1974.

Farago, Ladislas. *Patton: Ordeal and Triumph*. New York: Ivan Obolensky, 1963.

Frankel, Nat, and Larry Smith. *Patton's Best: An Informal History of the 4th Armored Division*. New York: Hawthorn, 1978.

Gabel, Christopher R. *The Lorraine Campaign: An Overview, September–December 1944*. Fort Leavenworth, Kans.: Combat Studies Institute, 1985.

———. *The 4th Armored Division in the Encirclement of Nancy*. Fort Leavenworth, Kans.: Combat Studies Institute, 1986.

———. *The U.S. Army GHQ Maneuvers of 1941*. Washington, D.C.: OCMH, 1991.

Garland, Albert N., and Howard McGraw Smyth. *Sicily and the Surrender of Italy*. U.S. Army in World War II: European Theater of Operations. Washington, D.C.: OCMH, 1965.

Giziowski, Richard. *The Enigma of General Blaskowitz*. London: Leo Cooper, 1997.

Graham, Dominick, and Shelford Bidwell. *Coalitions, Politicians, and Generals: Some Aspects of Command in Two World Wars*. London: Brassey's, 1993.

Greenfield, Kent Roberts, Robert R. Palmer, and Bell I. Wiley. *The Organization of Ground Combat Troops*. U.S. Army in World War II: European Theater of Operations. Washington, D.C.: Historical Division, 1947.

Grow, Robert W. *Brest to Bastogne: The Story of the 6th Armored Division*. Paris, 1945.

Guderian, Major General Heinz. *Achtung Panzer! The Development of Armoured Forces, Their Tactics and Operational Potential*. London: Arms and Armour Press, 1993, original publication in 1937.

Harkins, Paul D. *When the Third Cracked Europe: The Story of Patton's Incredible Army*. Harrisburg, Pa.: Army Times Publishing, 1969.

Hogg, Ian V. *British and American Artillery of World War 2*. London: Arms and Armour Press, 1978.

————. *The Biography of General George S. Patton*. New York: Hamlyn, 1982.

————. *German Artillery of World War Two*. London: Greenhill, 1997.

Howe, George F. *Northwest Africa: Seizing the Initiative in the West*. U.S. Army in World War II: European Theater of Operations. Washington, D.C.: Department of the Army, 1957.

Hughes, Daniel, ed. *Moltke on the Art of War: Selected Writings*. Novato, Calif.: Presidio, 1993.

Kemp, Anthony. *The Unknown Battle: Metz, 1944*. New York: Stein and Day, 1981.

Koch, Oscar W. *G-2: Intelligence for Patton*. Philadelphia: Whitmore, 1971.

Liddell Hart, B. H. *The Strategy of Indirect Approach*. London: Faber and Faber, 1941.

————. *History of the Second World War*. New York: G. P. Putnam's Sons, 1970.

Lucas, James. *The Last Year of the German Army: May 1944–May 1945*. London: Arms and Armour Press, 1994.

MacDonald, Charles B., and Sidney T. Matthews. *Three Battles: Arnaville, Altuzzo and Schmidt*. U.S. Army in World War II: European Theater of Operations Washington, D.C.: Department of the Army, 1952.

Mellenthin, Major General F. W. von. *Panzer Battles: A Study of the Employment of Armour in the Second World War*. Norman: Oklahoma University Press, 1971, original publication in 1955.

————. *German Generals of World War II: As I Saw Them*. Norma: Oklahoma University Press, 1977.

Millet, Allan R., and Williamson Murray, eds. *Military Effectiveness,* Vol. III, *The Second World War*. Boston: Allen and Unwin, 1988.

Nye, Roger H. *The Patton Mind: The Professional Development of an Extraordinary Leader*. Garden City, N.Y.: Avery Publishing, 1993.

Overy, Richard. *Why the Allies Won*. London: Johnathan Cape, 1995.

Palmer, Robert R., Bell I. Wiley, and William R. Keast. *The Procurement and Training of Ground Combat Troops*. U.S. Army in World War II: European Theater of Operations. Washington, D.C.: Government Printing Office, 1948.

Perret, Geoffrey. *There's a War to Be Won: The United States Army in World War II*. New York: Random House, 1991.

Phillips, Henry G. *El Guettar: Crucible of Leadership, 9th U.S. Infantry Division against the Wehrmacht in Africa, April 1943*. Penn Valley, Calif.: Henry G. Phillips, 1991.

Pogue, Forrest C. *The Supreme Command*. U.S. Army in World War II: European Theater of Operations. Washington, D.C.: Department of the Army, 1954.

Price, Frank J. *Troy H. Middleton: A Biography*. Baton Rouge: Louisiana State University Press, 1974.

Ruppenthal, Ronald G. *Logistical Support of the Armies*, Vol. I: *May 1941–September 1944*. U.S. Army in World War II: European Theater of Operations. Washington, D.C.: Department of the Army, 1953.

———. *Logistical Support of the Armies*, Vol. II: *September 1944–May 1945*. U.S. Army in World War II: European Theater of Operations Washington, D.C.: Department of the Army, 1959.

Semmes, Harry H. *Portrait of Patton*. New York: Appleton-Century-Crofts, 1955.

Spielberger, Walter J. *The Spielberger German Armor and Military Vehicles Series*, Vol. I: *Panther and Its Variants*. Atglen, Pa.: Schiffer, 1993.

———. *The Spielberger German Armor and Military Vehicles Series*, Vol. IV: *Panzer IV and Its Variants*. Atglen, Pa.: Schiffer, 1993.

Stanton, Shelby L. *World War II Order of Battle*. New York: Galahad, 1991.

Weigley, Russell F. *Eisenhower's Lieutenants: The Campaign of France and Germany 1944–1945*. Bloomington: Indiana University Press, 1981.

Wilmot, Chester. *The Struggle for Europe*. London: Collins, 1971, originally published in 1957.

Articles

Andidora, Ronald. "The Autumn of 1944: Boldness Is Not Enough." *Parameters: US Army War College Quarterly* XVII, 4 (December 1987): 71–80.

Berlin, Robert H. "United States Army World War II Corps Commanders: A Composite Biography." *The Journal of Military History* LIII (April 1989): 147–167.

Blumenson, Martin. "Bradley-Patton: World War II's 'Odd Couple.' " *Army* (December 1985): 56–64.

———. "America's World War II Leaders in Europe: Some Thoughts." *Parameters: US Army War College Quarterly* XIX, 4 (December 1989): 2–13.

Cottingham, Levin B. "Smoke over the Moselle." *Infantry Journal* (August 1948): 14–19.

Dietrich, Steve E. "The Professional Reading of General George S. Patton, Jr." *The Journal of Military History* LIII, 4 (October 1989): 387–418.

Deutsch, Harold C. "Commanding Generals and the Uses of Intelligence." *Intelligence and National Security* III, 3 (1988): 194–260.

Ganz, A. Harding. "Patton's Relief of General Wood." *The Journal of Military History* LIII, 3 (July 1989): 257–273.

———. "The 11th Panzers in the Defense, 1944." *Armor* (March–April 1994), 26–37.

Haislip, Wade H. "Corps Command in World War II." *Military Review* (May 1990): 22–32.

Hall, William C. "Bridging at Thionville." *Military Engineer* XL, 270 (April 1948), 169–173.

Nenninger, Timothy K. "Leavenworth and Its Critics: The U.S. Army Command and General Staff School, 1920–1940." *The Journal of Military History* LVIII (April 1994), 199–231.

Nye, Roger H. "Whence Patton's Military Genius?" *Parameters: US Army War College Quarterly* XXI, 4 (Winter 1991–1992): 60–73.

Walker, Fred L., Jr. "Siege Methods: 1945, Part I, Plans and Preparation." *Infantry Journal* (January 1945): 8–15.

———. "Siege Methods: 1945, Part Two, Assault and Exploitation." *Infantry Journal* (February 1945): 35–39.

Wilt, Alan F. "Coming of Age: XIX TAC's Roles during the 1944 Dash across France." *Air Force Review* XXXVI, 3 (1985): 71–87.

Woolley, William J. "Patton and the Concept of Mechanized Warfare." *Parameters: US Army War College Quarterly* XV, 3 (1985): 71–79.

Wright, Charles E. "Moselle River Crossing at Cattenom." *Armored Cavalry Journal* (May–June 1948): 50–53.

Index

About the Author

JOHN NELSON RICKARD is completing his Ph.D. in Military History in the Military and Strategic Studies Program at the University of New Brunswick. His specialty is World War II with particular emphasis on the campaigns in Northwest Europe.